PROGRAMME ON INSTITUTIONAL MANAGEMENT IN HIGHER EDUCATION

Quality
and Internationalisation
in Higher Education

ORGANISATION FOR ECONOMIC CO-OPERATION AND DEVELOPMENT

ORGANISATION FOR ECONOMIC CO-OPERATION AND DEVELOPMENT

Pursuant to Article 1 of the Convention signed in Paris on 14th December 1960, and which came into force on 30th September 1961, the Organisation for Economic Co-operation and Development (OECD) shall promote policies designed:

- to achieve the highest sustainable economic growth and employment and a rising standard of living in Member countries, while maintaining financial stability, and thus to contribute to the development of the world economy;
- to contribute to sound economic expansion in Member as well as non-member countries in the process of economic development; and
- to contribute to the expansion of world trade on a multilateral, non-discriminatory basis in accordance with international obligations.

The original Member countries of the OECD are Austria, Belgium, Canada, Denmark, France, Germany, Greece, Iceland, Ireland, Italy, Luxembourg, the Netherlands, Norway, Portugal, Spain, Sweden, Switzerland, Turkey, the United Kingdom and the United States. The following countries became Members subsequently through accession at the dates indicated hereafter: Japan (28th April 1964), Finland (28th January 1969), Australia (7th June 1971), New Zealand (29th May 1973), Mexico (18th May 1994), the Czech Republic (21st December 1995), Hungary (7th May 1996), Poland (22nd November 1996) and Korea (12th December 1996). The Commission of the European Communities takes part in the work of the OECD (Article 13 of the OECD Convention).

The Programme on Institutional Management in Higher Education (IMHE) started in 1969 as an activity of the OECD's newly established Centre for Educational Research and Innovation (CERI). In November 1972, the OECD Council decided that the Programme would operate as an independent decentralised project and authorised the Secretary-General to administer it. Responsibility for its supervision was assigned to a Directing Group of representatives of governments and institutions participating in the Programme. Since 1972, the Council has periodically extended this arrangement; the latest renewal now expires on 31st December 2001.

The main objectives of the Programme are as follows:

- to promote, through research, training and information exchange, greater professionalism in the management of institutions of higher education; and
- to facilitate a wider dissemination of practical management methods and approaches.

 THE OPINIONS EXPRESSED AND ARGUMENTS EMPLOYED IN THIS PUBLICATION ARE THE RESPONSIBILITY OF THE AUTHORS AND DO NOT NECESSARILY REPRESENT THOSE OF THE OECD OR OF THE NATIONAL OR LOCAL AUTHORITIES CONCERNED.

*
* *

Publié en français sous le titre :
QUALITÉ ET INTERNATIONALISATION DE L'ENSEIGNEMENT SUPÉRIEUR

Foreword

In a global economy, internationalisation is an increasingly important factor in the work of universities and other higher education providers. Internationalisation of higher education is understood here as both the concept and the process of integrating an international dimension into the teaching, research and service functions. As this concept becomes more widely understood and the process of internationalisation matures, it is increasingly urgent that institutions of higher education address the issues of quality assessment and assurance of the international aspects of their operations.

The OECD Programme on Institutional Management in Higher Education (IMHE) has taken a close interest in the international dimension of higher education over a number of years. Since 1994, it has led an activity focusing on a cross-country analysis of institutional level strategies, the Internationalisation Quality Review Process (IQRP) — a project in collaboration with the Academic Co-operation Association (ACA) in Brussels. The IQRP aims to help individual institutions of higher education to assess and enhance the quality of their international dimension according to their own stated aims and objectives. The review process includes procedures, guidelines and tools to be adapted and used in both a self-assessment exercise and an external peer review.

Two publications have already resulted from this activity: *Strategies for Internationalisation of Higher Education — A Comparative Study of Australia, Canada, Europe and the United States of America* (1995) and *Internationalisation of Higher Education in Asia Pacific Countries* (1997). This publication is the third one. Its purpose is to bring attention to the importance and complementarity of the various perspectives on the quality of internationalisation and to describe the IQRP. It presents two important issues and concerns that have emerged from the activity: quality assessment and assurance of the internationalisation strategies, and the contribution that internationalisation has made to enhancing the quality of higher education. It also analyses the project and the development of the process, shares its findings, looks at the implications and innovations, disseminates the results and aims to stimulate reflection and action.

3

The book provides an introduction to the concepts of internationalisation of higher education and quality assurance (Part I); an overview of the Internationalisation Quality Review Process and case studies in six countries in four different continents (Part II); and an analysis of the uses, benefits and issues related to the quality review of the international dimension in the broader context of quality assurance in higher education (Part III). The IQRP guidelines are included at the end of the volume.

Internationalisation quality issues are addressed from three perspectives:

- The first sees the inclusion of the international dimension as a key component in the general academic quality review systems operational at the institutional or system level. This is based on the premise that an international dimension is part of the university/college mission and major functions and is thus included as one of many elements addressed in the quality review procedures.
- The second looks at the quality of specific internationalisation policies, procedures and programmes (i.e. international students, work/study abroad, student/faculty exchanges, research, language instruction, and technical assistance).
- The third concerns the internationalisation of quality assurance procedures themselves. These procedures are in general nationally based. It is increasingly acknowledged that quality assurance procedures benefit from an international input and approach.

The IMHE Programme extends its gratitude to Hans de Wit of the Universiteit van Amsterdam, the Netherlands, and Jane Knight, Ryerson Polytechnic University, Toronto, Canada, for the work accomplished in their capacity as IQRP project leaders, as authors of several chapters in this book, and as editors of this publication.

This book is published on the responsibility of the Secretary-General of the OECD.

Dedication

On 5 August 1998, Jankarel Gevers, President of the Universiteit van Amsterdam and Chairman of the IMHE Directing Group passed away. During his long career in higher education in the Netherlands and within IMHE/OECD and other international associations, Jankarel Gevers was a strong advocate of internationalisation and of quality assurance in higher education. His support and views have been an inspiration, both for the Internationalisation Quality Review Project and for this publication. He is greatly missed.

Acknowledgements

The realisation of the project and the preparation of the IQRP guidelines resulting from the project, were done by a team of international experts, who were also involved in the peer reviews.

In addition to the editors, the project team included Marjorie Peace Lenn, Center for Quality Assurance in International Education/Global Alliance for Transnational Education, Washington, the United States; Outi Snellman, University of Lapland and Centre for International Mobility, Finland; Marijk van der Wende, formerly of ACA and the Netherlands Organisation for International Co-operation in Higher Education, NUFFIC, now University of Twente and University of Amsterdam, the Netherlands; and Leo West, Monash University, Melbourne, Australia (retired).

We would like to thank them and the nine institutions which volunteered to take part in the review process in the pilot stage.

We thank too the authors of the chapters in this book, not mentioned before: Tony Adams (Mcquarie University, Australia); Jerome Bookin-Weiner (Bentley college, United States); Paul Fogelberg (University of Helsinki, Finland, retired); Marian Geldner (Warsaw School of Economics, Poland); Joseph Koech and Peter Opakas (Moi University); Salvador Malo, Rosamaria Valle and Karin Wriedt (National University of Mexico); Grant McBurnie (Monash University, Australia); Bernd Wächter (Academic Co-operation Association, Belgium); and David Woodhouse (New Zealand Universities Academic Audit Unit). We also would like to thank the others not mentioned elsewhere who have participated in the peer review teams and who have contributed to the IQRP project, including Ian Anglis (Quality Assurance Services, Australia); John Davies (Anglia Polytechnic University, United Kingdom); Manuel Gil-Antón (Universidad Autónoma Metropolitana, Mexico); Kari Hypponen (Turku University, Finland); Jan Karlsson (IMHE Programme); John Mallea (Brandon University, Canada, retired); Miriam Mikol (University of Western Sydney, Australia); Knud Erik Sabroe (Aarhus University, Denmark); and Leong Yin Ching (Stamford College, Malaysia). We would like to thank them all for their role in the project.

It was the leadership and contribution of the IMHE Programme, in collaboration with ACA, that made this project and publication possible. We would like to thank them and the IMHE staff for their stimulating role in the project and in the realisation of this publication.

Jane Knight and Hans de Wit

Table of Contents

OECD 1999

OECD 1999

PART I
INTERNATIONALISATION
AND QUALITY ASSURANCE: CONCEPTS

1

Internationalisation of Higher Education
by
Jane Knight

The purpose of this chapter is to look at the concept and meaning of internationalisation and the strategies for integrating an international dimension into higher education institutions. This includes a discussion on the meaning and definition of the term, a description of the various approaches to internationalisation, an exploration of why it is important to internationalise the higher education sector and an analysis of which strategies are appropriate to integrate an international and intercultural dimension in a higher education institution.

Meaning and definition

Diversity in meaning of internationalisation

Due to the increased interest in, and understanding of, the international dimension of higher education, the term "internationalisation" is being used more and more. On the one hand, this can be interpreted as a sign that internationalisation is becoming more accepted and central to the provision of higher education. However, on the other hand, it is clear that internationalisation means different things to different people and as a result there is a great diversity of interpretations attributed to the concept.

There are a number of terms which are often confused with or used in conjunction with internationalisation. The term which is most often used interchangeably with internationalisation is globalisation and thus it is important to explore further the relationship between globalisation and internationalisation.

Globalisation can be described or defined in a vast number of ways. The description (Knight and de Wit, 1997) which is most relevant and appropriate to the discussion on the international dimension of the higher education sector is as follows:

- "Globalisation is the flow of technology, economy, knowledge, people, values, ideas ... across borders. Globalisation affects each country in a different way due to a nation's individual history, traditions, culture and priorities.
- Internationalisation of higher education is one of the ways a country responds to the impact of globalisation yet, at the same time respects the individuality of the nation."

Thus, internationalisation and globalisation are seen as different but dynamically linked concepts. Globalisation can be thought of as the catalyst while internationalisation is the response, albeit a response in a proactive way.

Related terms and concepts

As the attention to the importance and implication of internationalisation grows, there seems to be a new and differentiated vocabulary being developed to describe and denote some of the nuances in meaning. In many cases new terms are being used to describe new concepts, in other instances new terms are being attached to existing or traditional concepts. At the same time, old or existing concepts are also being given new meanings. The rather imprecise use of terminology illustrates the complexity and the evolution of the international, global/transnational/regional dimension of higher education. It is not the purpose of this chapter to elaborate on the meaning and use of the vocabulary of international education. Rather the aim is to highlight the need for further exploration of the diversity of related concepts such as internationalisation, globalisation, regionalisation or an even more complicated set of related terms such as transnational education, global education, world education, intercultural education, comparative education, multicultural education, international education.

Approaches to internationalisation

There are a number of generic approaches that institutions are using as they plan and implement an institution-wide internationalisation strategy. Table 1 provides a typology of approaches (Knight, 1994) to internationalisation at the institutional level. The purpose of the typology is to illustrate the different areas of emphasis that have been or are currently being given to internationalisation by different researchers, practitioners and higher education institutions.

The purpose of this typology is to stimulate reflection on the kind of approach that an institution has either implicitly or explicitly adopted. It is important to point out that these four different approaches are not necessarily exclusive.

Table 1. **Approaches to internationalisation**

Approach	Description
Activity	Categories or types of activities used to describe internationalisation: such as curriculum, student/faculty exchanges, technical assistance, international students.
Competency	Development of new skills, knowledge, attitudes and values in students, faculty and staff. As the emphasis on outcomes of education grows there is increasing interest in identifying and defining global/international competencies.
Ethos	Emphasis is on creating a culture or climate on campus which promotes and supports international/intercultural initiatives.
Process	Integration or infusion of an international or intercultural dimension into teaching, research and service through a combination of a wide range of activities, policies and procedures.

Source: Author.

The *activity* approach is one that has been most prevalent and is characteristic of the period when one described the international dimension in terms of specific activities or programmes. The most predominant types of activities include international students, development assistance or academic mobility. In fact, according to some professionals the activity approach was synonymous with the term international education in the 1970s and early 1980s.

The *competency* approach is more closely related to an outcomes approach to education where quality is thought of in terms of knowledge, skills, interests, values and attitudes of the students. In the competency approach to internationalisation the emphasis is placed on the human element of the academic community – the students, faculty and technical/administrative/support staff. The issue which is central to this approach is how does generation and transfer of knowledge help to develop competencies in the personnel of the higher education institution to be more internationally knowledgeable and interculturally skilled. Thus, in this approach, the development of internationalised curricula and programmes is not an end unto itself but a means toward developing the appropriate competencies in students, staff and faculty. There is a growing interest in the identification and measurement of competencies as outcomes of internationalisation. The preoccupation with competencies is interesting in that research and discourse is now taking place on defining competencies, sometimes called international or global or transnational competencies. Is there a fundamental conceptual difference between these terms? Or is it another indication of terms being used interchangeably and causing more confusion than clarity? The answers to these questions are not evident at this time but rigorous analysis and some

15

clarity on the definitions and relationships of these terms will help the study and practice of internationalisation move forward.

The *ethos* approach relates more to organisational development theories which focus on the creation of a culture or climate within an organisation to support a particular set of principles and goals. In the case of internationalisation, the focus is on establishing an ethos or which encourages and fosters the development of international and intercultural values and initiatives. This approach attempts to make the international dimension more explicit in the culture of the institution.

The *process* approach stresses the integration of an international and/or inter-cultural dimension into academic programmes as well as the guiding policies and procedures of an institution. A major concern in this approach is the need to address the sustainability of the international dimension. Therefore, emphasis is placed on programme aspects as well as organisational elements such as policies and procedures.

In summary, it is important to remember that these four different approaches to describing internationalisation are complementary and certainly not mutually exclusive. The typology reflects how dynamic the concept of internationalisation is and how internationalisation is shaping new directions for higher education and at the same time responding to current trends and needs of the sector.

Working definition of internationalisation

Given the variety of approaches to internationalisation of higher education, it is no surprise that there are also many different definitions applied to the term. The working definition adopted is as follows:

> "Internationalisation of higher education is the process of integrating an international/intercultural dimension into the teaching, research and ser-vice functions of the institution" (Knight, 1994).

There are several key concepts in this definition. The idea of internationalisation being a dynamic process and not a set of isolated activities has already been discussed in the previous section. Integration or infusion is also key to this defini-tion to ensure that the international dimension is a central part of programmes, policies and procedures and not a marginal and easily expendable element. Thus, integration contributes to the sustainability of the international dimension.

Both an international and intercultural dimension is included in this definition to emphasise the fact that internationalisation is not only oriented to countries or nation states but also includes the different cultural/ethnic groups within a coun-try. It is short sighted to think of internationalisation as only a geographically based concept (meaning outside our own borders or between/among different countries).

By design, this definition is also rationale neutral. That is to say, the motivation for an institution to internationalise is not included in the definition. A definition needs to be generic and to acknowledge the differences among institutions and the context and culture in which they operate. Institutions have different rationales for internationalisation which need to be made clear and explicit. A definition therefore, should not be linked to any particular set of rationales. Instead the definition is better associated with the primary and universal functions of an institution of higher education, namely teaching, research and service to society.

It is challenging to find a definition of internationalisation which is appropriate and sensitive to the higher education systems in a wide variety of countries and cultures. The working definition as outlined above is purposely oriented to the institutional level and attempts to build on the universality of the functions of an institution of higher education.

Rationale and motivation for internationalisation

Political, economic, academic and social rationales

Just as there are a variety of ways to describe and define internationalisation, there are also a number of different rationales or motivations for wanting to integrate an international dimension into higher education. This section will discuss four basic categories of rationales. These categories are not mutually exclusive, in fact, they are becoming more and more interrelated. Whether one is looking at rationale from a national policy level, a sector level or an educational institutional level there are bound to different perspectives and points of emphasis, and sometimes they are complimentary and in other instances they are contradictory. Furthermore, there seems to be major shifts in the motivations driving institutions to emphasise and be strategic about the international dimension of higher education.

A study of the various rationales for internationalisation is becoming more and more of a complex and challenging task because there are many different variables to consider (Knight and de Wit, 1995). In an attempt to bring a framework and some logic to the discussion on rationale, the first level of analysis categorises the reasons to internationalise into four groups: political, economic, academic and cultural/social. These are not necessarily clear and distinctively different categories. In fact, one of the changes that is occurring is that there is more integration or blurring of these categories. A second major trend is that there are changes happening within the categories as well. The following discussion will elaborate on these changes.

The reasons to internationalise from a *political* point of view are perhaps more relevant to a national perspective than an institutional perspective. Historically, international education was seen as a beneficial tool for foreign policy especially

17

with respect to national security and peace among nations. While this is still a consideration today, it does not have the importance it once did.

In the present era of increased globalisation of economies, technologies, communication, etc., there is a potential threat to the healthy survival of national identities and culture. The possibility for the homogenisation of cultures (often referred to the "MacDonaldisation" of culture) is a risk often cited by smaller and/or developing nations. In fact, globalisation has been referred to by some countries as synonymous with denationalisation and sometimes westernisation. Others would label globalisation as modernisation and a route towards finding solutions to global concerns such as environment, health and crime. However, if one does interpret internationalisation as a response to the denationalisation orientation of globalisation, then internationalisation can be considered and used by some countries as a way to strengthen and promote their national identity. This then becomes an important political rationale at the national level.

Likewise cultural, scientific and educational exchanges between countries are often justified as a way to keep communication and diplomatic relations active. However, there is a growing trend to see education in terms of an export product rather than a cultural agreement. With the massification of higher education increasing at an exponential rate, there is strong interest on the part of large and small countries to make the export of education products and services a major part of their foreign policy. In fact, we can see major shifts in foreign policies where education was primarily seen as a development assistance activity or cultural programme to one where education is an export commodity. This shift to a market orientation introduces the economic rationale for internationalisation of higher education.

The *economic* rationale has increasing importance and relevance. As a result of the globalisation of the economy, a growing interdependence among nations and the information revolution, countries are focusing on their economic, scientific and technological competitiveness. Effective ways to improve and maintain a competitive edge is through developing a highly skilled and knowledgeable work force and through investing in applied research. Both of these strategies involve the higher education sector. Thus at the national or regional level there is a closer and closer link between internationalisation of the higher education sector and the economic and technological development of the country.

Another important factor related to the labour market is the identification of competencies which are considered essential for new graduates to function in a more international work environment. The research to date has been sporadic at best and has served to highlight the need for further work to be done on this issue. Such work will require closer collaboration between the private sector and the education sector. This type of co-operation has not been very strong in the past and will require efforts and changes of attitude on both sides.

At the institutional level, the economic motive or market orientation is becoming more prevalent as well. Rationalisation of higher education systems and deep cuts in higher education budgets have made institutions look for alternative sources of funds. Many are looking to international markets for the export of products and services as an important revenue generating activity. This has resulted in a rigorous debate as to whether the export of education products to international markets is in fact contributing to the international dimension of teaching, research and service or is contributing income to the operating budget of the institution. Clearly, there can be a direct and beneficial relationship between an international market orientation and the internationalisation of the primary functions of a university/college or institute. However, the key phrase is "can be" which implies that this is not always the case. The more important issue is the need for an institution to be clear and explicit about its rationale for internationalisation and to ensure that the objectives, priorities and strategies are consistent with the stated rationale.

If one is to ensure that improving the quality of higher education is the primary goal of internationalisation, not the development of international export markets, it is essential to find the balance between income generating motives and academic benefits. Is the benefit of increased funding for international initiatives (given that a portion of the income earned is invested in other internationalisation activities) sufficient to describe a commercial international education activity as contributing to the international dimension of scholarship and research? Or are there other factors to be considered? How do we differentiate an international export/trade type of education activity which does *not* make a significant contribution to the international dimension of the exporting institution from those international activities which are income generating and *also* have a positive impact on the teaching, research, and service functions of the institution? These are questions which need further exploration and illustrate the close relationship (or confusion) which seems to be developing between economic and academic rationales.

The *academic* rationale for internationalisation is directly linked to the early history and development of universities. The fact the concept of universe is inherent in the name university illustrates this point. For hundreds of years there has been international mobility of scholars and an international dimension to research. At the same time, it is also important to take note of new trends, one of which is the influence of the market approach on higher education and the emphasis on quality both from an improvement and accountability perspective. One of the leading reasons cited for internationalising the higher education sector is the achievement of international academic standards for teaching and research. The pursuit of international standards is an increasingly controversial issue. Concern is expressed about the uniformity and homogeneity that can result from the excessive emphasis on internationally recognised standards. There are many complex factors at play in this debate, and it is prudent to be aware of concerns about a "cookie cutter" approach to education, yet, at the same time, try to achieve international standards of excellence in scholarship and research.

It can be rigorously debated whether internationalisation is an end in itself, as is often articulated, or as a means to an end, with the end being the improvement of the quality of education. It is assumed that by enhancing the international dimension of teaching, research and service there is value added to the quality of our higher education systems. This premise is clearly based on the assumption that internationalisation is considered to be central to the mission of the institution and is not a marginalised endeavour.

The *cultural and social rationale* for internationalisation appears to be of diminished importance and is taking on a different orientation than in the past. The preservation and promotion of national culture are becoming a strong motivation for those countries which consider internationalisation as a way to respect cultural diversity and counterbalance the perceived homogenising effect of globalisation. The acknowledgement of cultural and ethnic diversity within and between countries is considered as a strong rationale for the internationalisation of a nation's education system.

Related to this point is the need for improved intercultural understanding and communication. The preparation of graduates who have strong knowledge and skill base in intercultural relations and communications is considered by many academics as one of the strongest rationales for internationalising the teaching/ learning experience of students in undergraduate and graduate programmes. In fact, many would argue that attention to intercultural relations has to start much earlier than tertiary level of education.

In much the same way that the competency approach to internationalisation focuses on the development of international and intercultural abilities, the cultural and social rationales focus more on the development of the individual – the student, staff member or teacher – instead of the nation or the educational institution. The emphasis is on the overall development of the individual as a local, national and international citizen. Citizenship involves more than being a productive member of the wealth generation sector which the economic rationale clearly emphasises.

In summary it is important to repeat that these four groups of rationales are not distinct or exclusive categories. An individual's, an institution's, or a country's rationale for internationalisation is a complex and multi-leveled set of reasons which evolve over time and in response to changing needs and trends. Therefore, the purpose of using these categories is to try to illustrate the breadth and complexity of factors which need to be taken into account when one is trying to articulate the most important reasons for internationalising higher education. The interrelationship and sometimes integration of these four categories is increasing, thereby sometimes blurring the picture and making the need and task of identifying clear rationales ever more important but ever more challenging. The next section looks at the rationale from the perspective of different stakeholder or constituency groups.

Stakeholders' perspectives

In an attempt to clarify the rather complicated question of "internationalisation according to whose perspective" three major sectors are identified. They are called sectors because within each sector, there are many different stakeholder groups, all of whom have their individual and perhaps different viewpoints on why (and how) higher education should be internationalised. The three groups are the government, the education and the private sectors.

The *government sector* includes the different levels of government ranging from supra-national bodies to national, regional and local. Within the government sector there are, of course, many different stakeholder groups which have a vested interest in the international dimension of high education. The most obvious are the education departments. However, as the previous sections on rationale points out there are other governing units such as foreign affairs, culture, economic development and trade, science and technology which all have an interest in the international dimension of higher education.

The *education sector* is equally diverse because it is necessary to look at the sector from the system level, the institutional level and the individual level. Among the many stakeholder groups in the education sector are the different types of institutions (colleges, institutes, polytechnics, universities) which make up a system; the scholarly research and discipline groups; the professional and membership associations; the students, teachers, researchers, and administrators and of course other advocacy or issue groups.

The *private sector* is another heterogeneous group due to the varied interests of the manufacturing, service or trade companies, the nature of their products and services as well as their geographical interests. Another influencing factor is the size of the company and whether it is local, national or transnational in ownership. It is important to recognise that the private sector is much broader than private education providers.

Differences and similarities among sectors

The purpose of highlighting the different sector groups and the myriad of stakeholder groups within each sector is to illustrate that higher education is not the only group with a strong vested interest. Furthermore, each stakeholder group may have its own particular outlook on why it is important to internationalise higher education. The different rationales can imply different means and ends to internationalisation. Thus, it is extremely important for a national system and an institution to be aware of the explicit and implicit motives of different groups. This also may have important implications for quality assessment and assurance methods.

It is clear that different stakeholders will attribute different levels of importance to the four major rationale categories. However, what is most important to note is whether the difference in the level of importance is reason for conflict or collaboration among the stakeholder groups and whether it leads to a weakened or strengthened position for the international dimension. Therefore, it is important for an individual, institution or national body belonging to any of the sector groups to analyse the diversity and/or homogeneity of rationales and assess the potential for conflict of purpose or complementarity of purpose.

Table 2 provides a framework to analyse the level of importance that different sectors may attribute to the four categories of rationale. These cells of the chart have not been filled in as the importance attributed to the various rationales differs from country to country or even institution to institution. Therefore, there is not one universal or "right" chart. The purpose of including the framework is to encourage others to develop a similar type of grid system to help analyse the stakeholder perspectives affecting their institution or system and to identify similarities, differences and potential areas of conflict among the stakeholders.

This section on rationales has addressed the "why" of internationalisation. The next section will focus on the "how", or in other words, the strategies for integrating the international dimension into teaching, research and service. The "why" and "how" are (or at least should be) directly linked. The key motives which have been identified by the institution for internationalisation should direct the goals and objectives which in turn shape the types of strategies which are used to achieve these goals.

Table 2. **Stakeholders' perspectives on the level of importance (high, medium, low) of rationale for internationalisation**

Rationale	Government sector	Education sector	Private sector
Political			
Economic			
Academic			
Cultural/Social			

Source: Author.

Strategies for integrating the international dimension

The process approach and strategies

There are many ways to describe the initiatives which are undertaken to internationalise an institution. They are often referred to as activities, elements, components, procedures or strategies. Strategy is the preferred term because of the inherent notion of planned direction and the fact that it can be applied to academic types of activities as well as organisational types of procedures and policies.

In the process oriented approach to internationalisation, emphasis is placed on the concept of enhancing and sustaining the international dimensions of research, teaching and service. Integration is key to the process and strategies which focus on both academic activities as well as organisational factors are central to achieving a successful and sustainable integration of the international dimension. Therefore, two generic types of strategies are discussed in this section, programme strategies and organisational strategies. Both types of strategies are needed to internationalise an education institution. While they are very different in orientation they need to complement and reinforce each other.

Programme strategies refer to those initiatives which are academic in nature or are related to the teaching, learning, training, research, advising or supporting activities of the institution both at home and abroad. The organisational strategies include policies, procedures, systems and supporting infrastructures which facilitate and sustain the international dimension of the university or college.

Programme strategies

Programme strategies can be divided into four major categories: academic programmes; research and scholarly activities; extracurricular activities; external relations and services both domestically and abroad. Table 3 provides examples of internationalisation strategies in each of the major categories.

The first category of *academic programmes* is perhaps closest to what is considered by many to be internationalisation activities. Currently there seems to be the greatest amount of interest in this area. The different strategies included in this category illustrate the breadth of initiatives that can be undertaken to integrate an international/intercultural dimension into curriculum content and the teaching/learning process for undergraduate and graduate students.

The second category of strategies focuses on *research and scholarly collaboration*. The strategies included in this group can address the substantive nature of the research, the methodology, the research collaborators and the distribution of the research/knowledge. This provides a broad spectrum of ways to integrate an international, intercultural or comparative dimension.

Table 3. **Programme strategies**

Academic programmes	– Student exchange programmes – Foreign language study – Internationalised curricula – Area of thematic studies – Work/study abroad – International students – Teaching/learning process – Joint and double degree programmes – Cross-cultural training – Faculty/staff mobility programmes – Visiting lecturers and scholars – Link between academic programmes and research, training and development assistance
Research and scholarly collaboration	– Area and theme centres – Joint research projects – International conferences and seminars – Published articles and papers – International research agreements – Researcher and graduate student exchange programmes – International research partners in academic and other sectors – Link between research, curriculum and teaching
External relations and services (domestic and abroad)	– Community-based partnerships and projects with non-government groups or private sector companies – International development assistance projects – Customised/contract training programmes off-shore – Link between development projects and training activities with teaching and research – Community service and intercultural project work – Off-shore teaching sites and distance education – Participation in international networks – Alumni development programmes abroad
Extra-curricular activities	– Student clubs and associations – International and intercultural campus events – Liaison with community based cultural groups – Peer groups and programmes – Social, cultural and academic support systems

Source: Author

In terms of internationalisation the category of *external relations and services* has traditionally been oriented to international development activities and bilateral co-operation agreements between institutions. This is gradually shifting to more of a "trade" than "aid" focus. Commercial activities like contract training and the export of educational products and services to international markets are also increasing in frequency and importance. Networks and consortium among education institutions (and also with the private sector) are becoming more popular. Increase attention is now being given to the development of alumni groups in foreign locations. This category of internationalisation strategies is therefore one which seems to be fundamentally changing in orientation and increasing in importance.

Extracurricular activities can be an effective way to internationalise the total educational experience of both domestic and international students and help to bring a comparative perspective to the classroom.

The large number and diversity of internationalisation programme strategies are obvious and can be rather overwhelming. It is therefore essential that each institution be clear about why it wants to internationalise and what objectives it wants to achieve. When the rationale and objectives are articulated the next step is to ensure the programme strategies support and are consistent with the overall purpose and expectations for internationalising the education institution.

Organisational strategies

Organisational strategies include those initiatives which help to ensure that the international dimension is institutionalised through appropriate human resources, policies and administrative systems. The focus on organisational strategies is what distinguishes the process approach from the other approaches. By stressing the importance of integrating the international dimension into the institution's mission statement, planning and review systems, policies and procedures, hiring and promotion systems one is working toward ensuring that the international dimension is institutionalised.

Table 4 presents examples of organisational strategies (Knight 1994; Knight and de Wit, 1995). These strategies have been grouped into the following four generic categories: governance; operations; support systems; and human resource development.

This is a selection of organisational strategies, not a comprehensive list. Each organisation has its own organisational culture and governance/operating systems which affect the choice and success of different strategies. However, these organisational strategies are generic enough to warrant serious consideration as to how appropriate they are to achieve its stated purpose and goals for internationalisation.

Table 4. **Organisational strategies**

Governance	– Expressed commitment by senior leaders – Active involvement of faculty and staff – Articulated rationale and goals for internationalisation – Recognition of an international dimension in mission statement and other policy documents
Operations	– Integrated into institution-wide and department planning, budgeting and quality review systems – Appropriate organisational structures – Communication systems (formal and informal) for liaison and co-ordinator – Balance between centralised and decentralised promotion and management of internationalisation – Adequate financial support and resource allocation systems
Support services	– Support from institution-wide service units, *i.e.* student housing, registrariat, counselling, fund-raising, etc. – Involvement of academic support units *i.e.* language training, curriculum development, library – Student support services for international students studying on campus and domestic students going abroad, *i.e.* orientation programmes, counselling, cross-cultural training, student advisors, etc.
Human resource development	– Recruitment and selection procedures which reorganise international and intercultural expertise – Reward and promotion policies to reinforce faculty and staff contribution to internationalisation – Faculty and staff professional development activities – Support for international assignments and sabbaticals

Source: Author

The purpose of this chapter has been to introduce the key concepts behind what is meant by the term internationalisation of higher education; what are the different approaches to internationalisation; why is it important; what are the reasons why different stakeholder groups promote and support internationalisation; and what are the major strategies used to internationalise a higher education institution. This analysis is important as background information to the discussion of the assessment and assurance of quality and the international dimension of teaching/learning, research and service functions of higher education institutions.

Bibliography

AIGNER, J.S. *et al.* (1992),
   Internationalizing the University: Making it Work, CBIS Federal, Inc., Springfield, Virginia.

ARUM, S. and VAN DE WATER, J. (1992),
   "The Need for a Definition of International Education in US Universities", in C. Klasek (ed.), *Bridges to the Future: Strategies for Internationalizing Higher Education*, Association of International Education Administrators, Carbondale, Illinois, pp. 191-203.

BACK, K., DAVIS, D. and OLSEN, A. (1996),
   Internationalisation of Higher Education: Goals and Strategies, IDP Education Australia, Canberra.

DAVIES, J. (1992),
   "Developing a Strategy for Internationalisation in Universities: Towards a Conceptual Framework", in C. Klasek (ed.), *Bridges to the Future: Strategies for Internationalizing Higher Education*, Association of International Education Administrators, Carbondale, Illinois, pp. 177-190.

De WIT, H. (1993),
   "On the Definition of International Education", *European Association for International Education Newsletter*, No. 11, pp. 7-10.

De WIT, H. (1998),
   "Rationale for Internationalisation of Higher Education in Millenium", Revista do Instituto Superior Politecnico de Viseu, ano 3, No. 11, pp. 11-19.

HARARI, M. (1989),
   Internationalisation of Higher Education: Effecting Institutional Change in the Curriculum and Campus, Center for International Education, California State University, Long Beach, California.

OECD 1999

HARARI, M. and REIFF, R. (1993),
"Halfway There – A View from the Bridge", *International Educator*, Vol. 3, No. 1, pp. 16-19, 46.

HUNTINGTON, S. (1996),
The Clash of Civilizations and the Remaking of World Order, Simon and Schuster, New York.

KERR, C. (1991),
"International Learning and National Purposes in Higher Education", *American Behavioural Scientist*, pp. 17-41.

KLASEK, C. (1992),
Bridges to the Future: Strategies for Internationalizing Higher Education, Association of International Education Administrators, Carbondale, Illinois.

KNIGHT, J. (1994),
Internationalisation: Elements and Checkpoints, Canadian Bureau for International Education, Ottawa.

KNIGHT, J. (1995),
Internationalisation at Canadian Universities: The Changing Landscape, Association of Universities and Colleges of Canada, Ottawa.

KNIGHT, J. and de WIT, H. (1995),
"Strategies for Internationalisation of Higher Education: Historical and Conceptual Perpectives", in H. de Wit (ed.), *Strategies for Internationalisation of Higher Education – A Comparative Study of Australia, Canada, Europe and the United States of America*, European Association for International Education, Amsterdam.

KNIGHT, J. and de WIT, H. (1997),
Internationalisation of Higher Education in Asia Pacific Countries, European Association for International Education, Amsterdam.

MESTENHAUSER, J.A. and ELLINGBOE, B.J. (1998),
Reforming the Higher Education Curriculum: Internationalizing the Campus, The American Council on Education and Oryx Press, Arizona.

2

Quality and Quality Assurance
by
David Woodhouse

The issues of quality and quality assurance are of increasing importance in the higher education sector. The purpose of this chapter is to provide an introduction to the meaning of these rather complex concepts; to discuss the different approaches to quality assessment; and to identify some of the world-wide trends and concerns related to quality assurance and higher education.

The increasing preoccupation with quality

Many governments, believing that a large corps of highly educated people is essential for the prosperity of society, are committing a large percentage of the public funds to higher education, in order to provide places in degree and diploma courses for increasing numbers of students. With the increased funds comes an increased concern on the part of government to be reassured on three counts. Firstly, are the higher education institutions explicitly planning and organising to produce the graduates required by society, *i.e.* are their objectives appropriate? Secondly, is the money being spent well, *i.e.* are the higher education institutions operating efficiently? Thirdly, are the higher education institutions producing the desired graduates, *i.e.* are they operating effectively?

These concerns have led to new interpretations of the concept of quality. Traditionally, the word quality was associated with ideas of excellence or outstanding performance. Much has been written in recent years on the evolving meaning of "quality" in higher education, and many definitions suggested (Harvey and Green, 1993), but the most commonly now accepted is "fitness for purpose". This allows institutions to define their purpose in their mission and objectives, so "quality" is demonstrated by achieving these. This definition allows variability in institutions, rather than forcing them to be clones of one another. This at least is the theory, but whether it is achieved depends also on the culture. For example, systems based on the United States model tend to be comfortable with very differ-

OECD 1999

ent higher education institutions, but British-based systems often have policies that tend towards the reduction of variability.

These concerns have also led to a great increase in activities external to the higher education institutions that we might call external quality review (EQR), and the establishment of EQR agencies. These agencies are intended to hold higher education institutions accountable for the resources they enjoy, to provide independent affirmation of the quality achieved by the higher education institutions, and to assist higher education institutions to improve their quality. EQR can be related to national, regional or sectoral needs, but at heart it is an institutional issue. The specific purposes of EQR suggested by the above discussion are embedded in different rationales in different places. As a broad-brush categorisation, EQR in the United States (accreditation) was set up by the institutions themselves to permit an informed response to the transfer of students and the admission to graduate programmes across a large and diverse country. In mainland western Europe, governments have until recently tended to micro-manage higher education institutions, but have now backed off in return for the submission of the institutions to EQR regimes. In the United Kingdom, the move has been in the opposite direction, with hitherto highly independent institutions being brought under multiple EQR regimes. In eastern Europe, South America and to some extent in Africa a major impetus for EQR has been the need to handle a proliferating private sector; and in Asia, EQR is bringing some order to very large higher education systems.

Institutional attitudes to an EQR regime depend not only on the regime itself, but also on what preceded it (*i.e.* whether it is more or less stringent than the previous external controls) and on the cultural context.

The phrase quality assurance refers to the policies, attitudes, actions and procedures necessary to ensure that quality is being maintained and enhanced. It may include any one or more of the approaches described in the next section. Quality assurance is sometimes used in a more restricted sense, either to denote the achievement of a minimum standard or to refer to assuring stakeholders that quality is being achieved (*i.e.* accountability).

Approaches to quality

The different educational systems and the different stages of maturity of the institutions and systems mean that different approaches are taken by the EQR agencies in different countries. Some systems use more than one approach, either carried out by the same agency or by different ones.

Audit

It is a check on an organisation's explicit or implicit claims about itself. When an institution states objectives, it is implicitly claiming that this is what it will do, and a quality audit checks the extent to which the institution is achieving its own objectives. When the claims are explicit (as in financial reporting or if the institution has done a self-quality audit), audit becomes a validation (or otherwise) of those claims. Audit asks "are your processes effective?" (*i.e.* in achieving your objectives). The output of an audit is a description of the extent to which the claims are correct. An audit is sometimes called a review.

ISO (Standards New Zealand, 1994) defines quality audit as a three-part process, checking: 1) the suitability of the planned quality procedures in relation to the stated objectives; 2) the conformity of the actual quality activities with the plans; and 3) the effectiveness of the activities in achieving the stated objectives. That is, quality audit looks to find the following closed loop:

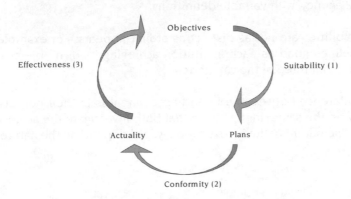

The following current variants can be distinguished:

- *Direct audit*: The EQR agency investigates whether the institution's processes are effective. In theory, the higher education institutions need provide no special documentation.
- *Validation audit*: The institution reviews its own processes (as it should do from time to time), and reports the results of the review in special documentation. In determining whether the result is valid, the EQR agency will inevitably do some direct auditing, *i.e.* it will check whether processes claimed to be effective in fact are.
- *Meta-audit*: The institution has quality assurance processes, and processes for checking their effectiveness. The EQR agency investigates the latter. In theory no special documentation is needed.

Assessment

Assessment is an evaluation that results in a grade, whether numeric (*e.g.* a percentage or a shorter scale of say 1 to 4), literal (*e.g.* A to F) or descriptive (excellent, good, satisfactory, unsatisfactory). There may or may not be a pass/fail boundary somewhere along the grade spectrum (or it may simply be a two-point scale). Assessment asks "how good are your outputs?". The output of an assessment is the grade. An assessment is sometimes called an evaluation.

The definition of assessment depends on the meaning of "good". Rather than trying to choose from the many definitions, it is more useful to ask "who has the responsibility and authority for defining 'good'?". This may be:

- The institution/department, etc.
- The EQR agency, with the same definition for all institutions/programmes, etc.
- The EQR agency, with variable definitions.

These possibilities are not as distinct as at first appears. For example, if an EQR agency defines good as each institution achieving its own objectives, the definition fits into all three of the categories.

The core difference between audit and assessment is in their outputs: their processes may be the same, in the sense that both investigate the achievement of objectives. (The nature of the investigation would depend on the nature of the objectives.)

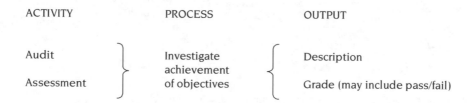

ACTIVITY	PROCESS	OUTPUT
Audit	Investigate achievement of objectives	Description
Assessment		Grade (may include pass/fail)

Accreditation

Accreditation is an evaluation of whether an institution qualifies for a certain status. The status may have implications for the institution itself (*e.g.* permission to operate) and/or its students (*e.g.* eligibility for grants). Accreditation asks "are you good enough (in various ways) to be approved?", that is, "are you fit to be approved?", where "approved" implies admission to some category.

In theory, the output of an accreditation is a yes/no or pass/fail decision, but gradations are possible, usually in the context of a transitional phase (towards or away from pass). Thus, both assessment and accreditation can result in one of several scores on a linear scale. Accreditation is also called licensing or registration.

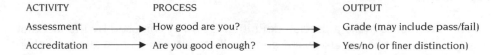

ACTIVITY	PROCESS	OUTPUT
Assessment ⟶	How good are you? ⟶	Grade (may include pass/fail)
Accreditation ⟶	Are you good enough? ⟶	Yes/no (or finer distinction)

These two activities have different emphases, but similar outputs.

Specialised or professional accreditation is an evaluation of whether an institution or programme qualifies its graduates for employment in a particular field (such as law or medicine).

The three concepts can be compared by reference to a natural five-point checking sequence:

- Are the higher education institutions' objectives appropriate?
- Are its plans suitable for these objectives?
- Do its actions conform to its plans?
- Are its actions effective in achieving its objectives?
- What is the measure of the objectives?

As usually applied, none of the three processes covers all five steps. Accreditation covers 1-4; audit covers 2-3; and assessment covers 5 and possibly 2-4. Thus we have:

Objectives Appropriate	Plans Suitable	Actions Conform	Actions Effective	Outcomes Measured

Although the definitions differentiate between the three concepts (audit, assessment and accreditation), according to some interpretations they can coincide. Following an audit, which has determined the extent to which the institution's claims are valid, this extent may be indicated by a percentage, which turns the audit into an assessment as defined above. Now, if qualifying for a certain status is defined in terms of achieving at least a certain percentage of one's claims, then the audit has also been an accreditation.

All these processes can be carried out by the institution or by an external body, but self-assessment and self-accreditation would not normally be seen as cred-

OECD 1999

ible. However, as with audit, an institution could self-assess or self-accredit initially, so the external process becomes a validation (or rebuttal) audit of the institution's own conclusions. Again, there is a situation in which the three concepts merge or mingle.

Any attempt to make a precise definition is further confused by the fact that most of these terms are also used generically to refer to any review or evaluation process.

Quality improvement

Whether from below or above the accreditation threshold, is a different issue to accountability, and many people believe that the two functions are incompatible, and cannot be achieved by the same EQR agency. However, they are so closely linked that it is more sensible to have the same agency sensitively attempting both than to try to separate them. Also, in checking for achievement of the threshold, an accreditor gains experience of what is good and effective, and can assist institutions to improve – whether up to or up from the threshold. However, quality improvement does not need the same investigative methods as accreditation or audit or assessment. Most external quality review is based on a site visit, but it may not be the best approach to combine quality improvement or strategic considerations with the accountability-oriented accreditation visit.

Other possibilities include:

- Use the visit for accountability, with separate consultation, training, and research activities for quality improvement.
- Use data checking by correspondence for accountability, with a variety of visits for quality improvement.
- Have temporal separation of the EQR agency's accountability and quality improvement modes.

Trends and issues

With the trend towards similar systems, and the commonality of concerns about the performance of higher education institutions, it is not surprising that there are many common threads running through the ways being used to address these concerns, and that similar issues emerge, independently, in different countries (Woodhouse, 1996).

International aspects

Fifteen years ago, there were few EQR agencies outside the United States. At about that time, the United States began to be concerned about the quality of its institutions overseas operations, and the regional accrediting agencies began to send teams abroad to accredit these. Unfortunately, although the various regional accreditors consider similar factors for accreditation, their approaches are sufficiently different that it has raised questions overseas about the quality and effectiveness of the process. An institution offering programmes from the United States institutions in three regions is subject to three slightly different American accrediting procedures. Some years ago, the United Kingdom became similarly concerned about its institutions overseas activities and now sends teams abroad to audit these.

Auditing or accrediting programmes offered abroad is always difficult, not only logistically but also philosophically. In the United States, the Center for Quality Assurance in International Education was set up in 1991 to address some of the concerns relating to international American education. With the rapid growth over the last ten years of the number of EQR agencies around the world, a new problem has emerged. If an institution in country A offers programmes in country B, should these programmes be subject to the external quality arrangements of country A or country B or both?

In 1995, an international organisation called the Global Alliance for Transnational Education (GATE) was established. Its central purpose is to ensure that quality issues are not overlooked when education crosses national boundaries, and to provide institutions with a mechanism for independent certification of quality that could avoid their having to undergo multiple review processes.

Another approach to avoiding multiple review is to provide a mechanism for mutual recognition of the work of external quality assurance agencies, and this is a current project of the International Network of Quality Assurance Agencies in Higher Education, which was established in 1991.

International comparability

Increasingly, interest and developments in this area are being driven by economic considerations, through trade blocs and professional associations. It has, for example, become a major pre-occupation in Europe. Although education was not well-addressed in the initial declarations setting up the European Community, the agreements on mobility across Europe have obvious consequences for the mutual recognition of graduates, programmes, etc., as do agreements such as GATS (the General Agreement on Trade in Services). Student mobility programmes such as ERASMUS have been popular and effective; and various professional associations are working on aspects of mutual recognition of qualifications.

Standards

Closely related to both quality and international comparability is the question of standards. Are your graduates at the same standard as my graduates? This has been a sleeper in a number of systems. The United Kingdom funding councils tried to assess teaching quality against absolute standards, and ended up doing it against each department's own objectives, but with a subjective excellence factor thrown in. The United Kingdom's Higher Education Quality Council (HEQC) was required to check institutional procedures for quality and standards, but it was not for several years that it addressed the latter aspect. It then embarked on an extensive project (the Graduate Standards Project) to investigate the general conception and understanding of standards, and to explore possibilities for establishing them more explicitly and achieving them more securely (HEQC, 1997). Preliminary conclusions are that academic standards do not have an objective existence, but could be established at minimum threshold levels. However, such an undertaking would be expensive, and might only be of short-term value as standards change over time. Nonetheless, the Quality Assurance Agency (QAA, the successor to the HEQC) is attempting to do this (QAA, 1998).

Autonomy

Quality is the responsibility of the individual institutions, and they are expected to be publicly accountable. Unfortunately, institutional autonomy and academic freedom are often confused, and both can become excuses for institutional failure to listen to what the world is saying. The latter can also lead academics to treat their jobs like voluntary work.

Ownership

EQR agencies are usually established either by the government, or by the higher education institutions themselves, often at the instigation or requirement of the government. There are various balances of ownership and governance. In the United States, the regional and general national accrediting agencies are owned by the groups of institutions they accredit. The country has a strong tradition of independent institutions, and accreditors would find it difficult to impose any requirements on them beyond what is agreed, jointly by the institutions' representatives on the governing boards of the accrediting agencies, as being essential to institutional quality. Elsewhere, the most common system is that the EQR agency is close to government, either as a statutory body answerable to the government, or as an arm of government. The former system is open to suspicions that the EQR agency may be an institutional defence mechanism and/or too lenient with its institutions. The latter system may emphasise funding and/or national priorities, and the agency may have less freedom of action. Professional (specialised) accreditors may tend towards caution and conservatism (Dill, 1998).

Number of agencies

In many cases, professional programmes are subject to two forms of external review, one by the relevant professional association and a more general one. In some higher education systems, all programmes and/or institutions are responsible to two or more review agencies. Where multiple agencies are used, the efficiency of the system needs to be considered very carefully: are activities being duplicated? Are conflicting requirements being applied? (Woodhouse, 1995).

Purpose of review

Reviews may have one or more purposes. Typical reasons for review include:

- Assessment: where are you now?
- Improvement: where can you get to?
- Accountability: what did you do with what you had?
- Professional certification/accreditation: what do your graduates know?
- Problem identification: what's wrong?
- Problem solving: what can you do about what's wrong?
- Funding: how much money do you need?

Not all purposes are compatible.

Improvement vs. accountability

These two purposes raise the question of incompatibility more often than any others, and there is an uneasy balance between them as objectives of EQR (Vroeijenstijn, 1995). It is a conflict observable more generally in the discipline of evaluation (House, 1978). Many people claim they are incompatible, as the openness essential for improvement will be absent if accountability is the aim. Others claim that they are inseparable, as accountability can always be re-phrased to focus on improvement.

The dual requirement is being addressed differently in different countries. In the United Kingdom, the HEQC had two groups, one of which carried out academic audits, while the other attended explicitly to quality enhancement (Middlehurst and Woodhouse, 1996). The latter group used the audit reports to design quality enhancement activities. It also developed guidelines on good practice and identified ways in which the audit process itself might be improved.

Focus: vertical

The focus of quality review may be on the institution as a whole, or on departments, programmes, the library, the careers office, etc. The need for some sort of explicit assessment at both institutional and programme or sub-unit level is being increasingly recognised. The United Kingdom has used separate agencies, but this appears to create an excessive load. In New Zealand (Woodhouse, 1994), universities are expected to initiate their own external programme-level reviews, and when the EQR agency audits the institution as a whole, it evaluates the scope

37

and effect of the programme-level reviews. A recent report has suggested that a more co-ordinated approach be adopted in the United States (Ewell *et al.*, 1997).

Focus: horizontal

The focus of quality review may be on aspects that cut across the whole institution, such as research, teaching, student support services, the international dimension or community outreach. There are clear dangers in piecemeal assessments, including duplication of activity, and the juggling of resources to bolster the function currently under review. On the other hand, a total, comprehensive review can be an unwieldy undertaking. Overlapping reviews must be carefully co-ordinated, and the information gathered used to help build a total institutional picture.

Scope

Some higher education systems have two sorts of institutions, namely universities and polytechnics (*technikons, fachhochschulen*, etc.). These may be functionally distinguished by awards offered, namely degree or sub-degree (diploma, etc.), or by the emphasis of all the courses, namely theoretical or applied. The scope of some EQR agencies is confined to one sort of institution, while other agencies cover all higher education institutions. Other agencies are restricted to considering only one of the types of award (*e.g.* degrees only), even if it means looking at only part of an institution.

Another categorisation of institutions is by fund source, namely private or public. In some jurisdictions, the government has set up EQR agencies to oversee the public institutions, while private ones are left to market forces. In other countries, the converse holds, namely private institutions are thoroughly checked, but for various reasons (*e.g.* political or traditional) the public institutions are not required to submit to such checks.

Methods

Most EQR agencies use the same basic sequence of processes, namely self-review and report, followed by an on-site investigation (visit) by an external group or team, that then produces a report. The depth and scope of the self-review varies greatly between systems.

Nonetheless, to the extent that systematic self-review is becoming widespread, institutions are experiencing many of the same problems and needs of EQR agencies (including the need for precise definition of purpose, selection and training of reviewers, decision-making, and implementation of review outcomes). The review of a department by the institution feels very much like an external review to that department.

In some systems, the agency seeks further information outside the self-review process. For example, the Danish *Evalueringscenteret* (evaluation centre) carries out extensive surveys of students, recent graduates and employers (Thune, 1993). These surveys are done by various sampling techniques and are relatively costly, taking up to one-third of the budget of an evaluation. These surveys are the first comprehensive discipline-based surveys carried out in Denmark, and the institutions find them to be one of the most useful outcomes of the review process.

In China, accreditation is even more heavily data-based. In Shanghai province, for example, after a self-evaluation report has been submitted, the Higher Education Bureau conducts extensive written surveys of graduates, employers, external examiners, students and staff (running into thousands of questionnaires) (Wei *et al.*, 1993).

Peer review

Investigation by the external team is commonly called peer review. This is a term with a long tradition in academia, and it has usually denoted an evaluation by another academic or academics, usually in the same discipline (Frederiks *et al.*, 1993). Increasingly, the membership of quality review teams is not restricted in this way, and in many systems they now include people outside academia and people from other countries [*e.g.* Denmark, Hong Kong, China, New Zealand, the European pilot projects]. Since, to the world outside academia, the term "peer review" has rather cosy connotations, it may be better to drop it in favour of, for example, "independent review".

Performance indicators

The factors for consideration in an evaluation must be clearly specified in advance, together with the criteria by which the factors will be judged and possibly performance indicators for the criteria. The extent to which performance indicators are used in EQR varies significantly (Cave *et al.*, 1997). Most commonly, institutions are invited to specify their performance indicators, indicating why and how they use them. The EQR agency, through its independent review team, then forms its own interpretation of the results. In other systems, however, higher education institutions are expected to report against a system-wide set of performance indicators, which are then available to the EQR process.

Review reports

The EQR agency produces reports on the institutions it reviews. In some systems, the reports are public, while in others they are not. In the latter case, summaries of or commentaries on the reports may be made public in various ways. In general, it is essential to consider the readership of any report, and the information desired by that clientele.

39

Funding

The link between the results in these reports and public funding (or other support) varies. Reviews of research often feed directly into the funding decisions, but there is a general view (inside academia) that basing funding for teaching solely on the basis of reviews of teaching would lead more to problems being concealed than solved. However, several countries (including Australia, England, Scotland, and many American states) have linked marginal funding to quality reviews. This can cause problems for external reviewers who are charged with reviewing for quality improvement, as the higher education institutions will fear that the information provided to the EQR body will inevitably reach the funding arm of government.

Enforcement and follow-up

The enormous amount of time and money being put into quality assurance activities (both external and internal) will be wasted unless these activities have a beneficial effect. Enforcement, which is about consumer protection, is a controlling function, while follow-up is a service function. It is noticeable that few EQR agencies have a thorough formal mechanism for following up the results of their reviews, and many do nothing about it, or simply ask the institution what it has done. Many EQR agencies are ambivalent about the possession of sanctions for enforcement of their recommendations, believing on the one hand that institutional improvement is not helped by threat of police action, while recognising on the other hand that some institutions are so weak that they are reluctant to even try to improve unless the EQR agency can insist on action.

Effect and impact of quality assurance activities

What are the effects of all these EQR activities? This is currently a live issue, subject to several major research projects.

EVALUE (Dubois, 1998) is a 30-month European Community project including 11 institutions in eight countries. It concludes that evaluation can cause improvement in university performance under certain conditions:

- Cognitive, learning, cultural, identity and legitimating effects during the evaluation.
- The nature and presentation of the evaluation results, and the presence or otherwise of sanctions relating to these results.
- The institution and its members take ownership of the evaluation results.
- Permanent mechanisms for internal evaluation are established.

An OECD/IMHE project is investigating the effect on decision-making in higher education institutions of the EQR practices to which they have been subjected over recent years (Brennan, 1995). A United Kingdom-based study (Brennan *et al.*, 1997) has investigated the effect of teaching quality assessments in 53 subject groups in 12 higher education institutions. The conclusion was that 65% of the recommendations had been acted upon, especially when the assessment results fell below institutional expectations, and especially when the recommendations were sensitive to the nature of the institution and programme. The self-assessment phase was also considered to have been most beneficial.

A research study of Dutch universities (Frederiks *et al.*, 1993) produced evidence of changes that appeared to be related to the discipline reviews, but there is another whole question of the relation between change and improvement. Another project is under way in South Africa to study the effect of the universities audit unit. In all these studies, the complexity of the system, the pace of change, and the myriad actors make it difficult to disentangle the effects of the EQR agency alone.

An audit approach is, in theory, the least intrusive, because it is based on the institutions own objectives. It is also better oriented towards improvement, as it investigates processes and comments on them. (Checking results only tells us what has happened, whereas checking processes tells us what will or may happen.) On the other hand, some discussions with staff in the United Kingdom institutions suggest that its effects are felt only by senior management.

Accreditation provides a cut-off or threshold, which can be low or high as desired. Accreditation is a gatekeeper role, and it is no criticism of an accreditor to observe that it has nothing to say to an institution that is very far above the quality threshold. A low cut-off leads to a caveat emptor situation, with many institutions that are well above the threshold, for which accreditation does nothing. A high cut-off is safer for users, but can deter innovation and new institutions. All the regional accrediting agencies in the United States are working on ways to make accreditation more relevant to institutions that are well above the threshold, and to build in a commitment to continuous improvement.

Assessment is usually carried out at programme level, so its effects are similar to those of specialised accreditation. The public impact of assessment can be affected by the number of dimensions used. Grading on a single dimension lends itself to the production of a ranking (of institutions, departments, etc.) with the associated results and problems.

By way of conclusion it needs to be said that quality assurance in higher education is being addressed in many ways and for many purposes, not all of them consistent. There are many similarities of structure, but many nuances which can result in wide differences in practice. Also, many differences between countries relate more to cultural, political, economic and social considerations, than to the technical aspects of quality assurance mechanisms.

41

Bibliography

BRENNAN, J. (1995),
"Authority, Legitimacy and Change: The Rise of Quality Assessment in Higher Education", OECD/CERI/IMHE Seminar on Institutional Responses to Quality Assessment, Paris, December.

BRENNAN, J., FREDERIKS, M. and SHAH, T. (1997),
"Improving the Quality of Education: The Impact of Quality Assessment on Institutions", Quality Support Centre, The Open University.

CAVE, M., HANNEY, S. and KOGAN, M. (1997),
"The Use of Performance Indicators in Higher Education", 3rd ed., *Higher Education Policy*, *Series* 3, Jessica Kingsley Publishers.

DILL, W.R. (1998),
"Specialised Accreditation: An Idea Whose Time has Come? Or Gone?", *Change*, 30, 4, pp. 18-25.

DONALDSON, J., OTTENWAELTER, M.O., THUNE, C. and VROEIJENSTIJN, A.I. (1995),
"The European Pilot Project for Evaluating Quality in Higher Education: European Report", European Commission.

DUBOIS, P. (1998),
"EVALUE: Evaluation and Self-evaluation of Universities in Europe, Final Report", European Community, TSER.

EWELL, P.T., WELLMAN, J.V. and PAULSON, K. (1997), "Refashioning Accountability: Towards a Co-ordinated System of Quality Assurance for Higher Education", Education Commission of the States.

FREDERIKS, M.M.J., WESTERHEIJDEN, D.F. and WEUSTHOF, P.J.M. (1993),
"Self-evaluation and Visiting Committees", Proceedings of 18th Meeting of ASHE, November.

FREDERIKS, M.M.J., WESTERHEIJDEN, D.F. and WEUSTHOF, P.J.M. (1994),
"Stakeholders in Quality: Improvement or Accountability in Quality Assessment in Five Higher Education Systems", in L.C.J. Goedegeburre and F.A. van Vught (eds.), *Comparative Policy Studies in Higher Education*, Lemma, Utrecht.

HARVEY, L. and GREEN, D. (1993),
"Defining Quality", *Assessment and Evaluation in Higher Education*, Vol. 18, No. 1.

HEQC (1997),
"Graduate Standards Programme: Final Report", Higher Education Quality Council.

HOUSE, E.R. (1978),
"Assumptions Underlying Evaluation Models", *Education Researcher*, March, Vol. 7, No. 3, pp. 4-12.

KALKWIJK, J.P.T. (1995),
"One Cycle of Quality Assessment of University Education in Retrospect", Third Meeting of INQAAHE, Utrecht, pp. 34-42.

MIDDLEHURST, R. and WOODHOUSE, D. (1996),
"Coherent Systems for External Quality Assurance", *Quality in Higher Education*: *Theory and Practice*, 1, 3, pp. 257-268.

QAA (1998),
"Quality Assurance: A New Approach", *Higher Quality*, No. 4, October, Quality Assurance Agency for Higher Education.

STANDARDS NEW ZEALAND (1994),
"Quality Management and Quality Assurance – Vocabulary", Australian/New Zealand Standard AS/NZS ISO 8402.

THUNE, C. (1993),
"Evaluation and Quality Assurance of Higher Education in Denmark", INQAAHE *Newsletter*, Issue No. 5, October, QAA, pp. 12-15.

VROEIJENSTIJN, A.I. (1992), "External Quality Assessment, Servant of Two Masters? The Netherlands University Perspective", in A.Z. Craft (ed.), *Quality Assurance in Higher Education*, The Falmer Press.

VROEIJENSTIJN, A.I. (1995),
"Improvement and Accountability: Navigating Between Scylla and Charybdis", *Higher Education Policy, Series* 30, Jessica Kingsley Publishers.

43

WEI, R., XU, B. and YANG, W. (1993),
"Specific Analysis on Qualification Evaluation for Shanghai Higher Education Institutions", Paper presented at HKCAA/PRC Joint Seminar on Accreditation, March.

WOODHOUSE, D. (1994),
"The Academic Audit Unit in Context", INQAAHE *Newsletter*, Issue No. 7, July, QAA.

WOODHOUSE, D. (1995),
"Efficient Quality Systems", *Assessment and Evaluation in Higher Education*, 20, 1, pp. 15-24.

WOODHOUSE, D. (1996),
"Quality Assurance: International Trends, Preoccupations and Features", *Assessment and Evaluation in Higher Education*, 21, 4, pp. 347-356.

3

An Introduction
to the IQRP Project and Process
by
Jane Knight and Hans de Wit

The first two chapters focused on the importance and nature of internationalising higher education and the necessity of assessing and ensuring the quality of the international dimension. This chapter builds on this discussion and has three objectives. The first objective is to provide information on the purpose, principles, and activities of the Internationalisation Quality Review Process (IQRP) project. The second objective is to present the internationalisation quality review process methodology and instrument which were developed and piloted during the project. The third objective is to introduce the case studies of the institutions which have piloted the IQRP methodology.

Description of the IQRP pilot project

Introduction to the IQRP pilot project

The IQRP project is an initiative undertaken by the Programme on Institutional Management in Higher Education (IMHE) of the Organisation for Economic Co-operation and Development (OECD) in collaboration with the Academic Co-operation Association (ACA).

Since 1994, IMHE has had an active programme focusing on a cross-country analysis of institutional level strategies for the internationalisation of higher education. Two important issues and concerns have emerged from this work: *i)* quality assessment and assurance of these strategies; and *ii)* the contribution that internationalisation has made to enhancing the quality of higher education. At the IMHE Seminar on Internationalisation Strategies held in October, 1995 it was decided to proceed with a pilot project on quality assurance and internationalisation and to co-operate with ACA. This organisation has established a Working Group on Research, Evaluation, Analysis and Quality Assurance and is working on the theme of quality in international academic co-operation, mobility and exchange.

During the first phase of the project, 1995-97, IMHE/OECD and ACA jointly developed the IQRP instrument and documents and tested the IQRP in three different institutions: University of Helsinki, Finland; Bentley College in Boston, the United States; and Monash University, Melbourne, Australia. Members of the IQRP project team participated in the pilots as external peer reviewers so that ways to improve the process could be noted.

Members of the team also presented the Internationalisation Quality Review Process at several international conferences in order to receive feedback from experts on the design and tools of the IQRP. Based on the experiences and lessons learned from the pilots and the feedback from experts, the team was encouraged to revise the IQRP documents and to pilot the process in a wider group of institutions and countries. Thus, phase two of the project, 1997-98, was planned and focused on two primary objectives: *i*) revising the original materials and *ii*) testing the IQRP in different types of educational institutions in a wider variety of country/cultural contexts. During phase two, the IQRP was piloted in six more institutions: National University of Mexico; Warsaw School of Economics, Poland; Tartu University, Estonia; Moi University, Kenya; Universiti Sains Malaysia; and Royal Melbourne Institute of Technology, Australia.

It was also recommended that a publication be prepared as a way to document and publicise the findings of the project and to ensure a wider distribution and potential use of the IQRP methodology and instrument.

Rationale for the pilot project

The key role of internationalisation and its contribution to higher education is gaining more recognition around the world, in both developed and developing countries. As internationalisation matures, both as a concept and process, it is important that institutions of higher education address the issue of the quality assessment and assurance of their international dimension.

If internationalisation of higher education is understood to mean "the process of integrating an international dimension into the teaching, research and service function of the institution", then it is critical to address the quality issue from three perspectives.

The first perspective refers to the inclusion of the international dimension as a key component in the general academic quality review systems operational at the institutional or system level. This is based on the premise that an international dimension is part of the university/college mission and major functions and is thus included as one of many elements addressed in the quality review procedures.

The second perspective looks at the quality of specific internationalisation policies, procedures and programmes (*i.e.* international students, work/study abroad, student/faculty exchanges, research, language instruction, technical assistance, etc.).

The third perspective concerns the internationalisation of quality assurance procedures itself. These procedures are in general nationally based. It is increasingly acknowledged that quality assurance procedures benefit from an international input and approach.

The purpose of the IQRP project is to bring attention to the importance and complementarity of the various perspectives and to develop a process which would guide institutions in undertaking a quality assessment and assurance review of their specific internationalisation initiatives.

Objectives of the IQRP pilot project

Three major objectives have governed the activities of phases one and two of the project:

- To increase awareness of the need for quality assessment and assurance in the internationalisation of higher education.
- To develop a review process whereby individual institutions can adapt and use a set of guidelines/framework to assess and enhance the quality of their internationalisation strategies according to their own aims and objectives.
- To strengthen the contribution that internationalisation makes to the quality of higher education.

Assumptions

There are a number of assumptions which have formed the foundation of the pilot project. They are listed below and complement a set of guiding principles which have guided and shaped the methodology and instruments of the IQRP.

The IQRP is based on principles of self-assessment and peer review and is guided by the institution's own mission and aims.

While the review process and framework is intended to be international in application, acknowledgement and recognition of differences among institutions and countries is essential.

47

The self-assessment and external peer review reports on the pilot institutions are for their use only. There is no intention to publish the reports or make any comparisons across institutions. The development and refinement of the process and the self-assessment guidelines is the primary objective and intended outcome of the project.

It is important to recognise that higher education quality review systems, even at the institutional level, benefit from an international perspective and input. This is especially true for the Internationalisation Quality Review Process and therefore importance was given to ensuring that the IQRP is developed by an international team, is tested in different countries and is international in application.

Pilot institutions

The IQRP project team worked with a small number of institutions from different countries in the testing of the IQRP instrument. With this group of selected pilot institutions the IQRP team members served as external peer reviewers in order to monitor the effectiveness of the document and guidelines. In choosing pilot institutions to test the IQRP, a number of factors were taken into consideration.

One element was the stage of the internationalisation process at the institution. It was important to test the IQRP at different levels of the development of the international dimension. It became clear that IQRP could also work well as a planning tool for those institutions in the initial phase of developing an institution-wide internationalisation strategy.

It was also important that there be a diversity of country and cultural contexts in which IQRP was piloted to ensure that lessons were learned from experience where there are different approaches and assumptions about evaluation. For instance, the fact that IQRP is based on the concepts of self-assessment and peer review may not be appropriate or successfully used in certain cultural contexts.

It was intended that IQRP be tested in institutions with different educational orientations or purposes, *i.e.* technical institutes, specialised colleges, comprehensive universities, undergraduate colleges, polytechnics, etc.

The testing of the IQRP in eight countries in five different parts of the world, provided valuable information for the design of the final guidelines. Three comprehensive institutions (Helsinki, Monash and Tartu) and two specialised institutions (Bentley and Warsaw) with well developed strategies for internationalisation used the IQRP to assess their strategies. Two comprehensive universities (Mexico and Moi) used the IQRP to assist in moving from a marginal and implicit international dimension to a central and explicit internationalisation strategy. One comprehensive university (Sains Malaysia) used IQRP to create awareness of the importance of an internationalisation strategy by assessing certain parts of the institution. The Royal Melbourne Institute of Technology used IQRP to further the mainstreaming of the international dimension throughout all functions of the university including their off-shore programmes.

The IQRP framework

The IQRP pilot project followed a framework for self-assessment and peer review, that was documented in project document "The Development of an Internationalisation Quality Review Process at the Level of Higher Education Institutions" (ACA, IMHE/OECD, March 1996) for pilot phase one, and project document "The Development of an Internationalisation Quality Review Process for Higher Education Institutions" (IMHE/OECD in consultation with ACA, March 1997) for pilot phase two. During the two phases changes were made in the framework, based on the experiences in the pilot institutions. Some of the more important changes are described in Chapter 10 of this publication. The framework is the outcome of the pilot project, and is part of the guidelines, as presented at the end of the book, p. 241. This section describes the principles of IQRP, its operational framework, the outline for self-assessment and the peer review.

The purposes and principles of the IQRP

The IQRP is a process whereby individual academic institutions assess and enhance the quality of their internationalisation efforts according to their own stated aims and objectives. The review includes procedures and guidelines to be adapted and used in both a self-assessment exercise and an external peer review.

Purpose of the IQRP

The purpose of the IQRP is to assist institutions of higher education to assess and improve the quality of their international dimension by focusing on the identification of:

- The achievement of the institution's stated policy (goals and objectives) for internationalisation, and its implementation strategy.
- The integration of an international dimension into the primary functions and priorities of the institution.
- The inclusion of internationalisation as a key theme area in the institution's overall quality assurance system.

Guiding principles of the IQRP

The starting point for the review is the institution's own stated aims and objectives. The review process assesses the extent to which institutions actually achieve the aims and objectives which they set for themselves. The assessment of the

49

relationship between objectives and actual achievement is the core of the quality issue.

The purpose of the self-assessment process is to provide a critical self-evaluation of a variety of aspects related to the quality of the international dimension of the institution. The more emphasis given to self-assessment, the more self-assessment will function as a means of training and assisting the institution to take responsibility for its own quality improvement. Self-assessment should not be seen as an exercise to produce information for the external peer review team, but rather as an opportunity to conduct an analysis of the extent and quality of internationalisation initiatives.

The purpose of the external peer review is to mirror the self-assessment process and to provide feedback and a complementary analysis to the self-assessment by the institution, from a different, external and international perspective. The emphasis is not on actual fact-finding, inspection or evaluation.

Whilst the review process is intended to be international in application, acknowledgement and recognition of differences among institutions and countries is essential.

The self-assessment and external peer review reports are for the use of the evaluated institution only. The reports are owned by the institution and can only be published by the evaluated institution or with its explicit approval.

The review process is not intended to prescribe practices or advocate uniformity or standardisation of internationalisation approaches or procedures. There is no explicit or implicit comparison with other institutions involved, it is an exercise for self-improvement. This does not exclude the possibility for an institution to combine the IQRP with other quality assurance procedures such as bench marking, ISO 9000, Global Alliance for Transnational Education (GATE) certification or Total Quality Management (TQM).

The review process is seen as part of an ongoing cycle process of advocating, planning, implementing, rewarding, reviewing and improving the internationalisation strategy of the institution.

Who should conduct an IQRP?

The IQRP guidelines and framework are designed in such a way that they are applicable in a great variety of circumstances. Experience of the use of IQRP has indicated that the IQRP can be used in:

- The university and the non-university sectors of higher education.
- Small and large institutions.

- Comprehensive and specialised institutions.
- Private and public institutions.
- Institutions wishing to assess an existing strategy for internationalisation but also institutions wishing to initiate such a strategy.
- Institutions in both developed and developing countries.

The specific circumstances of the institution and of the objectives have to be taken into consideration in the implementation of the IQRP. This implies a flexible use of the guidelines. Whilst the IQRP is guided by the institution's own goals and objectives for internationalisation, there are major areas which are common to many institutions and which the review process will address.

The operational framework of IQRP

The emphasis and orientation of the self-assessment exercise is on the analysis of the quality of the international dimension of the institution. It should not merely be a description of the various internationalisation initiatives. At the same time, it is recognised that, in particular for those institutions that intend to use the IQRP to initiate an internationalisation strategy, a qualitative and quantitative inventory of international activities will be an important basis for the assessment.

Self-assessment

a) Role and structure of the self-assessment team

A self-assessment team (SAT) is formed at the institutional level and is given the mandate to:

- Collect the necessary information.
- Undertake a critical analysis of the provision for and the quality of internationalisation, as well of the contribution of internationalisation to higher education.
- Prepare the self-assessment report (SAR).
- Engage the commitment of various parties inside and outside the institution to the whole process.

The institution chooses the members of the team to reflect the internal organisation and aims of the institution. Ideally, the SAT should consist of (central and departmental level) representatives of both the administrative and the academic staff as well as of international and domestic students. In order for the team to be functional and accomplish its task in a relatively short period of time the group should be relatively small and the members should be administratively supported to undertake the work.

51

The full endorsement and active involvement of the institutional leadership is essential for the success of the self-assessment team.

The SAT has a chairperson and a secretary. It is recommended that the key person in the institution responsible for internationalisation strategy and policy be the chair of the SAT. The secretary will be responsible for organising the work of the SAT and for co-ordinating the preparation of its report.

The SAT will exchange comments with the peer review team (PRT) on the self-assessment report prior to its visit, will prepare the programme of the visit in conjunction with the PRT and will discuss the draft peer review report with the PRT. The secretary of the SAT plays an important role in the liaison with the secretary of the PRT.

b) The design of the self-assessment process

It is important to emphasise that the whole purpose of the self-assessment is to analyse the international dimension, not merely to describe it. Collecting data to build a profile of all the different activities, programmes, policies and procedures related to the international dimension of the institution is only a first step. It certainly is an important and rather time-consuming step, in particular for those institutions that use the IQRP as an instrument to assist in the preparation of an internationalisation strategy and that do not yet have mechanisms in place to make a quantitative and qualitative description of these activities, programmes, procedures and policies. But the analysis of an institution's performance and achievements according to their articulated aims and objectives for internationalisation is critical to assess and eventually assure the quality of the international dimension and the contribution internationalisation makes to the primary functions of the institution. The process must indicate directions for improvement and change of the internationalisation strategy of the institution, which follows from the diagnosis itself.

The self-assessment report should give an adequate profile of the institution, reflecting its particular directions, priorities and effectiveness of its operations, and is aimed at giving directions for improvement and change. The self-assessment should recognise and reflect the potential diversity of rationales and strategies between faculties and schools.

This self-assessment should not primarily be regarded as a descriptive exercise, but rather as a critical analysis of the institution's performance and achievements in the field of internationalisation. Besides providing the necessary information, an analysis should be made of strong and weak points, indicating how well the various internationalisation efforts are being realised, and formulating potential avenues to improvement.

Terminology often differs from country to country and from institution to institution. Institutions should use the terminology which they find appropriate for their situation. It would be helpful to add a note of explanation so that the peer review team understands the use of terms in their institutional context.

c) General outline of the self-assessment

The self-assessment outline is designed as a template for the process of analysing the aims and objectives, the performance and achievements, the strengths and the weaknesses, and the opportunities and threats regarding the international dimension of the institution. It needs to be emphasised that it is the international dimension which is being reviewed and analysed. For instance in the case of curriculum activities and research initiatives, it is how the international dimension is addressed and integrated which is under review, not the curriculum or research itself.

The outline is a starting point and a guide for the institution to undertake the preparation of their self-assessment. It is not intended to be a coercive structure. There may be questions and issues included in the outline which are not relevant or appropriate to the mandate of the specific institution. In other instances, there may be important items which have not been included in the outline which the SAT wants to address and therefore these should be added.

The main categories of the outline for the self-assessment are as follows:

- Context.
- Internationalisation policies and strategies.
- Organisational and support structures.
- Academic programmes and students.
- Research and scholarly collaboration.
- Human resources management.
- Contracts and services.
- Conclusions and recommendations.

The complete outline, as part of the IQRP guidelines, is provided at the end of the publication, p. 241.

d) The self-assessment report

After the self-assessment exercise has been completed, the preparation of the self-assessment report is the next step in the IQRP. The report should be limited to a maximum 20-30 pages plus possible annexes. It would be most helpful if it followed as much as possible the general pattern of the self-assessment outline, with the caveat that not all the categories and questions in the outline may be appropriate or relevant for each institution. It is also important to stress that the self-assessment team may add issues not covered by the framework but considered relevant. Thus the self-assessment outline should be considered as a guide only, intended to introduce many of the areas and issues to be considered and to encourage the teams to undertake an analytical approach.

The self-assessment report will be much more than a description of the type and extent of internationalisation efforts; it is meant to critically assess and address ways to assure and improve the quality of internationalisation of the teaching, research and public service functions of the institution in the light of existing issues and forthcoming challenges.

The language of the self-assessment report will in part be guided by the make-up of the PRT. During the initial stages of the IQRP the secretary of the SAT will decide in collaboration with the secretary of the PRT the working language of the PRT site visit and also the language of the self-assessment report. If a language, other than the native language, is used for the SAT report and PRT reports, it is assumed that the supporting documents, such as data annexes, can be in the institution's national language.

The peer review team members are to receive the self-assessment report at least one month prior to the visit. The institution will send one copy of the SAT report for each of the PRT members plus two additional copies for the IQRP-archive to the secretary of the PRT.

The peer review process

a) Membership of the peer review team

The peer review team (PRT) can vary in size but requires a minimum of three members and usually consists of three/four members; all must be external and independent of the institution undergoing the IQRP. The experts appointed to the PRT will have a general understanding of quality assessment and assurance, will have a particular expertise in the internationalisation of higher education, and will be knowledgeable and experienced in higher education.

The PRT chairperson with preference should be a senior academic with expertise in higher education governance and preferably the development and management of international relations/programmes of institutions of higher education. Knowledge of recent developments in the internationalisation of higher education globally is also essential. The expertise and experience of the other members should relate to the priority areas of the institution's aims and objectives for internationalisation. They should be knowledgeable in academic culture and governance. It is considered an additional asset to have a team member with prior experience in quality assurance review exercises.

The composition of the PRT is primarily international, but it may include one member from the institution's home country or a member with considerable experience in and knowledge of higher education in the country (but not related to the institution itself). At least one member of the PRT should come from another continent than the institution's home country. The first person is likely to be able to provide the PRT with insight in the national context, the second person is likely to provide the PRT with a perspective beyond the regional context.

One member of the PRT will serve as secretary and be responsible for organising the work of the PRT and for co-ordinating the preparation of its report. The secretary of the PRT is also the liaison person with the secretary of the SAT for the response of the PRT to the self-assessment report, and the preparation of terms of reference of the site visit.

The secretary of the PRT prepares a written agreement with the institution on the terms under which the self-assessment and peer review reports will be placed in the IQRP archives of IMHE. The following options are available:

- The documents will not be included in the archives.
- The documents will be included but permission for use by parties other than the institution has to be granted by the institution on each occasion.
- The documents will be included and permission is granted by the institution to IMHE to provide a copy of the documents upon request.

In the last two cases, the SAT secretary is responsible for providing two copies of the self-assessment and peer review reports to IMHE.

The institution will be responsible for all costs related to the peer review. It is important to clarify and agree upon all the financial aspects of the review, before individuals are invited to become members of the PRT.

b) Responsibilities of the peer review team

The task of the PRT is to examine:

- The goals for internationalisation of the institution and whether they are clearly formulated.
- How these goals are translated into the institution's curriculum, research and public service functions and if the institution is providing the necessary support and infrastructure for successful internationalisation.
- How the institution monitors its internationalisation efforts.
- The institution's capacity to change; and its autonomy in order to improve its internationalisation strategies.

55

- The adequacy of its diagnosis and proposals for change and improvement.

The PRT members will receive the self-assessment report at least one month prior to the visit. After thoroughly reviewing it, the PRT may provide general comments to the self-assessment team prior to the site visit. Then the PRT will pay a two- to three-day visit to the institution and produce a detailed report (20-30 pages) for the institution no later than two months after the site visit.

c) Design of the peer review process

Ideally the PRT meets once before the actual site visit to discuss the self-assessment report, finalise the terms of reference for the visit and agree on the division of labour among the team members. It is preferable that such a visit takes place at the institution where the IQRP is carried out, and includes also a meeting with the self-assessment team to discuss the comments on the self-assessment report and to prepare the programme.

It is acknowledged that in many cases for reasons of costs and time such a preparatory visit will not be possible. In that case, the secretary of the PRT will establish active communication with the other PRT members to receive their comments on the self-assessment report and suggestions for the terms of reference and the programme of the site visit. Also, in that case it is recommended that the secretary will pay a preparatory visit to the institution to discuss the comments on the self-assessment report and finalise the terms of reference and the programme with the SAT.

The PRT will have on site a half or one day planning meeting prior to the commencement of the official PRT programme.

Based on the initial review of the self-assessment report and discussions of the PRT, a decision will be made as to whether additional information is needed before the site visit. Prior to the site visit a list of specific issues to be addressed, individuals/groups to be met will be prepared by the PRT and forwarded to the self-assessment team.

The institution prepares a detailed schedule for the PRT visit, which may vary in length between three and four days. The team should meet key persons among selected administrative and academic staff, students and graduates, and, if possible, representatives of other bodies (both inside and outside the institution) responsible for, or involved in international activities. Where appropriate, it may be useful to visit the units where students or staff receive assistance and service as well as other related facilities of the institution. In some cases it may be appropriate for PRT members to visit locations and programmes of the institution in other parts of the world. The schedule also includes meetings with the self-assessment team, the leadership of the institution, chief academic and administrative staff responsible for international activities and related support services.

At the end of the site visit, the PRT meets with the SAT to comment on the site visit and discuss the plans for the preparation of the PRT report and its presentation to the institution. The PRT also meets with the senior leaders of the institution to give a brief report, oral and preliminary, on the visit.

d) The peer review team report

The major issues to be addressed in the PRT report are the following:

- Is the institution's self-assessment report on internationalisation sufficiently analytical and constructively critical?
- Are the strengths and weaknesses of the institution's international activities clearly articulated and the plans for improvements clearly presented and realistic?
- Is the institution achieving the aims and objectives it has set for itself?
- How do the institution's vision and goals relate to the development and sustainability of its international activities within the totality?
- What action is required of the institution in order to monitor progress and provide continuing impetus?

The PRT prepares a draft report and sends it to the chairperson of the SAT within two months after the site visit. The draft version of the PRT report is meant for review and comment before the final version is submitted. This provides the institution with the opportunity to correct any factual errors and errors of interpretation. The institution provides feedback to the PRT within two weeks of the receipt of the draft version of the report. It is up to the PRT to decide whether to include the recommended changes in the report or not. Any required changes are made by the PRT and the final report is sent to the institution. The institution will receive five copies of the report. It is up to the institution to decide how many additional copies it will make for internal and external use. The institution has complete ownership of the report. The report is strictly confidential if the institution wishes to consider it as such.

The follow-up activities and other use of the PRT report is the responsibility of the institution. It is suggested that both the self-assessment report and the PRT report be made available at least internally. Given the self-assessment process has taken place with active participation by many individuals and groups in the institution, it is important that they are included in an open discussion or planning session about the comments and suggestions made in both the SAT and PRT reports. In other words, the use and follow-up to the reports is an integral part of the process of assessing, assuring and improving the internationalisation strategies.

57

Follow-up phase

The institution may add to the IQRP a follow-up phase, approximately one and a half to two years after the PRT report has been delivered. This is particularly important in those cases in which the IQRP is used to start a process for the development of an internationalisation strategy within an institution. This follow-up phase could take place with or without involvement of an external peer review. As part of this follow-up phase the self-assessment team will write a document analysing the progress in implementing the recommendations made by the SAT and PRT and the internationalisation strategy. It will make recommendations for further actions. This report is the basis for a one- to two-day site visit by the PRT to give their views on the progress and the recommendations for further action.

The decision to include a follow-up phase in the IQRP preferably should be taken at the beginning of the IQRP and at latest at the end of the PRT visit.

The case studies

Careful consideration was given to the selection of the institutions for the piloting of the IQRP methodology as it was important for the IQRP to be tested in a variety of situations. The experiences of six of the nine pilot institutions are described in this part of the publication. That does not imply that the three other cases were not illustrative for IQRP or not relevant projects. The timing of these reviews in relation to the preparation of this publication in combination with the potential overlap in types of institutions and strategies, resulted in the choice of these six. Each of the six cases is different, for geographic reasons, given the type and size of the institutions, their level of internationalisation and their motivation for using IQRP.

The case studies are: National University of Mexico, Bentley College, University of Helsinki, Monash University, Moi University and Warsaw School of Economics.

The case studies follow a general outline:

- Context; nature and extent of the international dimension.
- Reasons for taking part in the IQRP.
- Description of the self-assessment.
- Description of the peer review.
- Follow-up and impact of IQRP.

At the same time, each case study emphasises specific characteristics of the process.

The case of the National University of Mexico provides an insight in the way this institution has planned the quality review process. This case is also interesting for the fact that IQRP was used as a starting point for developing an explicit internationalisation strategy; and it shows how IQRP can be used within a extremely large and broad institution of higher education.

The case of Bentley College gives emphasis to the importance of the self-assessment exercise. As an illustration, an abridged version of the self-assessment report of Bentley College is included as an annex of this case study.

Helsinki University was the first institution that undertook IQRP. The impact of the review on the institution gets special attention in this case, as well as the peer review process. As an illustration, an abridged version of the peer review report is included as annex of this case study.

Monash University is an interesting case, because it shows how IQRP can be used in combination with other quality assessment instruments to direct their strategic planning process.

Moi University is an example of the use of IQRP in a developing country and how to use IQRP as a strategic planning tool.

The case of the Warsaw School of Economics emphasises the use of IQRP as an instrument to review the international orientation of a specialised institution of higher education in a context of radical political, economic and educational reforms.

The case studies presented in this publication not only are an interesting illustration of their own state of internationalisation, and of the opportunities that IQRP presented to them. They also have learned important lessons that have guided the formulation of the guidelines that are the product of this project – lessons that will be described in Chapter 10.

PART II
THE INTERNATIONALISATION QUALITY
REVIEW PROCESS:
OVERVIEW AND CASE STUDIES

4

Planning for the IQRP
The National University of Mexico

by

Salvador Malo, Rosamaria Valle and **Karin Wriedt**

Introduction

This chapter describes the way in which the International Quality Review Process (IQRP) contributes to the review of the international activities of a large, complex university and the formulation of a policy proposal for such activities.

The National University of Mexico (UNAM) is one of the largest and most complex universities in the world and the most important higher education institution in the country. It offers the widest range of undergraduate and graduate degree programmes, undertakes the largest share of the scientific research in the country and the activities involving cultural dissemination and the preservation of national heritage for which it is responsible are of national importance. Its organisational structure consists of authorities led by the Rector and collegiate bodies responsible for making decisions on the university's academic development. UNAM is characterised by its nationalism and Latin American vocation. Although it has not yet defined an explicit policy for its international activities, it has a long history of exchanges and agreements with institutions in other countries, particularly the United States and Western Europe.

The obvious differences between the educational model used in the Mexican higher education system and those of the United States and Europe, together with UNAM'S specific characteristics, suggest that the experience resulting from the use of the methodology and conceptualisation of the IQRP in this university could be of interest to other institutions and countries. Moreover, an intrinsic part of its value is the fact that it can be applied to various institutional and national contexts. This article therefore stresses the way in which the methodology was used and the changes that had to be made as well as its scope and limitations.

The chapter begins with a general description of UNAM in the context of the Mexican higher education system, the background to its international activities and the reasons behind the university's interest in the International Quality Review Process (IQRP). It describes the steps involved in the process, as well as the difficulties faced and the results obtained in both the quality review process and in its incorporation into university life. The document ends with a description of the actions deemed necessary to consolidate an institutional policy of international activities in the near future.

Mexico's higher education system

Higher education in Mexico consists of undergraduate and graduate degree programmes. Students wishing to enrol in undergraduate degree programmes must have proof of graduation from senior high school while those wishing to pursue graduate studies are required to have completed an undergraduate degree. Undergraduate studies in Mexico are the most important in higher education, since they prepare students for the exercise of a profession or discipline. Graduate studies include specialisation, master and doctoral degrees.

Undergraduate degree programmes, the first cycle of higher education, are completed in four or five years (with the exception of medicine which requires six years) with curricula that may be organised on a quarterly, half-yearly or annual basis. The undergraduate curricula (known in Mexico as *licenciaturas*) focus on training students for a particular degree course, or career as this degree programmes are known in Mexico.

In addition to passing the credits established in the curriculum, students at most institutions are required to complete the following in order to qualify for an undergraduate degree: *a*) perform social service, involving 480 hours of unpaid work that benefits society; *b*) submit a dissertation or some other kind of written work; *c*) sit a professional general examination of their knowledge of the area. A significant number of universities also require students to demonstrate reading proficiency in one or two languages other than Spanish, usually English and French. The undergraduate degree authorises legally the practice of the profession.

Undergraduate programmes are generally grouped into six areas, according to criteria established by the National Association of Universities and Higher Education Institutes (ANUIES): natural and exact sciences; education and humanities; agricultural sciences; health sciences; engineering and technology; and social and administrative sciences.

The higher education system in Mexico consists of various sub-systems that are co-ordinated and in some cases funded by the Ministry of Public Education (SEP): the university, technological and teacher training sub-systems, the latter providing training in pre-school, basic and special education. Universities and technological institutes offer undergraduate and graduate degree programmes, although some of these institutions also offer senior high school level studies (*bachillerato*).[1] Since 1984, teachers' colleges have been incorporated into the higher education level, although some teacher training is still given at the high school level.

Sixty per cent of the total number of students enrolled at the undergraduate degree level, and the majority of graduate level students in Mexico are enrolled at public universities. Technological institutions were established to offer students an alternative to undergraduate and graduate degree programmes that would be more closely linked to the job market and regional development. Private higher education institutions offer undergraduate degree programmes and in some cases, graduate studies. In 1991, technological universities were created, with short programmes to meet the requirements of regional development.

Nowadays, the higher education system consists of 748 institutions that grant undergraduate (*licenciatura*) degrees. They are generally organised academically as faculties or schools. Both may offer more than one undergraduate programme, but the term "faculty" is only used in institutions with at least one doctoral degree programme. In 1996, the higher education system had 1 523 956 students enrolled at the undergraduate level, and 77 764 at the graduate level, with 71% enrolled at universities; 6% at technological institutes, 7% at teachers' colleges and 16% at centres, schools and colleges. Private institutions accounted for a total of 24% of all students (SEP, 1997).

The National University of Mexico

The history of Mexican higher education has been closely linked to the history of UNAM. The types of academic organisation described earlier were initially implemented at UNAM and subsequently served as a model for other higher education institutions, both state and private. Its broad infrastructure, range of educational activities and the volume of research it conducts, together with the services it provides, and the fact that it has been used as a model for the creation of other higher education institutions make UNAM the country's leading higher education institution. It continues to play a leading role in the development of higher education in Mexico, although the current range of educational options has spawned a more diverse system of higher education.

---

1. In Mexico, the term *bachillerato* is used to describe the cycle of high school education, lasting three years, and following a nine-year cycle of elementary and secondary education, which is a requirement for enrolling in higher education.

65

UNAM seeks to generate and transmit new knowledge, prepare top-level professionals and preserve, strengthen and disseminate national identity and culture. It has a total enrolment of 267 486 students, 108 010 of whom are enrolled at senior high school, 139 881 in undergraduate programmes, 15 276 in graduate programmes, 910 in preparatory courses and 3 409 in technical and technical-professional levels. Its faculty and researchers total nearly thirty thousand academics (UNAM, 1996).

The main campus is located in Mexico City, with five other campuses in the metropolitan area and four graduate and research campuses in various states. These contain 15 faculties, 9 national schools, 26 institutes and 14 research centres. At the undergraduate level, UNAM offers a choice of 69 programmes; at the graduate level, it offers 81 specialisations, 113 master's degrees and 45 doctoral programmes. It also provides over two thousand continuous education programmes annually (UNAM, 1997).

The principal function of the faculties and schools is to train students at the undergraduate, specialisation and master's degree level, and in the case of faculties, at the doctoral level. They also undertake research and continuous education activities as well as providing services that link faculty and students to society.

The research institutes and centres are primarily concerned with generating knowledge to contribute to the development of their disciplines and the solution of social problems. They also assist faculties and schools in the training of students.

International activities at UNAM

Since its inauguration in 1910 as national university, the institution has been open to other countries. Proof of this was its inauguration sponsored by the Universities of Salamanca, Paris and California, on behalf of 24 other universities of world renown. Since then, the university has been linked to the rest of the world, as shown by the huge diversity of international actions in its teaching, research and cultural dissemination activities.

All the university departments currently have international links with the member countries of the North American Free Trade Agreement (NAFTA) and Latin American countries and, to a lesser extent, with European countries such as Spain, France and Great Britain.

In most of UNAM'S faculties and centres, international activities initially focused on faculty and student exchanges. Nowadays, however, they all, to a greater or lesser extent, have research, academic and technological collaboration agreements with peer institutions, which in turn has enabled them to organise and participate in events, research networks, publications and international consortiums. Some faculties have incorporated new concepts of teaching and knowledge into their curricula that have contributed to the reform of professional and graduate training and attracted students from other countries, especially Latin America.

Recently, and with increasing frequency, faculties, institutes and centres have begun to incorporate international criteria for accreditation, basic bibliography in other languages, mainly in English, and global means of communication such as Internet into their curricula. Scholarship programmes are also available for students pursuing studies abroad.

By their very nature, the two extension centres at UNAM have an international component in their basic functions. The Centre for Foreign Students, which began its activities in 1921 with the opening of a summer school for foreign students, offers students from other countries Spanish language, history, art, and Mexican literature courses. Its extension units in San Antonio in the United States and Hull in Canada disseminate the Spanish language and Mexican culture. The Centre for Foreign Language Teaching provides teaching in 14 languages for students and staff members of the university's faculties, schools, institutes and centres, although English and French courses are in greatest demand.

However, this vast range of activities is offered in an isolated fashion at each of the university's faculties or schools, often at the personal initiative of individual academics, rather than as part of an internationalisation plan. Formal procedures for the management and periodic assessment of these international activities at either individual academic units or the university as a whole have as yet to be implemented.

The social, political, economic and cultural effects of the recent processes of globalisation have led to significant changes in higher education throughout the world, from which Mexico has not been exempted.

One of the main concerns of the present UNAM Rector, Francisco Barnés, is that the university should be transformed in order to maintain its leading position in the country and that this transformation should respond to the profound changes in the international context, including the rapid growth of knowledge and the development of new technologies in information management and communications, as well as the increasing demand for a high degree of specialisation in the labour market.

As a result of the university's openness to an increasingly interconnected world, and the growing internationalisation of education, one of the aims of the current administration is to turn the university into an active participant of the international academic community over the next few years. Consequently, UNAM has had to redefine its role vis-à-vis a new, more complex context. In order to gain support for the desired changes, the current university administration opened for

67

discussion its strategic plan and started a process to integrate an institution-wide work-plan with the consensus of the community.

The IQRP at the National University of Mexico

Within this context, the institution decided to participate in the International Quality Review Process (IQRP) for a number of reasons, including the following: IQRP was regarded as a useful means of evaluating the international dimension while at the same time encouraging the analysis of the quality of the university's main functions; it was thought to be flexible enough to adapt itself to the complexity and scope of UNAM; it would stimulate critical and reflexive analysis; it could enable comparisons to be made between the various university faculties, schools, institutes and centres, and eventually with other institutions; and it was regarded as a useful instrument for reviewing the guidelines, policies and plans for the internationalisation of the university.

From the point of view of IMHE/OECD and ACA, the aim of implementing the IQRP at UNAM was to review the methodology and the instrument used for self-assessment.

Implementation of the IQRP at UNAM was divided into two phases, the first of which consisted of three stages. During the first stage, a pilot group was formed, self-assessment guides were drawn up, and two working sessions were held to prepare for the implementation of the process. The second stage involved the self-assessment process of each participating unit, reports on the exercise, the overall report, a search conference and the incorporation of the results of this conference and the self-assessment guide into the final self-assessment report. During the third and final stage of the first phase at UNAM, a peer review team (PRT) visited the university, and drew up and submitted a report on its visit (Chart 1).

Stage 1: preparation of the self-assessment

Composition of the pilot group

It was decided that the pilot group for the first phase should have both academic faculties and schools and central administration departments, in a way that would reflect the complexity and scope of the university and its various international activities. Eight faculties were selected: architecture, accountancy and administration, engineering, medicine, veterinary medicine and animal husbandry, dentistry, psychology and chemistry. These faculties were chosen because they offer degree courses with a professional orientation that also involves professional certification. The Open University and Distance Learning Co-ordinating Offices (CUAED) were included since they co-ordinate educational modules that are crucial to the internationalisation process. Three institutes and a research centre (the

Institutes for Anthropological Research, Biomedical Research and Materials Research and the Centre for University Studies) represented the four areas of knowledge covered by the disciplines taught at the university: humanities and the arts, biological and health sciences, physics-mathematical sciences and engineering and social sciences respectively. The two extension centres (the Centre for Foreign Language Teaching and the Centre for Foreign Students) organise international extension activities, while the two central administration offices (the Academic Personnel Affairs Office and the Academic Exchange Office) assist academic units in the management of international activities. This group of faculties, institutes and centres have 56 638 students (39% of the total student body) and employ 11 746 academics (45% of the total academic staff).

Self-assessment guides

Self-assessment guides were drawn up using the same guidelines specified in the instrument proposed as a result of the International Quality Review Process carried out at Helsinki University, with certain modifications to adapt it to the specific characteristics of UNAM and the participating units. As a result, five self-assessment guides were prepared, one for each type of unit.

In the guide for the faculties, particular emphasis was placed on the international dimension of the curricula, the teaching and learning processes and the academic activities concerning faculty and students. The guide for the research institutes and centre placed greater emphasis on academic and research collaboration, and the curricula. The guide formulated for the CUAED stressed the international dimension of open, continuous and distance learning. In the guide for the extension centres, greater importance was placed on the activities and characteristics of the students, the exchange agreements with other institutions, their infrastructure and their co-ordination with the academic units. Finally, the guide for the central administration offices was oriented towards the scholarship programmes, activities involving academic support and the management procedures used to support the academic units. All the guides included questions on the procedures used to evaluate the international activities that were not considered in the original instrument.

Statistical analyses

Computer programmes were written to create databases with information on Mexican students and academics abroad and foreigners at the university, scholarships for studying abroad and research programmes and projects in collaboration with foreign universities and institutions. These data were used for the statistical analyses included in the self-assessment report.

OECD 1999

Chart 1. **The Internationalisation Quality Review Process at UNAM**

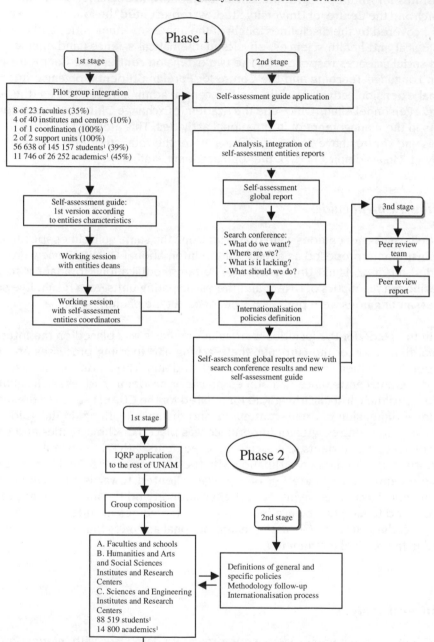

1. Only faculty and students in graduate and undergraduate programmes were considered.
Source: UNAM (1997).

Working sessions

Afterwards, two working sessions were held. During the first session, the group in charge of co-ordinating the process at the university met with the directors of the participating academic units and administration offices, and during the second session they met with those responsible for the self-assessment exercise, designated by the directors.

The aim of the meeting with the directors was to have them become personally involved in the project, explain them the bases and objectives of the process for evaluating the quality of international activities and their importance for higher education institutions, and agree on the organisation of the self-assessment process in each unit, and on the schedule.

Preparatory meetings

Once the directors had agreed to participate in the project, the operational details of the self-assessment and peer review processes were discussed with the peer review team co-ordinator, who paid a visit to UNAM for that purpose. That visit provided an alternative for inviting the whole peer review team for a preparatory visit, and helped to clarify expectations on both sides with respect to the implementation of IQRP at UNAM.

Subsequently, a meeting was held with those in charge of the international self-assessment exercise at each of the participating units to explain the importance, bases, purpose and objectives of the International Quality Review Process, as well as the procedure for conducting the self-assessment exercise and the use of the guides. At these meetings, the general co-ordination mechanisms and the activity schedule were also established. The co-ordinating group maintained close contact with the directors of the units, clarifying doubts and helping to compile data where necessary.

Stage 2: the self-assessment exercise

Preparation of the self-assessment report

During the second stage, the self-assessment exercise was carried out, databases were created and the units' self-assessment reports drafted. The co-ordinating group analysed and incorporated the reports from the various faculties and centres into a single report with statistical analyses, and a search conference was held, the conclusions of which were incorporated into the final self-assessment report together with the new guide. The self-assessment exercise took from six to eight weeks, while the final report and statistical analysis took approximately five weeks to complete.

Below is a description of some of the main difficulties encountered during this stage:

- The time required for the units to conduct the self-assessment exercise was underestimated, since having to compile non-systematised information took longer than anticipated.
- The two aforementioned activities were carried out simultaneously, and in some cases the database was drawn up after the self-assessment exercise; ideally the database should have been drawn up first.
- Formulating five separate guides proved unnecessary, since by clarifying some of the instructions and eliminating others that were redundant it was possible to use a single guide.
- The self-assessment reports tended to consist of lengthy descriptions of the units involved, with a history of their international activities, rather than a critical analysis resulting from group reflection.
- The co-ordinating group found it difficult to provide a summary of the information provided by a complex variety of units without ignoring the essence of their particular features.

Search conference on internationalisation

Due to the fact that it was thought necessary for the directors and those responsible for the self-assessment exercise to have the opportunity of analysing together the results obtained, and fostering reflection on the present and future of internationalisation, a "search conference" (Emery and Trist, 1973) was organised. The aim of this conference was to answer the following questions: what did we want regarding internationalisation? what was our current status? what did we need to do? and what steps should we take?, and to use the answers from these questions to formulate objectives, strategies and goals for the internationalisation activities at UNAM, as well as a policy for incorporating the international dimension into the university's main functions.

In keeping with the methodology used in search conferences, participants were divided into several groups working separately yet simultaneously, each of which discussed in different stages various aspects of internationalisation and its relationship to the university (Chart 2).

The conference began with an introduction describing the methodology to be used, analysing the concept of internationalisation according to Davies (1992) and Knight and de Wit (1995), and stating the general objective of the conference. During the first stage of the conference, the groups analysed what international activities should contribute in order to improve the main functions of the university and formulated an ideal vision of these international activities in both the context of the mission of each of the individual units and in that of the university as a whole.

Chart 2. Search Conference Stages

Introduction

1. Ideal Vision
> groups A, B, C, D

2. Confrontation of Ideal Vision and Present Situation
> general discussion, conclusions

3. Strategic Objectives
> groups A, B, C, D

4. Goals and Proposed Institutional Agenda
> general discussion

During the second stage of the conference, following a reflection on the status given to the internationalisation of the university by each of the various participating groups, the results of the self-assessment were presented, thereby enabling the differences between the university's present situation and an ideal vision of the latter to be confronted.

During the third stage, the groups discussed ways of achieving this ideal vision of internationalisation on the basis of current conditions. They then proposed the objectives, strategies and goals they regarded as necessary for their aim to be achieved.

Finally, during the fourth and final stage of the search conference, the various groups merged into a single group to incorporate their objectives, strategies and goals and propose an institutional policy of internationalisation.

During this day-and-a-half-long meeting, conclusions were reached and key proposals put forward to continue both the stages of the second phase of the process and to formulate an institutional policy of internationalisation:

- Greater awareness was achieved of the importance of the internationalisation activities carried out in the units and of their lack of co-ordination.
- It was decided that these should be systematised by the university and incorporated into its institutional strategic plan, while continuing to regard the needs of the country, the institutional development plan and its own plans as top priority.

73

- It was stressed that the internationalisation of the university should not lead to its academic dependence on other countries.
- A preliminary proposal for an institutional policy was defined with objectives, goals and strategies: "UNAM will implement a series of measures to link its main functions to the international environment in a context of quality that will enable it to compete successfully in a globalised world. This process should also take into account the defence and consolidation of national cultural values and the critical analysis of values stemming from the international context" (UNAM, 1997).

Concern for the defence of national cultural values led to a definition of the phrase "internationalisation of higher education" which includes the term intercultural, as an attempt to highlight the importance of preserving national and institutional values in the process of internationalisation:

"The internationalisation of higher education involves the process of incorporating an international and intercultural dimension into university teaching, research and services." (UNAM, 1997).

Stage 3: the peer review

In preparation for the peer review team (PRT) visit, the PRT co-ordinator was sent a copy of the "Report on the International Quality Review Process at the National University of Mexico". This final report incorporated the conclusions and proposals of the search conference. The document contains six chapters on the mission and national and international contexts of UNAM and each of its units, as well as their internationalisation activities and the conclusions from the search conference. The statistical data on the internationalisation activities, the institutional profiles of UNAM and its units and the new self-assessment guide are contained in the appendices.

The visit by the peer review team to the university marked the start of the third stage of the IQRP at UNAM that ended with the PRT report. The group was made up of four experts: Professor John Mallea, Emeritus Professor at the University of Brandon, Canada, member of the OECD Review Committee for Higher Education in Mexico (1997) and Chairman of the UNAM's PRT; Dr. Manuel Gil-Antón, professor of the Universidad Autónoma de Metropolitana de México; Dr. Marjorie Peace Lenn, Executive Director of the Center for Quality Assurance in International Education, Washington, DC; and Drs. Hans de Wit, Vice-President for International Affairs at the University of Amsterdam, IMHE consultant and co-ordinator of the PRT.

One of the innovations incorporated into the PRT review was the inclusion of a local committee member, Dr. Manuel Gil-Antón, chosen at the suggestion of UNAM because of his experience in the field of the sociology of higher education and in various international research projects on that area and not a member of this university. His contribution to the peer review proved extremely valuable in placing the international dimension of UNAM in a national and regional context.

The work schedule for the PRT visit was drawn as a result of joint consultation between UNAM and the team itself, and the visit was based on the UNAM self-assessment report. The PRT was divided into two groups to visit the various units. Since the PRT was unable to arrange a meeting prior to the visit, the team co-ordinator met with each group member separately, before the team visit. In combination with his preparatory visit to UNAM in the first stage, this proofed to be helpful in the preparation of the peer review.

After the interviews with the directors, academics and students at each of the units, the PRT and the Rector of UNAM analysed the university's international activities. The Rector pointed out that in the past, these activities had been oriented more towards Latin America but that these relations had declined. He concluded that one of the problems that UNAM will face in the near future will be its active incorporation into the international academic community.

The visit concluded with a meeting between the PRT and the directors at which key issues for both parties were discussed.

In short, the visit was extremely fruitful, since the level of communication between the PRT and the directors of the units was such that it permitted the exchange of ideas and information and led to the team's acceptance of the proposal by the UNAM group to add the term "intercultural" to the concept of internationalisation. Moreover, the peer team acquired more information on and a better understanding of the university.

At the same time, as the PRT pointed out in its final report, despite the fact that the team was unable to hold a preparatory meeting to discuss the central aspects of the visit and was not given the assessment report earlier, "these facts were satisfactorily compensated by the review, the information provided by the university, the quality of the self-assessment report and the excellent organisation of the visit by the co-ordinating group of the International Quality Review Process at the National University of Mexico" (Gil-Antón et al., 1997, p. 5).

The first phase ended with the conclusion of the PRT report, "The International and Intercultural Dimension of the Universidad Autónoma de México: Current Realities and Future Perspectives" (Gil-Antón et al., 1997). It concluded that the current international dimension of UNAM operates in a fragmented fashion, which can be defined as *ad hoc* and low priority. The report adds that it is essential to develop a proposal for a plan to incorporate the internationalisation activities, both at the level of central administration and in each of the faculties and research centres; make the objectives and strategies of the programmes more explicit and develop a high level of co-ordination and cohesion between the various

75

programmes and organisational structures of the university and each of its component parts "in order to be able to continue to serve as the academic and cultural engine of a nation in the current context of globalisation" (Gil-Antón et al., p. 14). The report adds that conditions are ripe for UNAM to assume a leading role in the internationalisation of higher education in Mexico.

Conclusions

Regarding the process

The IQRP was a useful experience for UNAM which, as mentioned in the PRT report (Gil-Antón et al., 1997), highlighted its rich international history and wide range of international activities, while affording a critical analysis of its current situation and a definition of the changes needed to enable it to meet future challenges.

The self-assessment process proved to be a useful device for analysing the strengths and weaknesses of UNAM's international activities. It demonstrated its value during the first stage of the IQRP, while in its modified form it could also be used during the next phase.

The self-assessment exercise produced a descriptive and quantitative document on the current status of the university's international activities, which will undoubtedly be extremely useful in conducting a critical analysis of the current state of internationalisation in the university. At the same time, the search conference, instigated by the UNAM, proved to be a valuable strategy, serving as a complement to the self-assessment exercise which led to a critical analysis of the internationalisation activities conducted in the past, as well as those currently being undertaken and of the desirable objectives for the immediate future.

In short, as a result of the IQRP at the National University of Mexico, several important goals were achieved. These included a) a critical self-assessment of the university's internationalisation; b) the systematisation of quantitative information on the current status of its international activities; c) highlighting the importance of the internationalisation of UNAM for its current and future development; d) defining policies, objectives and goals for the future development of internationalisation; and e) carrying out a complementary analysis from an external, international perspective, through the peer review process.

The final self-assessment and peer review team reports, both conclude that the university has programmes that promote the mobility of students, professors and researchers, both Mexican and foreign, the exchange of academic and cultural experiences with institutions from other countries and collaboration agreements and research networks. However, these activities have not as yet been incorporated into an institutional policy aimed at strengthening the internationalisation of UNAM. This is why the peer team rated UNAM's global international strategy as both ad hoc and low priority.

Immediate effects

When the IQRP was being carried out at UNAM, the university was in the process of defining the lines of action, objectives and goals of its strategic plan. In the process implemented for this purpose UNAM opened for discussion its strategic plan, and comments were requested from the directors, collegiate bodies and the whole university community. Therefore, the resulting final document included the most important proposals from the IQRP, legitimising the inclusion of international and intercultural aspects as an important mean to support the university's main objectives and mission.

UNAM's 1997-2000 Institutional Development Plan states that "an unmistakable sign of the times is the internationalisation of ideas, systems and institutions, together with the establishment of exchange and co-operation networks between individuals and institutions" (UNAM, 1998, p. 68). Therefore, "the globalisation and growing internationalisation of education means that UNAM's actions, its international and intercultural alliances and collaborations are instrumental in strengthening and enhancing its main functions" (UNAM, 1998, p. 69).

In addition to statements such as those quoted, UNAM's Institutional Development Plan establishes various goals related to the internationalisation process. Thus, one of the 11 strategic objectives of the plan is to develop more flexible undergraduate and graduate programmes that will be better suited to a more competitive world environment. This increased flexibility will allow the university to offer students greater mobility, thereby enabling them to complete part of their training at other national or international institutions.

In addition, the university has committed itself to the reinforcement of foreign language learning and English proficiency. One of the university's immediate aims is to have all students due to begin their undergraduate courses in 1998 take an English proficiency examination.

The plan also aims to strengthen the internationalisation of research at the university's institutes and centres and expand its academic collaboration and exchange programmes with the best educational and research institutions in other parts of the world.

As far as cultural dissemination is concerned, the university aims to expand its international collaboration and exchange activities in order to foster the knowledge and appreciation of other cultures among its students and disseminate Mexican cultural values abroad.

77

Finally, as part of its institutional planning and evaluation objectives, the plan aims to promote the exchange of national and international experiences concerning these two areas, develop a system of information on the various internationalisation activities and establish indicators that will reflect the diversity of UNAM and incorporate national and international standards.

Future actions

UNAM's participation in the IQRP undoubtedly had positive effects on defining the role of international and intercultural aspects of the institution. However, an institutional policy of internationalisation has yet to be designed. Several actions will be undertaken to achieve this end, including the second phase of the IQRP at the university.

In June 1998, the National University of Mexico was to begin the second phase of the quality review of its international and intercultural dimension, with the participation of the remaining academic units. This stage will entail the self-assessment of the university's remaining academic units organised into three groups. The first comprises faculties and schools, including those outside the university city campus; the second consists of research institutes and centres in the areas of humanities and arts and social sciences, while the third is composed of institutes and centres in the areas of biological and health sciences, physics, mathematical sciences and engineering.

On the basis of the results obtained, the information gained in the earlier stages and the IQRP report, an institutional plan for the international and intercultural activities of UNAM will be elaborated.

Bibliography

DAVIES, J. (1992),
"Developing a Strategy for Internationalization in Universities: Towards a Conceptual Framework", in C. Klasek (ed.), *Bridges to the Future: Strategies for Internationalizing Higher Education*, AIEA, Carbondale.

EMERY, F.E. and TRIST, E.L. (1973),
Towards a Social Ecology. Contextual Appreciation of the Future in the Present, Plenum Press, London.

GIL-ANTÓN, M., MALLEA, J., PEACE LENN, M. and de WIT, H. (1997),
"The International and Intercultural Dimension of the Universidad Nacional Autónoma de México: Current Realities and Future Perspectives", PRT report, October-December, Universiteit van Amsterdam.

KNIGHT, J. and DE WIT, H. (1995),
"Strategies for Internationalisation of Higher Education: Historical and Conceptual Perspectives", in H. de Wit (ed.), *Strategies for Internationalisation of Higher Education: A Comparative Study of Australia, Canada, Europe and the United States of America*, EAIE, Amsterdam.

SECRETARÍA DE EDUCACIÓN PÚBLICA (SEP) (1997),
Datos Básicos de la Educación Universitaria 1995-1996, Dirección General de Educación Superior, SEP, México.

UNIVERSIDAD NACIONAL AUTÓNOMA DE MÉXICO (UNAM) (1994),
La Universidad en el Espejo, México.

UNIVERSIDAD NACIONAL AUTÓNOMA DE MÉXICO (UNAM) (1996),
Agenda Estadística, Dirección General de Estadística y Sistemas de Información Institucionales, México.

OECD 1999

UNIVERSIDAD NACIONAL AUTÓNOMA DE MÉXICO (UNAM) (1997),
"Reporte de Autoevaluación del Proceso de Revisión de la Calidad de la
Internacionalización de la Universidad Nacional Autónoma de México",
Dirección General de Evaluación Educativa, México.

UNIVERSIDAD NACIONAL AUTÓNOMA DE MÉXICO (UNAM) (1998),
Plan de Desarrollo 1997-2000, Secretaría de Planeación, México.

5

The Importance of the Self-assessment Exercise
Bentley College, United States

by

Jerome Bookin-Weiner

Introduction

The Bentley College case is a case where the impetus for involvement in quality review and assessment of the international dimension came from within the institution and specifically from its international education professionals. This chapter introduces the institutional self-assessment undertaken as part of its participation in the IQRP pilot project. The self-assessment report (abridged version), provided as annex to this chapter, illustrates this crucial aspect of the quality review of the international dimension of higher education institutions.

The college and its international mission

Bentley College is an independent, non-sectarian institution of higher education located in the Boston suburb of Waltham, Massachusetts. Approximately 90% of the undergraduate students and 100% of the graduate students are in business fields. Today, the college enrols nearly 3 300 full-time undergraduate students and about 1 850 graduate students, 85% of them part-time. The faculty consists of approximately 200 full-time members – two-thirds of them in business disciplines. Bentley College is accredited by the New England Association of Schools and Colleges to offer bachelor's and master's degrees, and all of its business and accounting programmes are accredited by AACSB.

Today, in the late 1990s, there are approximately 550 international students enrolled in Bentley degree programmes, but since the mid-1920s, Bentley has enrolled students from outside the United States. Nevertheless, as late as 1963 the presence of a mere eight international students led the student newspaper to trumpet in a banner headline "Bentley Goes International". It was not until the mid-1980s that the number of international students exceeded 100 and staff was added to service their needs. In 1985, the Internationalising Bentley Committee was established, which issued a report in August 1986 calling for a comprehensive plan of action. The guiding principles enunciated in that report remain the central international mission of Bentley College:

> "Internationalising a college means internationalising each individual. A Bentley College education should provide each student with a broader, deeper appreciation for other cultures and peoples. Internationalising Bentley is not an add-on programme, it is an attitude. The liberally educated professional in an interdependent world must work at understanding the many and diverse components of that world."

Among the recommendations in the 1986 report was establishment of an international centre at the college to focus attention on issues related to faculty development, internationalisation of the curriculum, faculty exchange and study abroad programmes. In 1995, the Office of International Student and Scholar Services was merged with the Office of International Programmes to become the Bentley College International Centre, with the first Dean of International Education. This brought all of Bentley's international activities (with the exceptions of student and faculty recruitment) together under one umbrella for the first time.

The need for self-assessment

While the overall international education mission remained unchanged, the environment had changed substantially over the ten years since the Internationalising Bentley Report. As a result, the college's President and Provost charged the Dean with undertaking a comprehensive strategic planning process for the future of international education at Bentley during the 1996-97 academic year. In the context of that strategic planning process, Bentley hoped to measure its international dimension and future plans against international standards. Therefore, it was logical for Bentley to become involved in the IQRP pilot project in 1996.

During the spring semester 1996, the International Affairs Committee – seven faculty members appointed to two-year staggered terms by the Faculty Senate – conducted a series of seven focus groups involving faculty, students and administrators. The focus groups were homogeneous in that each one consisted of faculty, students or administrators exclusively and each group consisted either of people heavily involved in international activities or relatively uninvolved. The data collected from these focus groups, which were not attended by members of the International Centre staff and were conducted by faculty in management and marketing familiar with focus group techniques, formed an important part of the "raw material" used by the self-assessment team when it began to assess the strengths and weaknesses of Bentley's international activities.

At the end of the spring semester 1996, Bentley received the IQRP framework and organised its self-assessment team (SAT). Dr. Marylee S. Crofts, Associate Dean of International Education, headed the SAT, which also included three faculty members, the Dean of International Education and two other professional staff members of the International Centre, the Administrative Director for Academic Affairs in the Provost's Office, and representatives of both the Undergraduate and Graduate Admissions offices. Because the work of the SAT was to take place during the summer, it was not feasible to include students.

The SAT divided the sections of the framework amongst themselves and each undertook the project independently. For example, the sections dealing with institutional organisation and policy were drafted by the Dean, those relating to the curriculum, research and faculty development by the faculty members (who divided up this work amongst themselves), those relating to student recruitment by the admissions officers, those relating to study abroad by the Director of Study Abroad, and those relating to international students and scholars by the Director of International Student and Scholar Services. In each section the members of the SAT were asked to pay particular attention to analysis and assessment and to make concrete recommendations for future initiatives and improvements on current activities. This was done in part to be responsive to the IQRP framework and in part to make the exercise as useful as possible to the overall international strategic planning process at Bentley of which participation in IQRP was a part.

As a concrete example of the kind of data assembled, the faculty members divided the academic departments among themselves and each took responsibility for reporting on internationalisation of the curriculum in those departments. They gathered data on the courses with an international focus offered in each department, on the inclusion of international cases and other content in courses that do not have a clear international focus and on enrolment patterns in those courses. They also looked at the involvement of faculty in each department in international activities, including faculty development programmes, institutional development projects, and research.

During the summer of 1996, Dr. Crofts spent approximately 50% of her time working on IQRP related matters – attending meetings of the SAT (of which there were a total of four), prodding members of the SAT to complete their sections of the report, and, most importantly, editing and rewriting the sections into a report that was a complete and coherent document to be forwarded to the members of the peer review team that would visit Bentley in mid-September 1996. Other members of the SAT spent considerably less time on the task than did Dr. Crofts. In part, this was a result of the fact that much of the data needed for the SAT report was already available in the International Centre and in part because the entire IQRP participation was part and parcel of the larger strategic planning process.

OECD 1999

The self-assessment report that was the result of this process provided an important instrument to develop the strategic planning process of the institution. The annex provides the text of the report in an abridged version. The next sections will look at the way the peer review took place and how IQRP has impacted on the strategic planning process of Bentley College.

The peer review

Because Bentley was one of the three pilot institutions in the first phase of the IQRP project, time constraints played a significant role in the process. The IQRP framework did not become available until late in the spring semester 1996. This forced most of the SAT work into the summer when many faculty and staff take vacation time. Then the PRT visit was scheduled in mid-September, meaning that only a broad outline of the first draft of the institutional strategic plan was ready.

In addition to the above constraints, the institutional context was in the process of changing during the period in question. In April 1996, Dr. Joseph M. Cronin, Bentley's president since 1991, announced that he would be leaving the college at the end of the 1996-97 academic year. He immediately became a "lame duck", with most of his responsibilities devolving to Dr. Philip Friedman, the Vice-President for Academic Affairs and Provost. Cronin had made internationalisation a cornerstone of his strategy for the college and Friedman strongly supported this thrust.

Despite the constraints of time and institutional transition, the PRT visit proved to be the most valuable part of the exercise for Bentley international education administrators. Vice-President Friedman met with the three-person team – Marjorie Peace Lenn of the Center for Quality Assurance in International Education, Outi Snellman of the University of Lapland in Finland, and Leo West of Monash University in Australia – at the outset of their two-day visit and posed to the team a basic question: "Is there something clearly missing or awry in our international activities, or are we basically on track and need only to stay the course and improve certain aspects of what we are doing?"

During the two-day visit, the PRT met with a wide variety of faculty, staff and students in a series of very intense sessions. In fact, two days probably were not sufficient for the team to meet and assess effectively, and one of the consequences was that the team's report was not delivered to Bentley until nearly three months after the visit – the team had insufficient time to meet together to draw conclusions, given the intensive schedule of sessions with faculty, students and staff during their two days at Bentley.

However, during its visit and in exit discussions with Vice-President Friedman and the Dean and Associate Dean of International Education, the PRT identified a clear problem area for the future development of international education at Bentley.

Over the preceding five years a considerable amount of time and energy had gone into the college's involvement with projects in Estonia. These projects were funded by more than $1.5 million in United States government grants. More than 30 faculty members had visited Estonia to teach and give seminars, and many more had been involved with visiting Estonian faculty and students at Bentley. The projects had become the most significant engine for faculty involvement in international education. In some cases it had become a major professional commitment, altering teaching and research directions, while in others it had been a first introduction to involvement in international activities and the catalyst for further involvement in Estonia and elsewhere. But, by the time of the PRT visit, it was clear that the United States government funding for Bentley's involvement in Estonia was coming to an end – Estonia was deemed to be so successful in making the transition to a market economy that further funding was not to be provided for transition projects.

Impact of IQRP

Consequently, the PRT strongly recommended that Bentley find another avenue (or other avenues) for faculty to become actively involved in international activities – a new engine was necessary. This insight became a major thrust of the strategic plan that emerged over the succeeding months as one of its most important components became the search for new avenues to involve faculty in international activities. In keeping with the PRT reports observation that Bentley had accomplished significant internationalisation over the preceding ten years and was "on the right track" in other respects, the strategic plan otherwise consists largely of efforts at continuous improvement and quality enhancement.

Within six months of the PRT visit, Bentley had appointed a new president, Dr. Joseph Morone. His vision of the college's future is different from his predecessor's in that he sees international education as an essential element in fulfilling the goal of "moving Bentley to the next level", but he does not see it as the defining characteristic that is central to that goal. As a result, the strategic emphasis on international education has been subordinated to an emphasis on the intersections between information technology, business, and leadership/citizenship development. Within that triad, international education has an important role to play, and so the international strategic plan has had to be reformulated to speak to those issues while maintaining the important elements present over the previous decade and the insights gained from participation in the IQRP pilot project. In that process, the self-assessment played a crucial role, reason why the report is presented in an abridged version as annex to this chapter.

85

Annex
The 1996 Bentley College Self-assessment Report
Abridged version

Preface

Bentley College, located in the Boston suburb of Waltham, Massachusetts, United States, is one of a handful of speciality business schools in the United States. The college was founded in 1917 as the Bentley School of Accounting and Finance by Harry C. Bentley, former chairman of accountancy at Boston University and former dean of what is now the business school of Northeastern University. Bentley College offers bachelor of science degrees in eight business disciplines (accounting, business communications, business economics, computer information systems, economics-finance, finance, management, and marketing), bachelor of arts degrees in five fields (English, history, international culture and economy, liberal arts, and philosophy), a bachelor of science in mathematics, the master of business administration (MBA), and master of science degrees in six fields (accounting, business economics, computer information systems, finance, personal financial planning, and taxation). Bentley enrols approximately 3 200 full-time undergraduate students, 1 400 part-time undergraduates, 250 full-time graduate students, and 1 800 students pursuing graduate degrees on a part-time basis.

Bentley first admitted international students as early as the 1920s, but only began a serious commitment to international education in the mid-1980s. In 1985, the college's Vice-President for Academic Affairs and Provost at the time convened a campus-wide Internationalising Bentley Committee to examine ways and means of enhancing international education at the college. The Committee's Internationalising Bentley Report, issued in August 1986, has served as the guiding document for the development of the philosophical and programmatic aspects of internationalisation over the past decade. Developments since 1986 have included expansion of the number of international students nearly five-fold to almost 600 from more than 75 countries, establishment of Bentley-sponsored study abroad programmes for undergraduates and study tours abroad for graduate students, expansion of faculty international competence through college-sponsored faculty development efforts, establishment of linkages for faculty and student exchange with institutions in 20 countries, and securing of nearly $3 million in grants to support a range of different international activities. The focus of much of Bentley's international programme development has been in the business areas, a reflection of the fact that the college is a speciality business school. Staff to implement and oversee the college's international commitment has grown from a half-time foreign student advisor in 1985 to nine full-time staff members in 1996.

Governance and organisation systems

Mission and purpose

The Internationalising Bentley Committee developed the international mission statement of Bentley College:

> "Internationalising a college means internationalising each individual. A Bentley College education should provide each student with a broader, deeper appreciation for other cultures and peoples. Internationalising Bentley is not an add-on programme; it is an attitude. The liberally educated professional in an interdependent world must, throughout his or her lifetime, work at understanding the many and diverse components of that world." (*Internationalising Bentley Committee Report*, 1986).

As a business college, Bentley has a special international focus within the global community of industry, trade and commerce. The mission statement adopted for the International Centre in 1994 states: "As American business responds to the challenges of the international arena, so must American education. If the United States businesses are to survive and prosper in a global economy they must have managers who are comfortable working with foreign executives and living in foreign cultures. If world peace is to be an achievable goal, people of different races, religions and languages must interact with a tolerance and appreciation of diversity."

The need to understand other people and to coexist and compete with them require an international dimension in a student's academic experience. The centre works in collaboration with the rest of the Bentley community to achieve the goal of internationalising each individual.

These educational goals are accomplished through internationalised curricula and faculty, through study abroad programmes and study tours, through faculty and student exchanges, and aided by the presence of an international student body. In addition to the educational goals of the college, the presence of international students provides Bentley with a broad global base for the development of contacts to recruit students, conduct research, and promote faculty and student involvement overseas in a variety of projects. Because the international students at Bentley receive no financial aid, they also provide an important source of revenue for the college.

The mission is valued by the college as a whole – indeed, "globalisation" is identified as one of the college's "core values" in the college mission statement. Internationalisation

87

is supported and respected and seen as a worthy, advantageous and self-enlightened mission. The Dean of Faculty and the Undergraduate College and the Dean of the Graduate School of Business support the international mission. For example, they make it possible for faculty to teach in study abroad programmes and to offer courses with embedded study tours. The deans make their decisions openly and fairly regarding the interests of the International Centre, weighing them within the needs of the college as a whole. They have allowed, for example, important, under-enrolled international classes to be offered and have permitted faculty to devote needed time to International Centre programmes and projects.

The Vice-President for Academic Affairs and Provost is a firm supporter of the international mission and, thus, of the initiatives and work of the International Centre. One of his important contributions is to facilitate reciprocal agreements with institutions overseas, which broaden the scope of study abroad, provide additional faculty opportunities for overseas teaching and bring international transfer students to the college.

Policies and strategies

In 1985-86, the college went through an intensive planning process resulting in the Internationalising Bentley Report. That, together with the international sections of the college-wide strategic plan, serve as the basis of Bentley's policy and strategy. In essence, the approach is a broadly based effort to internationalise the student body – both through the recruitment of international students for the undergraduate and graduate programmes and by providing international experiences for American undergraduates through study abroad, student exchanges, study tours, and co-curricular activities.

In 1996, the college has undertaken a comprehensive strategic planning process for the future of international education at Bentley. This internationalisation strategy is part and parcel of the college's overall strategic thinking and planning. All decisions are made in that context.

As at most academic institutions, decision-making at Bentley is a collaborative process. For the most part, decisions originate in the International Centre and from its staff. Within the centre there are weekly meetings of the staff as a whole and of the four senior international education professionals (Dean of International Education, Associate Dean, Director of International Student and Scholar Services, and Director of Study Abroad). New policies tend to evolve from those meetings and are taken to administrators (Deans' Executive Council) and faculty committees (International Affairs Committee, standing Faculty Senate Committees) for discussion and approval. The Dean of International Education is a member of the Deans' Executive Council (which also includes the Vice-President for Academic Affairs and Provost, Administrative Co-ordinator for Academic Affairs, Vice-Provost and Dean of Enrolment Management, Dean of Faculty and the Undergraduate College, Dean of the Graduate School of Business, Dean of Continuing Education, Associate Dean of the Undergraduate College, and Dean of Students). The International Affairs Committee is a faculty advisory committee, appointed by the Faculty Senate. It meets regularly during the academic year and has been actively involved in reviewing policies and procedures and in the academic programme review of study abroad and the strategic planning process. The other faculty committee which is frequently involved is the Curriculum Committee, particularly with respect to curriculum issues in study abroad programmes and academic affiliations. Finally, during the summer of 1996, the Dean of the Graduate School of Business established an International Opportunities Action Team headed by the Director of Graduate Admissions and including the Dean of International Education, Director of International Student and Scholar Services, Co-ordinator of the MBA International Business Concentration, Graduate Registrar, and Director of Field-based Learning for the Graduate School. This new body will play a key role in identifying and pursuing international opportunities in the graduate programmes.

Organisation and structures

Ultimate responsibility for policy rests with the Dean of International Education who reports to the Vice-President for Academic Affairs and Provost. The President and the Board of Trustees oversee general policy, which affects the programmes of the International Centre as it does every other unit on campus.

The International Centre has direct operational responsibility for international activities. The centre works with institutions overseas and, in some cases, retains support personnel to facilitate study abroad and other linkages with sister institutions.

The Dean of International Education serves on the Deans' Executive Council, which is a formal channel of communication with the college. Additionally, the International Centre communicates with college departments and faculty through the International Affairs Committee (IAC) composed of faculty representatives appointed by the Faculty Senate. The IAC serves in an advisory capacity to the centre.

Planning and evaluation

At the institutional level, internationalisation is an integral part of the institutional strategy, with "globalisation" listed in the college's mission statement as one of Bentley's "core values". As a member of the Deans' Executive Council, the Dean of International Education is a participant in the annual academic affairs planning process, which is part and parcel of the annual budget process. At the departmental level, evidence of how internationalisation is integrated into the planning processes is much more difficult to identify in a coherent manner. It is largely a function of the degree to which a department feels that its needs lie in that area as hiring decisions are made.

Overall assessment of the internationalisation process is taking place as part of the strategic planning process for international education that began in the spring of 1996 and will continue throughout the 1996-97 academic year.

89

The American Assembly of Collegiate Schools of Business (AACSB) and the New England Association of Schools and Colleges (NEASC) both examine international aspects in their accreditation reviews. AACSB requires that the curriculum include international elements, and NEASC examines the overall international efforts of the institution, with particular reference to credit bearing activities.

Study abroad programmes are evaluated on an on-going basis by the International Centre through surveys of returned students and through focus groups. In addition, the overall study abroad programme was reviewed in 1995-96 in preparation for a report to the Curriculum Committee that is being submitted in September 1996.

Financial support and resource allocation

Internally, the college budget supports basic operations and programmes to serve international students and scholars, a staff of nine (six professional and three support), faculty development, campus awareness programming, etc.

Externally, the college has been successful in attracting federal grant support for a variety of faculty development, curriculum development, student exchange, and development assistance projects (especially in Estonia). Over the past decade nearly $3 million in grant funding has been secured.

Efforts are now beginning to approach international alumni and parents of international students as a potential source of support.

Allocation of funds to the International Centre is determined by the college's regular allocation procedures through the Division of Academic Affairs, with account being taken of the revenue potential of new ventures and the impact on the educational programme of faculty and curriculum development activities.

Most funding for internationalisation comes from within the institution through processes described above. External funding is sought from the United States government grants primarily, although this source is dwindling.

Support services and facilities

Services and infrastructure to support and develop international activities at Bentley are located primarily in the International Centre, which occupies approximately 2 000 sq. feet of space in the Adamian Graduate Centre. In addition to the offices, the centre includes a resource library for students interested in studying, working or pursuing internships abroad, lounge space for students, and a small conference room.

On the whole, support from institution-wide service departments is good.

The library director has been very supportive of the internationalisation process. His staff has been very good about adding international materials to the collection, and has actively participated in the college's projects in Estonia. Other facilities, such as the residence halls and cafeterias, also have made strides in recent years, although there is still room for improvement in cross-cultural programming in the residence halls. Other extra-curricular activities are internationalised to the degree that student demand will support – there is a World Affairs Club that meets sporadically, a Model United Nations programme that facilitates student participation in Model United Nations for college students in the United States and abroad and runs a Model United Nations for secondary school students each May, an International Business Association and International Graduate Association of Business and the active International Club primarily for international students. In addition, last winter a chapter of Phi Beta Delta was established to recognise international accomplishments of Bentley students, faculty and staff. Nine years ago a group of students established a chapter of AIESEC, the international organisation of business students that focuses on obtaining traineeships for exchange students and send students to participate in such exchange traineeships abroad. However, the group's founding coincided with a very deep recession in the local economy and it was disbanded three years later after failing to obtain a single traineeship.

Self-assessment of the governance and organisation systems for internationalisation

Generally, the SAT evaluation is positive concerning this area, for two basic reasons: the merger of the Office of International Programmes and the Office of International Student Services, in January 1995, has brought better communication among the parties and stronger support for student services. Secondly, the change in the appointment of the Director to Dean of International Education has broadened the purview of the internationalising process and mandate and has made this mandate more central in the eyes of the college.

The SAT deems necessary the following issues for further action:

- Revisit the structure and role of the International Affairs Committee. Can/should it be a standing Senate committee, with elected members, or remain an appointed committee? Should the purpose of the committee, now advisory, be altered?
- To what extent can/should the issue of internationalisation be factored into department-level decision making regarding programme and departmental reviews?
- How can improvements be made with those units on campus with which the centre has direct contact: admissions, career services, library, food service, financial aid, registrar, undergraduate dean's office, etc.?
- Is it now appropriate to revive the AIESEC chapter at Bentley?
- How can the college position itself better to involve international alumni in programming and develop a plan for fund raising internationally?

The SAT recommends that the suggestions in this report be considered in the development of the college's international strategic plan, due in revised draft form in early 1997.

Academic programmes

Area, language and interdisciplinary studies

All bachelor of arts (BA) students are required to achieve intermediate competency in a foreign language. Bachelor of science (BS) students have arts and science electives, a humanities elective, and two or more free electives which they can dedicate to study of a foreign language, should they desire. Both BA and BS students may minor in a foreign language, although the somewhat inflexible nature of the business curriculum makes this difficult for BS students. A pending curricular reform proposal would, if adopted, provide greater curricular flexibility and accommodate more language study for BS students.

Language courses give strong emphasis to communication skills and cultural content, and oral proficiency is emphasised in testing. The multimedia learning centre offers computerised instruction as well as standard taped language lessons. The department also has developed courses in business communication in French, Spanish and Italian.

Area studies are offered in a number of arts and sciences departments. History, for example has courses in pre-Columbian America, Early Modern Europe, Twentieth-Century Europe, Modern Germany, The Soviet Union and After, Latin America (1 800 present), History of China, History of Japan, Modern Japan, Modern East Asia, Middle East: Islamic and Contemporary, and The Past and Present in Africa. In addition, the English Department offers courses in the British Tradition, Literature and Culture I and II, the European Tradition, Intercultural Communication, African American Literature and Culture, Literature of the Caribbean, and Selected Topics in World Literature.

With regard to "international" courses, the Government Department offers International Politics, International Organisation, World Order: Crisis Management and Conflict Resolution, and the Model United Nations. International courses on the business side include International Economics, International Economic Growth and Development, Modern Economic Systems, International Business Law, Management of International Operations, International Marketing, International Accounting, and International Finance. In addition to these offerings at the undergraduate level, there are "international" courses in the graduate programmes in all the key disciplines – accounting, economics, finance, law, and marketing, with two offered in the management area.

Four years ago the college inaugurated a new interdisciplinary BA degree in International Culture and Economy (ICE). The ICE programme requires study of a modern language as well as courses in intercultural communication, global issues, international economics and a senior seminar. Students are also allowed to choose electives from a broad group of internationally oriented courses in a number of academic departments such as history, government, behavioural sciences and economics.

Beyond the ICE programme, the college also offers to undergraduate students minors in International Business and International Culture and Economy. At the graduate level, there is also an International Business Concentration within the MBA programme which allows students to take courses from several disciplines. Finally, the Graduate School offers several International Study Tour Courses: International Treasury Management (at the Royal Melbourne Institute of Technology in Australia), European Business Environment (at Maastricht, Netherlands), Japanese Culture and Business Practice, and Studies in the Transforming Economies of Europe: The Case of Estonia.

Language studies are developed in the Department of Modern Languages. Area studies are developed in particular departments as well. In addition, however, the faculty director of the ICE programme and the Dean of International Education are collaborating to promote the development of area studies options for students and the development of new courses for undergraduates.

Courses and instructors are evaluated by students through the Student Evaluation of Teaching (SET). This evaluation instrument includes a computerised section as well as written feedback to faculty. It is administered in every course section taught each semester. Departments individually evaluate courses by reviewing syllabi, peer classroom visits of junior faculty, monitoring enrolments, and through periodic departmental self-study reviews (every five years or sooner).

In the immediate future, the ICE programme will be a major focus for the development of new area studies courses in conjunction with various academic departments. The ICE programme is not, however, an international "ghetto" where all international course development is located. The International Centre will also work with individual departments to develop new area studies courses and also business courses with an international dimension.

As regards research, Bentley has no specialised research or graduate centres with an international focus in the strict sense. However, the Centre for Business Ethics has been quite active internationally, and the soon-to-be-established Centre for Securities Analysis and Trading (based in a computer simulated trading room being constructed on campus) will have a strong international profile once it is up and running.

At the institution level, the International Centre has established a number of exchanges which send Bentley faculty abroad to lecture and conduct research at partner institutions and bring international faculty to Bentley for periods ranging from several weeks to a full academic year.

International curricula

All degrees (BA, BS, BA/MBA, BA/MSA) allow for language and area studies courses as an option through free electives, arts and sciences electives, and humanities electives. Some majors encourage such courses: English, history, and business communication, for

93

example. All students can minor in languages or in other fields such as history where area studies are part of the curriculum. The ICE programme is built upon the premise that students will explore the various language and area studies courses available throughout the curriculum.

Integrating the international dimension has been an institutional priority for a number of years. Inclusion of adequate international content in the curriculum is encouraged by the standards of both of Bentley's primary accrediting groups, AACSB and NEASC.

Rather than requiring a specific "international" core course for all students, Bentley has tried to broadly integrate international material across the curriculum. In many business disciplines, a required undergraduate survey course includes an international component as one of many topics covered. Finally, all study abroad courses (see below) are carefully reviewed and are given Bentley College rather than transfer credit.

At the graduate level the same pattern holds: an international component in a basic course is supplemented by the opportunity and/or requirement to take other specifically international courses. In addition, the MBA requires a two course capstone sequence for all students: GR 601 "Competing in the Global Marketplace: Analysis of the Business Environment" and GR 602 "Competing in the Global Marketplace: Strategy and Implementation".

While the college offers no joint or double degree programmes at this point, Bentley currently does have two formal partnerships at the undergraduate level with Spanish institutions. Catalonia International College in Barcelona has designed its undergraduate programme based upon the Bentley model. Bentley has also recently entered into a similar arrangement with the College for International Studies in Madrid, a two-year institution.

Internationalised curricula are developed within various departments or task forces. All new courses are reviewed by the college Curriculum Committee. New course development is encouraged primarily through faculty interest. Funding is sometimes available in the form of Rauch grants, initiatives sponsored by the office of the Vice-President or Undergraduate Dean. The International Centre also receives some funding used to develop courses and programmes.

Teaching and learning process

Because of the attention given to internationalisation for well over a decade, a significant amount of material of this sort is used throughout the curriculum. A few examples will show the nature of what is being done and its spread across the curriculum:

- Cross-cultural consumer behaviour is discussed in all sections of MK 264 "Consumer Behaviour".
- Cross-national examples, case studies and writing assignments are used in MK 160 and 162.

- International negotiating is a key topic in MG 360 "Negotiating" and in the graduate course, MG 635 "Negotiating".
- An Internet and WWW module explores international possibilities and issues in information technology in CS 301 "Information Technology in Organisations".
- Ethical cases having international dimensions are used in GR 509 "Information Technology in the Business Environment".
- Case studies of specific countries and regions are integrated into classroom discussions and student assignments in EC 321 "International Economic Growth and Development".
- Students prepare country studies/analyses in ICE 260 "Global Issues and Interdependence".

Because the number of international students has increased greatly in recent years, the volume of interaction has naturally increased. Students enrol in courses based on the requirements of their major and their personal scheduling preferences. They may or may not interact extensively with students from other countries during a specific semester.

The Associate Dean of International Education has written "International Students in the Classroom", a guide for faculty to help them integrate domestic and international students effectively in the classroom and the Centre for Excellence in Teaching has also held a number of seminars for faculty on this topic.

Only in the study of modern languages and in some study-abroad sites is instruction given in a language other than English. Study abroad students whose site is a non-English-speaking country are required to study a language of that country.

Study abroad and student exchange programmes

The Study Abroad Office at Bentley College is responsible for the advising, administration, operation, marketing, recruitment and placement of both graduate and undergraduate study abroad programmes for fall, spring, summer, year-long, embedded, short-term, spring break, and winter break programmes in 10 different countries, as follows:

- Melbourne, Australia. Operating since 1990, Melbourne is one of Bentley's two most successful programmes. Students take three courses taught specifically for Bentley's study abroad programme and take two additional courses at either the Royal Melbourne Institute of Technology or Monash University.
- Brussels, Belgium. This is the other most popular programme at Bentley. Since 1989, Bentley has been sending students to Vesalius College, an English-medium, American style division of the Vrije Universiteit Brussel. Its primary attraction is its European location. Students are required to study a language (French, Dutch or German from the beginner to advanced levels), and to take two required courses. One required course is a European arts course which includes field trips to Paris, Amsterdam

95

and various other cities and museums, and the other required course is on the Origins and Development of the European Union.

- Tartu, Estonia. The spring of 1996 was the first semester that Bentley sent students to the University of Tartu. Students take all of their classes at the University of Tartu in the Baltic Studies Division.
- Paris, France. Bentley is in the process of developing a programme in Paris for the fall of 1997. We are currently reviewing two universities in Paris.
- Puebla, Mexico. This programme has been offered since 1991 at the Universidad de las Américas in Puebla (UDLA). Students are required to have at least one year of college level Spanish, because most courses are taught in Spanish at UDLA. UDLA offers a large variety of courses but unlike the other study abroad programmes, very few courses are offered in English.
- Madrid, Spain. This programme was also new for spring 1996, offering students the opportunity to study in Madrid at the College for International Studies, an institution with which Bentley has an articulation agreement.
- Florence, Italy. This is Bentley's newest programme located in Florence, at Instituto Lorenzo de Medici. Students are required to study Italian (offered at all levels, including intensive) and to take one culture course selected from a choice of four.
- Graduate study tours. Bentley's graduate study tour destinations include: Tokyo, Japan; Maastricht, the Netherlands; and Melbourne, Australia. The Tokyo programme offers credit in GR/MG 790 "Japanese Culture and Business Practice". The Maastricht course is GR 790 "European Business Environment: Competing in the Global Economy in the 21st Century". The Melbourne programme, GR/FI 790 "International Treasury Management", is designed for students in finance.
- Summer programmes. Where possible, Bentley offers summer programmes at institutions that host the semester or year long programmes. Summer programmes emphasise language study and are offered at the following sites: Spain, Mexico and Italy.
- Embedded programmes. Currently, two embedded programmes are offered, in London and Estonia. Both study tours take place during spring break and form an integral part of the course work in the regular semester class.

Bentley markets its study abroad programmes externally and accepts students from other academic institutions throughout the United States. Bentley offers business students the opportunity to study abroad while taking upper level business courses towards their degree requirements. Bentley's study abroad programmes are primarily taught in English, requiring collateral study of the host country language. In addition, it is far less complicated for business students to transfer business course credit (to be used for degree requirements) to their home institution from an AACSB accredited college or university. Because every course taken on a Bentley sponsored study abroad programme is approved as a Bentley course, assigned a Bentley course number, and transcripted by Bentley, students are transferring credit from an AACSB accredited business programme.

Bentley College offers internships on a regular basis through the MBA Internship Programme. The purpose of the MBA Internship Programme is to provide appropriate work opportunities for MBA candidates who have had little practical, professional experience. Since the programme began in the spring semester of 1991, 104 students have participated. Half of these were international students.

Bentley currently does not offer work abroad or internship programmes overseas for undergraduate students, although several have arranged international internships on their own.

Study abroad and student exchange programmes are evaluated by students at the close of their academic study abroad, by personnel on-site who are responsible for the administration of the programmes and by the staff of the International Centre.

Self-assessment of the internationalisation of academic programmes

Generally, the SAT is pleased with the development of internationalisation in the academic programmes of the college because significant growth has occurred in the past few years. Successes include development and implementation of:

- International modules in most business core courses.
- Undergraduate history requirement with coverage of non-western areas included.
- An MBA International Business Concentration.
- Three graduate study abroad opportunities.
- The International Culture and Economy BA major.
- Minor fields of study in international business and international culture and economy.
- Expansion of undergraduate study abroad opportunities.
- Exchange opportunities for study abroad.
- Business foreign language courses.
- Sustained commitment to international faculty development.

The following issues arose during the course of the SAT's work:

- As the number of faculty positions grows, 25-30 new positions are anticipated in the future, how can departments be encouraged to seek faculty with international interest and experience?
- How can the departments be encouraged to increase the importance of international perspectives in their programme development?
- How can the study abroad programmes attract more students of ethnic minorities?

The SAT recommends that:

- International faculty development funds remain stable for programme planning.
- A review be made of the MBA International Business Concentration and of the minors in international business and international culture and economy at the undergraduate level.

- A senior faculty member be hired with an international business specialisation to provide academic leadership to the MBA International Business Concentration and undergraduate international business minor.

Research and scholarly collaboration

This is an area of internationalisation in which Bentley has taken a very limited institutional role. In this regard, Bentley is similar to most United States business schools, in large measure because little in the way of external funding is available in the United States to support such research.

Students

Domestic students

Bentley's goal for student participation in study abroad programmes has been to maintain a level of 10% of each undergraduate class to participate in overseas programmes.

Feedback from students is collected through programme surveys sent out by the Study Abroad Office at the end of each semester. In addition, surveys are often distributed by on site staff who forward feedback to this office.

In the spring of 1996, a local chapter of Phi Beta Delta, an international honour society, was inducted at Bentley College. Students at Bentley who had studied abroad and maintained a minimum grade point average of 3.4 (undergraduate) and 3.6 (graduate) were invited to join.

The International Centre encourages, supports and provides opportunities for both international and domestic students to participate in international activities. The Study Abroad Office works with both faculty and the various administrative offices on campus to provide community outreach to all students.

The Office of Academic Advising assists students with obtaining the necessary approval to transfer course work from overseas. The Financial Aid Office has designated a special staff member to handle all inquiries about study abroad.

There are several co-curricular and extra-curricular activities designed specifically to involve students who do not study abroad in international activities. The most extensive is the Model United Nations programme. For the past nine years the group has sponsored a Model United Nations for high school students from the eastern US; held in late May each year it attracts 300-350 students.

Other internationally oriented co-curricular and extra-curricular activities include the International Club, International Graduate Association of Business, International Business Association, and Phi Beta Delta. Each of these groups seeks to promote an international perspective among domestic students by involving them in club activities and providing programmes with an international focus.

Foreign students on campus

As part of the strategic planning process for international education, a previous target figure of 18% international students is now under review, and is likely to revised downward to 15%. At present, international students make up about 13% of the undergraduate student body and 9% of the graduate student body.

A new professional position was created to put more emphasis on recruitment, admission and retention of international students in the freshman class. The important element in this process is to sustain diversity and encourage applications from different parts of the world, while working towards the quantitative goal.

Although it is important to have representation from different nationalities and ethnic backgrounds, the institution does not have quotas based on national or ethnic origin. Students are selected based on their merits and admissibility.

The Graduate School of Business at Bentley College seeks to enrol an internationally diverse class. All admission professionals in the admission office are trained to review international applications and assist international students (the Graduate School classifies international students as those who are studying on a F or J visa).

Admission standards for international applicants are essentially the same as for domestic applicants with the addition of a TOEFL score of approximately 580 or better. International students may compete for Graduate Assistantships which offer tuition remission in exchange for providing assistance to a faculty member or administrator.

The current informal Graduate School goals with respect to international students is to keep the total number relatively stable and work to increase the diversity of countries and major areas of the world represented in the student population.

In order to achieve institutional goals for an increased international student population on campus, as well as to create a good network of international ties, some short and long term strategies have been developed.

Current recruitment and election guidelines for the next two years include:

- Increased site visits and participation in recognised college fairs and exhibitions, and forums.
- Increased level of communication with the prospect pool.
- Direct contacts and enhanced relationship with overseas advisory centres.
- Recruiting via "word of mouth" through alumni, parents, and special projects.

- Encouraging faculty exchange programmes with other institutions, arrange articulation agreements with foreign institutions, encourage study abroad, student exchange programmes.
- Enhancing the ESL programme on campus.
- Establishing Alumni Admission Committees.
- Introducing "focus groups" for self-evaluation.
- Encouraging campus visits.
- Bringing international-oriented events to the Bentley campus.
- Updating publications, video, Internet and Web Page information to make information easily accessible world-wide.

The Graduate School provides academic and recruiting information to the United States education and advising centres, listing or advertising in graduate level guide books and publications that have international readership.

For the last several years the Graduate School has actively recruited in Asia (Japan, Hong Kong, China, Singapore, Thailand, Indonesia, India, China) and Europe (Turkey, Germany, France and the Netherlands). The Graduate School has been instrumental in establishing formal college alumni/ae chapters in Turkey and Thailand and has plans to start clubs in Bombay, Tokyo and Frankfurt.

In addition to measures undertaken by the Undergraduate Admissions Office, the Bridge Programme attracts a number of students every year via word of mouth.

Requirements have been set at 475-550 TOEFL scores for Bridge, 550 and above for regular admissions; the ESL staff may reject or recommend Bridge students to the programme. The ESL staff also make recommendations concerning mainstreaming Bridge students.

Support for international/second language students at this time appears adequate:

- Bridge students have access to personal tutors, the ESL tutorial centre manned by ESL faculty, advisory sessions with the Bridge Director, selected academic advisors, and special social activities.
- Undergraduate ESL students have access to the ESL tutorial centre, ESL administration, and the International Centre and a multitude of activities.
- Graduate ESL students have special access to the graduate ESL tutor and the International Centre.

International students' academic performance is in keeping with the general student population due to the fact that these students are recruited under comparable admission requirements. The Selection Committee reviews each individual's credentials, taking into consideration his or her previous educational background, the educational system of the country and curriculum. English proficiency is always measured through the TOEFL exam to give a relatively accurate assessment of the student's language knowledge level. The

Admissions Committee's goal is to make sure that accepted candidates have high potential for academic success in the programmes to which they are admitted.

Student services

Study abroad

A comprehensive catalogue of Bentley sponsored study abroad programmes is published annually. A team of peer advisors, in conjunction with study abroad staff offer weekly information sessions concerning specific study abroad sites. Faculty also take an active role in speaking to students about study abroad opportunities. Periodically, overseas staff come and speak to students about their institutions. There is also a complete study abroad library, with books, magazines, videos and various other reference materials.

Study abroad students are prepared for their international academic experiences through a series of pre-departure orientation and advising sessions.

Bentley offers language instruction from beginner through intermediate levels in the following: French, Spanish, German, Italian, Japanese, and Chinese. In addition, Bentley offers advanced level course work in Spanish, French and Italian.

English as a Second Language (ESL)

Bentley offers ESL classes to students who need further work in language skills. In all ESL classes (Bridge and freshman composition) there is an emphasis on diversity. This emphasis is reflected in assignments, group work, and other classroom activities. Comparisons and contrasts are made constantly among the cultures represented in the classroom and American cultures.

The ESL Undergraduate Tutorial Centre serves as a primary academic support. ESL staff teach the freshman composition classes, which offers students who need it help from professionals trained in ESL.

The ESL administration maintains personal contact with each student throughout their time in ESL courses.

The Bridge Programme admits and prepares conditional students to continue at Bentley if their language skills become adequate. Bridge attracts international as well as United States American students whose mother tongue is not English.

In the Bridge Programme, there are personal tutors (academic and personal advising), a thorough orientation programme, workshops in using computers, academic skills preparation, registration workshops and advising sessions.

International students

The International Centre provides assistance on a wide range of issues to all international students enrolled or planning to enrol at Bentley College, and serves as the primary resource and advocate for these students on campus. Although an international student's *first* contact with Bentley is usually with the Office of Admission, the International Centre staff seeks to have an *ongoing* relationship with each international student during his or her time here.

The International Centre provides information to students and scholars before their arrival on campus, sponsors an International Orientation Programme, and works with other offices across campus to present a variety of programmes and activities throughout the year. Personal counselling and advising on immigration, employment, tax, insurance, financial, academic, housing, and adjustment issues are available.

Self-assessment of internationalisation with respect to students

Creating the International Centre was a wise decision on the part of the college; this organisational change, which increased staffing and pooled resources, has had great positive impact with respect to students. The centre has a high level of service, a growing number of activities for international students, an extensive international handbook not found at most colleges, a professional-looking newsletter, a new peer advisor programme, and an expanded hosting programme. A steady improvement has been seen, and although there is still much room for growth, the centre is clearly moving in the right direction.

According to the SAT, the following topics are of particular concern from the point of view of services to international students:

- *Orientation*: We support the combining of international and general new student orientations to allow international students and domestic students to get to know one another before the start of classes.
- *Retention*: Retention of international students, particularly men, is a concern. The revision of the freshman year experience – including joint orientation – should help retain international students. A second effort designed to improve retention is the new International Peer Advisor (IPA) programme which will provide every new international student with a continuing student – international or domestic – as a sort of mentor.
- *Academic advising*: Academic advising should be instituted in a rigorous fashion before classes begin. Waiting until two or three weeks into the semester is not adequate; new students need academic advisers early on.
- *Freshman courses*: Could there be a required "Bentley 101" – a revamped "Freshman Seminar" course – to introduce new freshmen to the college? Could there be a "USA 101" in lieu of the United States government for international students? This would be an introduction to the United States history, society and contemporary life.

- *English Language Issues*: Should we develop a pre-matriculation ESL programme along with more ESL support for matriculated students?
- *Food service*: This is a problem for many international students who, day in and day out, are not able to eat foods they prefer or to which they are accustomed. We would like to see a greater commitment on the part of Marriott to incorporating foods from different countries into their daily menus, rather than only providing these foods for special dinners or catered events.
- *Residence life*: The current policy of matching international and United States students as roommates is supported by the International Centre. Could there also be an international floor or dorm that would house equal numbers of United States and international students who are interested in being more involved in programming activities? International students frequently want single rooms, but there are too few single rooms available.

For study abroad students, the SAT recommends that:

- Specific target numbers be set for Bentley student participation.
- Further recognition be given to student participation.
- More exchange options or more creative variations on exchange opportunities be developed.
- A review of the financial aid policy be undertaken to increase the amount of institutional aid applicable to study abroad.
- Study abroad scholarship opportunities be developed.
- The programme fee structure be re-examined.

For English as a Second Language students, the SAT recommends that:

- Bentley develop an intensive ESL programme to attract undergraduate and graduate students who could not otherwise be accepted to matriculate at Bentley.
- Options be explored to expand the scope of the Bridge Programme to add a one-semester academic preparatory programme for students intending to enrol at institutions other than Bentley.
- Full-time rather than part-time professors be hired for the ESL programme.
- Workshops and seminars in American business be held for international students.
- Profession development opportunities be offered to increase faculty inter-cultural awareness and competence to work in cross-cultural ways.

In addition to the above comments, which focus on student services, study abroad and the ESL programme, the following specific recommendations were made by the SAT:

- That creative ways be found to bridge the gap between wealthy students, many of whom are international, and students of modest means.
- That the college calendar recognise a broader spectrum of religious observances and holidays.

103

- In publications, when naming an institution or place in a foreign country, that the spelling of those words be in the national language.
- That a new recruitment video be developed with an international student community as its focus.
- That the International Centre undertake a review of the needs of students for appropriate space for religious observances.
- That the library be encouraged, especially under budget constraints, to continue to subscribe to foreign newspapers.

Orientation, retention and academic advising are the most critical issues relating to international students on campus. It is the SAT's recommendation that all of the above areas be addressed, to the extent possible, in the international strategic plan. And more should be done to recruit students for the Bridge Programme.

Faculty and staff

International activities and mobility of staff

Over the past decade approximately half of the Bentley faculty (196 full-time) has been involved in some form of international activity. Twelve different faculty members have led summer, winter break, or spring break study tours, and five faculty members (four in accountancy and one in information systems) have taught in Brussels. A total of 35 individuals from Bentley have been involved in the college's extensive efforts in Estonia alone – including teaching assignments ranging in length from a few days to a full academic year, joint research, joint publications, and institutional development assistance. Bentley conducted a series of two-week faculty development opportunities in Europe that involved a total of 25 faculty members, and five more participated in a three and a half week faculty development programme in Brazil and Mexico in 1996. And 19 different faculty members have designed new or revised courses to include international components, with funding from a variety of institutional development grants.

An annual $40 000 budget allocation supports international faculty development, including biannual plans for group programmes abroad and self-designed opportunities for faculty development in alternate years.

While no formal policies exist to encourage faculty to undertake assignments abroad/sabbaticals, there is a very clear, de facto three part strategy: assistance from the International Centre in making arrangements prior to departure; support during the assignment abroad; and administrative recognition of overseas assignments.

Foreign staff

There is a steady flow of international visitors to campus for periods ranging from a few days to a full academic year. Visiting faculty from abroad are brought to Bentley either by the relevant department or through an initiative of the International Centre. Over the past decade visiting foreign faculty from the United Kingdom, Portugal, Australia, the Netherlands, Belgium, Germany, Egypt, and China have taught at Bentley in economics, finance, accountancy, and modern languages. In addition, visiting faculty from Brazil, Estonia, China, Japan, and Germany have visited Bentley to conduct research.

Recruitment and selection procedures

Faculty are sought and selected by the academic departments based on the need within the discipline, not on the origin of the faculty member.

Normally, appointments in most departments do not require faculty who are internationally experienced or active. The academic needs of that department are met; an international perspective is an asset in most cases, but not essential.

Procedures for selecting faculty for international education assignments are, basically, informal. Individual faculty members inform the International Centre of their interests, and the centre suggests their names to the inviting institution. Likewise with the study abroad programmes. Individual faculty express their interest in teaching in an overseas programme, and the centre investigates the possibility.

Staff development and promotion procedures

Bentley College faculty are carefully recruited by the academic departments in a process involving close collaboration between the department chair and the tenured faculty members of that department. The process is monitored by the Dean of Faculty who approves all hiring and issues faculty contracts. This careful process has resulted in Bentley having a faculty in which 87% possess the terminal qualification of a doctoral degree in their academic discipline.

Summer faculty development programmes regarding the EU and European business have been held on a number of occasions and have in each case included travel to Europe as part of the programme. This past summer a three week development programme involving five faculty members was held in Brazil and Mexico to support international teaching initiative at both the undergraduate and graduate levels. Other examples of faculty development programmes sponsored by the International Centre include opportunities to undertake research while teaching in countries where study abroad programmes are held.

The college has a number of arrangements with foreign institutions that allow faculty to teach and lecture overseas. Faculty have travelled to China, Estonia, Spain, France, Belgium, England, Australia, Germany, and Egypt.

In addition, a very generous sabbatical policy has been used to support faculty research and study abroad in recent years. Faculty members have taken sabbatical leave in France, Australia, Israel, Germany, India, the United Kingdom, and elsewhere. Overall, faculty have had very significant opportunities for development in the international dimension in recent years and there is an institutional commitment in both programmatic and budgetary terms to continue it in the future. Approximately 50% of the overall faculty has participated in international activities of one type or another at least once in the past decade.

International activities have clearly been, de facto, an increasingly important part of that agenda in recent years. There is at present, however, no formal weight given de jure to this dimension of a faculty member's portfolio of activities.

Self-assessment of internationalisation with respect to staff

In general, Bentley has performed well in this area, particularly with regard to international faculty development and identifying possibilities for faculty to spend periods abroad lecturing and teaching. De facto there has been very strong support given to faculty involvement in these areas, almost to the point where one wonders if de jure weight needs to be given to international involvement in the tenure, promotion and merit raise process. Where there is still a gap, however, is in departmental and institutional policies regarding international competence in new hires.

The SAT recommends that the strategic plan provide for continuation of international faculty development opportunities and that it address the issue of including international competence as a criterion in the hiring process for new faculty.

External relations and services

Partnerships and networks

Bentley has established a broad range of formal and informal international affiliations over the past decade. At present there are 27 institutions in 18 countries with which the college has such links.

The "International consortium" is a grouping of ten institutions that came together in 1989 at Bentley's initiative to form the International Consortium for Business and Management Education. The initial membership consisted of institutions in Australia, Belgium, Brazil, Egypt, Estonia, France, Mexico, New Zealand, and Spain, in addition to Bentley. The aim of the consortium is to foster the development of faculty and student exchanges and assist member institutions in implementing their internationalisation strategies.

The "Estonian consortium" is a group of institutions that has come together to assist in the creation of an Estonian International Graduate School of Management.

New partnerships and linkages are established after evaluation by the staff of the International Centre and other relevant bodies on campus – the Graduate School in some cases, individual departments in others, and the International Affairs Committee in all instances. Following this evaluation and approval of the agreement, it is submitted to the Vice-President for Academic Affairs and Provost and President for their approval and signature. Agreements are managed by the staff of the International Centre. Evaluation is undertaken on an on-going basis by the Dean of International Education and the Associate Dean who meet with participants to solicit their input, and by the Director of Study Abroad.

Development assistance

Bentley has been actively involved as contractor in a series of development projects in the field of management education in Estonia. These have included provision of faculty development seminars both in Estonia and on the Bentley campus over a period of five years beginning in the summer of 1991 as well as provision of teaching and library materials to Estonian business faculties as they have made the transition to teaching market economics.

Bentley's Estonian involvement has been a direct outgrowth of its other internationalisation activities and a direct contributor to the process as well. Initial contact with Estonian institutions took place in the process of organising the International Consortium for Business and Management Education, which itself has been a tool of internationalisation at Bentley. The projects themselves have contributed to the process by involving a large number of faculty – approximately 15% of the total faculty of the college – who have brought their Estonian experiences into the classroom. In addition, the project has led directly to creation of the spring break study tours to Estonia, which have been held for three consecutive years and enrolled a total of 40 students, a summer study/internship programme in 1995 for a group of 15 students, and inauguration of a study abroad site in Estonia.

Essentially these are handled in the same manner as institutional affiliations, with the International Centre staff playing the key role in evaluating possibilities and preparing grant proposals to support such activities.

Community services and project work

Bentley College has no education department; hence, there is no automatic entree into the schools through practice teaching programmes. The International Centre, however, has developed a strong network with local area schools through the Massachusetts Global Education Programme and the Economic Education Council of Massachusetts – both active, pre-collegiate teacher in-service education agencies, which have collaborated with the centre in teacher education programmes. The most extensive of these was funded through the United States Department of Education under the Centre for International Business Education and Research (CIBER) grant in the early 1990s.

External communication

If Bentley's external communications are geared to an international audience it is usually by accident rather than by design. Some steps have been made in the past few years

107

with the publication of a small international recruitment piece, but much needs to be done in this area.

Self-assessment of internationalisation with respect to external relations and services

This is an area where the institution's performance has been uneven. In some areas it has been superior – creation of linkages, involvement in the development assistance process in Estonia, and (within limits) outreach to the K-12 education community. However, in others there has been little activity – off-shore teaching, outreach to the business community, and internationalisation of external communications. In the area of consortia, promising starts have, to date, not yielded the kind of results anticipated.

The Estonian programme has been a model of integrated development of internationalisation at Bentley. However, because federal government funding for such projects in Estonia is reaching its end, special attention is required to either find the ways and means of sustaining the involvement or planning a careful and orderly exit strategy.

The SAT deems further action necessary on the following issues:

- Reinvigorating outreach to the K-12 education community.
- Developing international outreach to the business community through involvement in international executive training programmes both at Bentley and off-shore.
- Giving greater attention to international audiences for certain college publications.
- Putting greater emphasis on maximising the benefits of involvement in consortia.
- Developing a strategy for either a) continued involvement in Estonia or b) an orderly exit from involvement in the country.

All of these areas mentioned above should be taken into consideration in the development of the college's strategic plan for the future of international education at Bentley.

Conclusions

Bentley College has established a comprehensive set of goals for internationalisation, including clear targets for international enrolments and a mission to "internationalise" every faculty member and student. While major strides have been made in the decade since the Internationalising Bentley Report was issued, significant challenges remain. These include:

- Integrating international students more thoroughly into the Bentley community, both in and out of the classroom.
- Improving the international coverage in the curriculum so that graduates will possess the knowledge they will require for successful business careers in the 21st century.

- Involving a broader range of faculty members in the process so that the goal of thoroughly internationalising the educational process at Bentley becomes a reality.
- Finding external resources to support special projects and new initiatives in an era of declining federal spending for educational exchange.
- Building stable and effective networks to facilitate recruitment of high quality international students, and effective support services to retain them once they have been recruited.
- Selecting from among the many new programme initiatives that are presented so that those with the greatest potential for long term benefit.

The most important steps that the institution should take are embodied in the development of the international strategic plan.

Bentley College is at an important juncture in its history. The current president, Dr. Joseph M. Cronin, announced last April that he will step down at the end of the current academic year. He has been a major supporter of the internationalisation process since his selection to assume the presidency in 1991. The rest of the core administrative team of the college, starting with Vice-President for Academic Affairs and Provost Dr. Phil Friedman, also have been extremely supportive of internationalisation. Clearly, the selection of a new president who is as supportive as Dr. Cronin has been and the maintenance of a senior administrative team which is as supportive as the current incumbents have been, are of great importance to the future of internationalisation at Bentley.

6

Using the IQRP in a Comprehensive University University of Helsinki, Finland

by

Paul Fogelberg

The setting

As a university serving a small national population, the University of Helsinki has for hundreds of years had the ambition of being international. University researchers and teachers have followed international developments in their fields, and literature in the world's major languages has been widely used in teaching and research. At first the language of academic publication was Latin that was also used as the language of instruction during the 17th and 18th centuries. Subsequently, besides Latin, Swedish, later German and occasionally French came into use as publishing languages. At present English is the main language in scholarly publishing, with the exception of those fields with a strong national focus, in which Finnish and Swedish are widely used. Foreign language teaching forms a significant part of Finnish secondary education, and Finnish university students have always assumed that they would have to read and pass examinations on books written in languages other than their mother tongues.

For these reasons, internationalisation is nothing new at the University of Helsinki, for the university has a long and deep history of developing international activities. In this respect, a university serving a smaller national language and culture differs from those serving larger nations or operating in one of the major world languages.

Today, international activities at the University of Helsinki are manifested especially through international co-operation in research; researcher, teacher and student exchanges; the widespread use of English as language of instruction; publishing in international journals and series; and the wide-ranging linguistic abilities of both teachers and students, along with their active participation in international co-operation projects.

111

National context

There are 20 universities in Finland, of which ten are multi-faculty institutions, and ten are specialist institutions. Of these specialist institutions, three are universities of technology, three are schools of economics and business administration, and the remaining four are art academies. Over 140 000 students are enrolled in institutions of higher education, over half of whom are women.

Finnish institutions of higher education use the *numerus clausus* system; degree students are selected on the basis of matriculation and/or entrance examinations. A small number of places are also reserved for students who have not completed the matriculation examination.

Finnish degrees correspond to bachelor's, master's and doctor's degrees, though some degree programmes do not include a lower academic degree and thus the initial degree is a master's. In most fields students can also take a voluntary licentiate's degree after the master's and before going on to the doctorate. The bachelor's degree requires at least three years of full-time study; the higher, master's degree requires five years, *i.e.* two years after the bachelor's degree. Full-time studies for a doctor's degree take approximately four additional years. In general, however, Finnish students take much longer to complete their degrees, and therefore the average age of university graduates is older than in the rest of Europe. The independent nature of university studies in Finland allows for considerable freedom of choice, and in most fields students are able to choose from a wide range of options, including their choice of minor subjects.

Higher education in Finland is funded mainly through the national budget, and students do not pay tuition fees. Degree students at the University of Helsinki are required to join the Student Union, which entitles them to various discounts and services, including the services of the local Student Health Care Centre, reduced travel costs, and subsidised meals at student restaurants.

The Finnish higher education system underwent considerable expansion from the 1960s to the 1980s, and there are now universities in all parts of Finland with the exception of the extreme north. By contrast, the 1990s have been defined by cuts in higher education funding, mandated by the national government's need to cut spending. In 1997 the Ministry of Education introduced a new model for the state funding of universities, based on target numbers of degrees to be taken at each university within a certain period. These targets are decided upon in negotiations between the ministry and each university.

The largest change in the system of higher education has been the creation in the 1990s of polytechnics. By the year 2000 there will be 20 institutions on the polytechnic level in Finland.

International context

The Nordic countries share a long tradition of co-operation; in the university sector the main channels for mobility and co-operation have been the NORDPLUS and NORFA programmes. In addition, NUAS (Nordiskt universitetsadministratörssamarbete) facilitates co-operation between Nordic university administrators, and NUS (Nordiskt universitetssamarbete) between rectors.

As a close neighbour of Russia and the Baltic countries, Finland has naturally cultivated ties with universities in these areas. This co-operation has especially deepened in the aftermath of the area's recent political changes. Co-operation is arranged both bilaterally as well as through Tempus projects. Because of its geo-political position as the easternmost of the western European countries, Finland can function as a gateway to Russia, although Russian language skills have been nearly as rare in Finland as they are in the rest of western Europe.

Finland's joining the EU in 1995 has brought a number of new international opportunities, particularly the opportunity to participate fully in EU research and development framework programmes and various projects promoting the mobility of researchers, teachers and students. Since 1992, Finland has been able to participate in the EU's ERASMUS programme.

Institutional profile

The University of Helsinki is the oldest university in Finland. Founded in Turku in 1640, and transferred to Helsinki in 1828, the University of Helsinki is the country's largest and most multidisciplinary university.

In 1997, there were 33 419 students studying in the University of Helsinki (23% of the total number of university students in Finland). In the same year, 2 309 basic academic degrees were taken (21% of the total number for Finland), and 311 doctoral degrees (33% of the total number for Finland). There were 37 559 students attending continuing education courses, 19 626 students participating in Open University courses.

The teaching staff of the university comprised 1 712 persons in 1997 and the other staff 4 477 persons, totally 6 189 persons.

The University of Helsinki is the country's only bilingual multi-faculty university, with Finnish and Swedish as the languages of instruction. About 100 of the teaching posts are intended for instruction in Swedish; approximately 7% of the student body is Swedish-speaking. Education of Swedish-speaking doctors and lawyers, for instance, is also part of the university's national responsibility.

The university is composed of nine faculties: theology, law, medicine, arts, science, education, social sciences, agriculture and forestry, and veterinary medicine. The latter became a faculty in August of 1995, when the former College of Veterinary Medicine became incorporated into the University of Helsinki. Also included in the operations of the faculties are five field stations and two research farms. Teaching is provided in approximately 270 subjects.

The university contains 15 independent institutes and departments operating under the supervision of the University Senate and a few others operating under the supervision of the faculties. Some of these independent institutes and departments provide services for the entire university (such as the University Language Centre); others are research institutes.

The Centre for Adult Education operates in various units situated in Helsinki and in six other locations. The university provides one quarter of the adult education provided by institutions of higher education in Finland.

In 1997 the University of Helsinki's total budget was Mk 2 202 million, of which Mk 1 620 million came from the national budget.

On December 31, 1997 there were 1 384 foreign students studying at the University of Helsinki, which is approximately 4% of the student population; of these, 715 were studying for basic academic degrees and 291 for postgraduate degrees. The rest, 378, were exchange students and other students admitted for a short-term study at the university without the right to take a degree.

The university's mission

The mission of the University of Helsinki is defined by law:

> "The university is charged with promoting independent academic research and scientific knowledge, providing the highest quality instruction based on research, and educating young people to serve their country and humankind."

The law specifies and further regulates university autonomy, granted by the Constitution, and guarantees academic freedom in both teaching and research.

In the late 1990s, the university's priority areas are to:

- Promote high quality research and education of researchers.
- Develop teaching and its assessment.
- Promote international activities through enhancement of interaction and by taking advantage of international research funds.

- Increase interdisciplinary co-operation in research and teaching.
- Promote the university's impact on the external community.

The history of internationalisation at the University of Helsinki

International co-operation was originally based on personal contacts between individual researchers rather than on official agreements, and such contacts still form the basis for international co-operation. European universities have a long tradition of mutual co-operation.

International co-operation in Finland has also taken the form of government cultural exchange agreements and various stipend programmes.

The University of Helsinki concluded its first official bilateral co-operation agreement with a foreign university in 1974; since then the number of official agreements has grown and approaches 60.

Student exchanges, in particular, have expanded in the 1990s. In 1988 new exchange programmes sponsored by the Ministry of Education were started with France, Germany and Great Britain, and the university joined the NORDPLUS programme sponsored by the Nordic Council of Ministers. The university has taken part in the American ISEP programme since 1984.

Since the university joined the EU's ERASMUS programme in 1992, the number of exchange students has increased dramatically. Finland's joining the EU has opened up many new opportunities for international co-operation; for example, the EU's Tempus and Alfa programmes support projects with non-EU countries. The SOCRATES programme, which continues out of the ERASMUS programme, includes other forms of co-operation besides student exchange. In addition, many Finnish researchers have actively participated in EU research programmes.

Further development of student exchanges demands increasing reciprocity of exchanges. In order to stimulate such reciprocity, the University of Helsinki has from year to year increased the number of courses given in foreign languages (by and large, in English), put a greater emphasis on marketing itself internationally, and further developed services supporting exchanges.

Several administrative measures have supported internationalisation. In 1991, an International Relations Office (including Swedish Language and Nordic Affairs) was created in the central administration; today it is part of the Department of Strategic Planning and Development. In 1990, the first post of Faculty International Affairs Secretary was established; at present, all faculties have an employee with this specialisation. A post of Research Liaison Officer was established in 1994 mainly to handle EU research programmes. In addition, several departments in the different faculties have appointed specific staff members, normally people working in either teaching or research, to co-ordinate international affairs. These administrative reforms have proved beneficial, though there is a need to develop the co-operation between the various units.

In 1992, the University Senate appointed a Committee for International Affairs to replace the former International Relations Steering Committee and the Foreign Admissions Committee. The Committee for International Affairs prepared an internationalisation strategy which was approved in 1993. Subsequently it was thoroughly revised, partially in light of the changes resulting from Finland's joining the EU, and the University Senate approved the new strategy in 1996.

In summary, internationalisation is one of the University of Helsinki's priority areas. According to the Strategy for International Operations, international contacts are a key way of maintaining a high level of teaching and research and of preserving their international competitiveness. The strategy document also states that through international co-operation the university fulfils its responsibility as set out in the University Act to educate students to serve their society by promoting peaceful and sustainable development in the world (a new frame law for all Finnish universities came into force on August 1, 1998). The university's regional perspective, specifically its European focus, can be seen in the strategy documents related to European co-operation. The EU strategy, approved on 19 October 1994, sets the guidelines for developing administrative support structures and the European Policy Statement accompanying the university's SOCRATES application, submitted on 1 July 1996, ties the university's general internationalisation principles to the activities of the SOCRATES programme. Both of these strategies have parallel objectives and support the development of the university's internationalisation process.

The self-assessment process

In the beginning of 1996, the University of Helsinki was asked to be one of the three pilot institutions for the implementation of the first phase of the IQRP project. The final decision to participate was made in early spring. After that a full-time project co-ordinator was employed, which became possible through a grant from CIMO (Centre for International Mobility, Helsinki), and a self-assessment team (SAT) was set up according to the guidelines given, consisting of Vice-Rector Paul Fogelberg as the chairperson, Ms. Anna Luikko (Director of International Relations), Professor Jari Niemelä, Dr. Kari Takamaa, Ms. Elina Ussa (a student), and Ms. Kaija Pajala (project co-ordinator, secretary).

The IQRP checklist for self-assessment was distributed to all nine faculties of the university together with a number of questions prepared by the SAT. Other recipients were a number of separate institutions, and the Student Union. Most of these responded to the questions, and then the SAT, or more correctly a group consisting of members of the SAT, visited every faculty for an interview with the deans, faculty secretaries and other leading officials. This exercise took place mainly during the first half of June. The replies, the interviews and statistical information formed the basis of the self-assessment report that was written by the project co-ordinator in co-operation with the chairman of the SAT, mainly in July. The date fixed for delivering the self-assessment report to the project team was the beginning of August, and this deadline was adhered to.

One problem in the self-assessment was caused by its timing: at the University of Helsinki the end of May and June are difficult months with respect to the annual rhythm of faculties. Nevertheless, all faculties responded to the questionnaire and were also willing to have a discussion with the self-assessment team. One severe drawback related to the tight schedule of the exercise and the time of the year was that it was not possible to extend the evaluation down to the department level. It is of course clear that the replies received from the faculties were quite general. However, the discussions between faculty representatives and members of the self-assessment team were very useful, and they complemented the information received from the written replies. It must be admitted that the self-assessment report more became a descriptive inventory of the international operations of the university than a real assessment of them. It was very much steered by the IQRP pilot checklist that was then in use. This checklist was also subject to criticism during the discussions mentioned, *inter alia*, for its very fragmented character including too many questions. Anyway, the self-assessment report served as the principal document for the peer review, but its further use within the university has probably been quite restricted, because the report more or less has the character of a general presentation for outsiders.

Based on the Helsinki experience, the following critical observation can be made: there should be more time available for the preparation of the self-assessment report than was the case in the application in the University of Helsinki, and the time of the year should be chosen so that students and faculty are not intensively preparing for their holidays. A good self-assessment report should not be merely a description of the international activities, but it should aim at being a real evaluation in order to be of value also inside the university. When preparing the report, one should really go into depth and ask the departments, at least a representative selection of them, not only the larger units such as the faculties.

The self-assessment process was considered useful in the faculties, and one important effect, at least in certain faculties, was to open their eyes for many aspects of internationalisation. Thus, not only the outcome of the exercise, *i.e.* the resulting report, but also the process itself was considered to have a value in its own. However, a general opinion was that internationalisation should not be assessed separately from other academic activities, since it is integrated in them as a mainstream. There was also an opposition against too frequent quality assessments.

117

The peer review

Between 9 and 11 September 1996, the visit of the IQRP peer review team (PRT) took place, during which the members of the team met with the SAT, the rector, the vice-rectors, the deans, other administrative and faculty staff, and students who represented the Student Union. After that, the PRT prepared the report, a draft of which was sent to the SAT for checking, and the final PRT report was received in November, 1996.

The peer review team report was based on the self-assessment report, the international strategy of the university (a revised version of which had just been approved by the Senate), and discussions with groups and persons. The idea of having a team consisting of outsiders to assess the university is of course that they may note and observe such things that need improvement but are too familiar for the insiders to be noted. On the other hand, the risk inherent in a very brief visit of the team is that the impressions remain on a merely superficial level. Also, the opinions and views transferred by single interviewees may be biased and merely personal; for the members of the peer review team it may be difficult to judge whether this is the case.

For practical reasons the members of the PRT in this case neither had the possibility to meet before the review process to evaluate the written information, nor after it to digest the impressions received against the background of the documents. This being the case, the result is easily a fragmented report, particularly if it is compiled in accordance with the very tight time schedule that is recommended. There is also a risk for actual errors and misunderstandings. To avoid such shortcomings, the draft report shall be sent to the SAT for checking. This was the case, and a few errors and a number of misunderstandings were noted and submitted to the PRT; however, not all these remarks were taken into consideration in the final report. The readability of the report would also have profited from a more efficient final editing that would have lessened the fragmentation, and some repetitions could also have been avoided. Consequently, the PRT report is to be seen more as an impressionistic overview than a profound analysis; anyway, also as such it has an undeniable value and interest for the university assessed. The report also contains a lot of information and many interesting views.

It would be most advisable for the PRT to meet both before and after the site visit, first to evaluate the information obtained in written, then to collect all the impressions and to outline the report. For practical and financial reasons this is, however, difficult and utopian. Also, the interaction between the PRT and the SAT in preparing the final report should be more functioning than was the case in the Helsinki assessment. In addition, a careful editing of the report would have eased its further use.

On the whole, the PRT report is very positive with respect to the quality of internationalisation within the University of Helsinki. It is to be noted that the university's strategy for internationalisation was in preparation and almost ready when the university decided to join the IQRP process; it was finally approved by the Senate about one month before the visit of the PRT. This timing was criticised by the PRT, who would have recommended a final updating of the strategy only after receipt of the final PRT report. However, the PRT understood the reasons behind the acting of the university, particularly when it was emphasised from the side of the university that the strategy document is not a static policy document, but a guideline to be adapted in the light of new circumstances and continuous self-assessment; also the PRT report will contribute to this process.

The report by far supports the international strategy of the university. However, it also contains criticism against certain principles of the university's strategy, against the way of managing certain things, or against the state of some issue. It also in a few cases suggests priorities differing from the strategy. The Committee for International Affairs of the university is continuously monitoring and developing the implementation of the international strategy; in this work the IQRP report is also included.

In the following overview those suggestions and views of the PRT report that complement the university's strategy or are in conflict with it will be presented with respect to how they are further processed in the implementation of the international strategy. The PRT report itself is included as an annex to this chapter, in an abridged version.

The most important PRT suggestions and their impact

There are few suggestions in the PRT report that could be said, at this stage, to have been directly applied to change the administration, research, teaching or academic life. As pointed out above, many of the suggestions and ideas underline elements of the university's international strategy and thus support the implementation of it. The PRT report hardly contains anything in direct conflict with the strategy, even if several views and suggestions complement it and introduce new views that have been and still have to be carefully studied by individuals and groups elaborating policy documents and planning activities.

European and global co-operation

The PRT notes the strategical emphasise on European co-operation and very active participation of the university in European Union's academic exchange and research financing programmes. It expresses some concern for an over reliance on the EU and a narrowing of internationalisation to Europeanisation.

119

Concerning the good success in raising funds through the EU IV Framework Programme the PRT states that it may be a double-edged knife: research priorities may become influenced by the programmes to a greater extent than by university strategies, and the EU funds become concentrated to restricted areas particularly in the field of natural sciences, whereas areas such as social sciences and humanities have much less opportunities for receiving EU funds. Certain special measures should be taken to guarantee the long-term funding from both institutional and national sources for fundamental research and research in areas that are not priority for the European Commission. Another problem is that of sustainability: the external funds for research, such as those from the EU, are short-term funds. The PRT suggests a certain level of buffer funding to ensure the continuation of excellent research projects after the external money has dried up.

The university has recently founded a new committee, the Scientific Council, whose primary tasks are to promote research and its funding and to develop the structure of academic positions. The problems mentioned above fall into the tasks of this council and will no doubt be on its agenda. The council also grants the universities own research funds on the basis of applications. The need for buffer money can often be catered for through these funds.

In academic mobility, according to the PRT, too much emphasis has been laid on the European programme ERASMUS and the Scandinavian programme NORDPLUS. The mobility based on bilateral agreements should be increased and, particularly, exchange with non-European countries, such as Pacific Asia and Latin America, should be developed in this way. The PRT is worried about its interpretation that achieving a balance between incoming and outgoing students would be the main motivator for attracting foreign students and scholars, and it points to the enriching effects students and researcher from abroad have on the quality of the academic environment.

To this it must be said that the Ministry of Education emphasises the quantitative aspects of student mobility, and that it is an imperative for the university to actively raise the amount of both incoming and outgoing students and to strive at a balance. Achieving a balance is a necessary goal, but it is by far not the main motivator. Most students and staff at the University of Helsinki can be supposed to appreciate the presence of foreigners in their immediate surroundings. Since at least some degree of fluency in English is widespread among staff and students, and many also speak other languages, there should not be any contact difficulties either.

When dealing with the regional dimensions the PRT has also pointed out the importance of consultancy, training, and institutional building in the Baltic States and Russia. Important is the observation of the PRT about potential EU funding for these purposes. With, *inter alia*, this in mind, the Committee for International Affairs has formed an *ad hoc* working group to find out about what academic co-operation with these countries there has been, what would be needed, and what are the future prospects. The group finished its report at the end of July, 1998, and its results will form the basis for the strategical discussions about this issue.

Internationalisation of curriculum

Among potential sources for further internationalisation of curricula are:

- The presence of foreign students could be considered more explicitly as sources for internationalisation of the teaching and learning process through highly interactive course designs with both domestic and foreign participants.
- International research projects could be made use of in teaching, particularly at the postgraduate level, and reward of staff performance in international education could be created.
- Internationalised curricula should not be too narrowly defined as courses taught in English, but an international dimension in both content and learning processes is necessary. All courses taught in other than the domestic languages should be attended by both foreign and domestic students.
- A more structured approach to the offering of courses taught in English would help in making the curriculum more attractive to foreign exchange students. At present the impression is that there is a fragmented offer of isolated courses (but there are master's programmes and coherent course entities offered in English).

All these issues have been noted at the university. The Committee for International Affairs has set up an *ad hoc* working group on developing international education that has reached certain recommendations, very much in line with the PRT comments. The faculties are encouraged to take measures for improving the present situation.

The PRT noticed a dualism in the university policy with respect to foreign students: there is a strong emphasise on recruiting exchange students, whereas foreign degree students according to the PRT seem to be considered more a burden than an asset of the university.

This is a problem, one of the backgrounds of which is the Finnish legislation: there shall not be any tuition fees for education leading to a degree. The foreign degree students need a lot of more work in the departments than the domestic students (such as introductory and language courses), and since the financing of the departments greatly depends on the number of degrees taken the international degree students do not benefit the departments economically, since most of them study more slowly than most Finns. This is particularly the case with students from developing countries. The Committee for International Affairs set up a working group and employed a researcher entrusted with the task to make an account of the interaction between the university and countries of the Third World, and to suggest possible solutions. The report was finished in late July, 1998. One possibility suggested is the attempt to raise funds from development aid agencies, and to offer education as development aid. The report will form the basis for further discussions on this issue.

Marketing strategies

The PRT encourages the university to pay more attention to marketing its strengths in teaching and research to the international community. Elements to be emphasised include:

- Information on excellent research groups in general.
- Niche research areas (such as epidemiology).
- Unique resources (such as the Russian Library).
- IT based international co-operative network.
- Excellent research conditions and traditions.

It is true that the marketing strategies need to be developed. This should take place as a co-operation between the Committee for International Affairs, the Public Relations Department, and the Research Services Department.

The PRT was intrigued and puzzled by the role of the university companies (Helsinki University Development Services Ltd, Helsinki University Knowledge Services Ltd, and others) in marketing and internationalisation. They found them to be separate and marginal. Also the highest administration of the university has had similar feelings, and at present the role of these companies is being scrutinised.

Organisational issues

The PRT attempted an analysis of the sustainability of the internationalisation effort, first along an axis with marginal and peripheral effort at one end, and high priority and centrality at the other. The university was found to move rapidly towards the latter position. Another axis stands for the degree of systematisation of the efforts, running from an *ad hoc* attitude to a very systematic approach. With respect to this axis the PRT was not quite convinced: are arrangements as systematic as they should be, without weakening that entrepreneurial urge which is essential to operate effectively in the international arena, in research grants or student marketing?

On the basis of the analysis the PRT wanted to recommend attention to the following issues.

Personnel politics

- Attraction of high quality overseas academics (competitive salaries and a permanent basis).
- Better integration of visiting teachers.
- Adequate budget for staff travel and international sabbaticals.
- Broadening promoting criteria including high quality teaching and work abroad.
- Staff development country briefings.
- EU briefings.
- Language skills.
- Teaching multinational classes.
- Development of distance learning materials.
- Contractual issues relating to work abroad.

The university has adopted a programme for developing politics on personnel, but most of the above items are missing from it. Some of the items have been discussed, but a number of them do not seem realistic in the present economic conditions, even if they would be most interesting.

Financial management

- Visibility of income and expenditure flows.
- Developmental/pump priming funds.
- Accurate costing and pricing of international services and optimum fee recovery.
- Financial incentives to operate internationally.
- Stability, sustainability and diversification of international income sources.
- Liability and risk cover for international projects.
- Adequacy of intellectual property arrangements.

The visibility of the flows is something that is soon being achieved at the university. Financial incentives have existed since 1993, and based on the experiences gained they were in late 1997 suggested by the Committee for International Affairs to be revised. A revision has taken place and was implemented during the latter half of 1998.

Convergence and compatibility of university and faculty plans

- The way in which some unconvinced departments may be activated to perform adequately on the international scene.
- Closer articulation of goals and budget priorities.

These items are reflected in the annual agreements between the departments and the dean, and between the deans of the faculties and the rector.

Consistent quality assurance processes across the whole domain of international work

Research evaluation works well, since there is an old tradition of peer review. In teaching, much has been done to create relevant methods of evaluation. In this context reference can also be made to the self-assessment exercise, in which several interviewees would prefer to integrate the assessment of internationalisation in a general evaluation.

The question of centre/faculty/department relations

- Articulation of central policy priorities.
- The roles of central units.
- A close integration of effort between the International Relations Office and other central units.
- The continuing proactive role of central units, but in an entrepreneurial rather than a bureaucratic spirit.

At present, the central administration is going through a process of restructuring, in which all these issues are being discussed.

Final remarks

The application of the IQRP in the University of Helsinki was an experiment and a pilot project, aimed at collecting experiences. What could be particularly criticised was the too tight timetable for the collection of data from the faculties and their departments, and the point of time that was problematic in the faculties. Also, the checklist then in use more steered the self-assessment towards an inventory than an assessment. For this reason the SAT report more became a base document for the peer review than a document to be used parallel with the PRT report in implementing and developing the international and other strategies. Very much based on the criticism received from Helsinki, a new questionnaire was elaborated. It can be assumed that a self-assessment based on the new questionnaire leads to much better and analytic self-assessment report.

According to the guidelines of the IQRP every participating university has the right to publish the results or to treat them as confidential, or anything between these. The University of Helsinki preferred a total transparency, which was also thought to benefit the future development and application of the IQRP, and in consequence with this published the PRT report, the checklist used, and the SAT report together in one volume (Fogelberg and Pajala, 1997).

This publication has awaked great interest all over the world to the extent that a new printing of it was needed. The Helsinki IQRP has been presented at international fora, such as the EAIE conference in Barcelona in November 1997. One reason for the great interest in the Helsinki case may be that the other pilot institutions have hardly given any publicity to their assessments.

The Helsinki experience has had a significance not only for the university itself but for the international community and for the development of the process. Information about it has been largely disseminated thanks to the publication.

Bibliography

FOGELBERG, P. and PAJALA, K. (1997),
"An Internationalisation Quality Review Process: University of Helsinki, 1996", *Evaluation Projects of the University of Helsinki* 5.

Annex
The 1996 University of Helsinki Peer Review Report
Abridged version

Peer review team members

- John Davies, Anglia Polytechnic University, UK/La Trobe University, Australia (Chair).
- Jane Knight, Ryerson Polytechnic University, Canada.
- Outi Snellman, University of Lapland/Centre for International Mobility (CIMO), Finland.
- Marijk van der Wende, Academic Co-operation Association (ACA), Belgium/Netherlands Organisation for International Co-operation in Higher Education (NUFFIC), the Netherlands.
- Hans de Wit, University of Amsterdam, the Netherlands (Secretary).

Self-assessment team members at the University of Helsinki

- Paul Fogelberg, Vice-Rector (chair).
- Anna Luikko, Director, International Relations.
- Jari Niemelä, Professor, Faculty of Science.
- Kari Takamaa, Assistant, Faculty of Law.
- Elina Ussa, Student of Food Technology, Student Union.
- Kaija Pajala, Project Co-ordinator, International Relations.

Introduction

This report has been written according to the framework of the "Pilot Project on the Development of an Internationalisation Quality Review Process at the level of Higher Education Institutions", a project of the Programme for Institutional Management in Higher Education (IMHE) of the Organisation for Economic Co-operation and Development (OECD) in co-operation with the Academic Co-operation Association (ACA).

The peer review team (PRT) visited the university of Helsinki on 9-11 September 1996. The PRT based its report on an elaborated self-assessment report, dated August 1996, and on the document "Strategies for International Operations at the University of Helsinki, 1996-2005", prepared by the Committee for International affairs for approval by the Senate of the University of Helsinki in August 1996. In addition to these two documents, the PRT received before and during the visit several other background documents. The PRT had an extensive programme of meetings and discussions with the rector and vice-rectors, the Director of Administration, the heads of several central administration units, the deans, a delegation of the Faculty of Social Sciences, the Foreign Student Advisor, the Research Liaison Officer, and representatives of student organisations. Also, the PRT had two intensive meetings with the self-assessment team, at the beginning and at the end of the visit.

The PRT in its composition reflected the intentions of the pilot project and has executed its role according to the tasks stated in the project document, which are, to determine:

- What the goals for internationalisation of the institution include and whether they are clearly formulated.
- How they are translated into the institution's curriculum, research and public service functions and how the institution is providing the necessary support and infrastructure for successful internationalisation.
- How the institution knows that its internationalisation works (how it monitors its efforts).
- How the university needs to change in order to improve its internationalisation strategies.

The PRT was impressed, not only by the dedication but also by the commitment within the university to internationalisation and to the quality review process of its internationalisation strategy. The time and energy put into the self-assessment, not only by the team but also by the central administration, the students, the faculties and their deans and international secretaries, was clear, from the documents and from the intensive participation in the meetings with the PRT.

The PRT welcomes the statement of the authorities of the University of Helsinki, that quality review of the internationalisation strategy will be integrated into the overall quality review process of the University of Helsinki, thus facilitating positive interaction between the two processes.

Also, the PRT welcomes the observation by the SAT that in several faculties there has been a catalytic effect of self-assessment, putting internationalisation higher on their agenda. Their involvement has been stimulated by the self-assessment, and several new ideas have emerged, mainly for the implementation, rather than on the goals and objectives of internationalisation. "Transparency" and "interchange" were key elements of the self-assessment process. It confirms the impression of the PRT that in quality review the most important element is the actual process of self-assessment itself.

127

General observations

Overall, the PRT is impressed with the results of the internationalisation strategy of the University of Helsinki in a relatively short period. The International Relations Office of the university has only been established in 1991, the Committee for International Affairs in 1992 and a first policy document, "Developing International Operations at the University 2 of Helsinki", was produced in 1992 (and approved by the Senate in autumn 1993). The participation in ISEP dates from 1984, in NORDPLUS programmes from 1988, and in the EU programmes only from 1995 (partially in 1992). In 1994, the post of a Research Liaison Officer was established, and the success rate of this post is the most clear indication of the effective way the University of Helsinki has implemented its internationalisation strategy. The presence in most faculties of full-time or part-time (combined with academic positions) international secretaries, and the creation of an ERASMUS student network, are indications that this strategy reflects itself at all levels of the university.

The general objectives of the internationalisation strategy of the University of Helsinki, as formulated in the latest strategy document, are:

- To maintain high standards in teaching and research by making use of international interaction and by promoting the mobility of Finnish and foreign researchers, teachers and students.
- To increase international research co-operation and international funding for research.
- To take the demands of present-day internationalism and European unification into account in teaching and course content.
- To encourage the development of versatile language and communication skills. Students will also be encouraged to study in languages other than their own.
- To promote the teaching of Finnish, Swedish and of the Finnish culture to foreign students and staff members.
- To disseminate throughout the world information on Finnish cultural and scientific achievements.
- To promote respect and tolerance for foreign cultures.
- To strengthen the Finnish national identity by emphasising Finland's role and contribution to Nordic, European and world-wide co-operation.

In reaching these objectives, the University of Helsinki has passed the stage in which it reacted primarily to imperatives from the government. In the opinion of the PRT, the strategy of the university gives the impression that to a certain extent the national imperatives have been replaced by European Union imperatives. The PRT understands the argument, that, given their history and location, the nation and the university see the participation in the European Union and its programmes more as a natural attitude than as an imperative. But there is an inherent danger of over reliance on the EU and a narrowing of internationalisation to europeanisation. Overall, it would be too optimistic to conclude that the University of Helsinki has reached a state where it is basing its strategy on its own funds and plans more than on reactions to other funds and plans from national and international sources. However, the new policy reflects the fact that the University of Helsinki is heading in that direction.

Regionalisation and internationalisation

Related to the participation in the EU programmes is the issue of sustainability and degree of influence. In other words, are the European programmes used to enhance and provide resources for internationalisation plans or are they shaping and driving the strategy? Clearly the former is most desirable but at this stage of participation and support from the EU it is important to prevent the latter. The PRT wishes to raise questions about finding the optimal balance and role that the EU programmes and funding play in the internationalisation of the research, teaching and service functions of the University of Helsinki.

Participation in the EU programmes has clearly been beneficial to the internationalisation/regionalisation of the University of Helsinki. For instance, the success rate for funded research projects is very impressive and to be applauded.

Also, the importance of consultancy, training, and institution building in the Baltic States and Russia, is, given the location of the university, an important element of the international policy of the university. In this area further opportunities are available, with potential financial support from the EU and other international funds.

However, the new opportunities and increasing emphasis on participating in EU funded programmes also raise new questions and issues regarding the long-term internationalisation strategy for the university. One of these issues relates to geographic priorities and balance of the internationalisation plan.

The new long-term internationalisation plan for the University of Helsinki astutely includes objectives for the national, Nordic, European and international levels of co-operation. The current increase in European level co-operation is occurring at the same time that development and technical assistance projects supported by FINNIDA are decreasing. This is a result of reduced government support for work with developing countries which can in turn have a negative impact on university co-operation with several partners in the southern hemisphere.

Thus special attention may need to be given to alternative types of international co-operation with countries outside of the Nordic and European region. Interest in Pacific Asia and Latin/South America was expressed by students, administrators and academics. It may be prudent to invest in developing closer linkages with countries in these regions of the world. Allocation of resources is always a challenge when developing new international linkages and partnerships and therefore, income generating joint projects such as in-country contract education and training with the overseas partners may need to be considered in order to support other kinds of international academic activities.

129

External relations and services

Opportunities for new technologies and electronic/information exchange and distance education are increasing exponentially. A thorough analysis of these opportunities from a cost benefit (academic/economic) point of view may also help in the implementation of the internationalisation strategy especially related to the best geographic and cultural balance and mix of countries.

Local Partnerships for International Co-operation are, in the perception of the PRT, providing interesting opportunities for internationalisation of the university. The Helsinki Summer Academy Project is an excellent example of local partnerships for international programming. This model may lead to other co-operative programmes with non-government organisations, private sector companies and other public sector institutions in Finland. International co-operation involves developing new linkages with local partners, an area that needs further development. It requires clarity of purpose and goals as partners often have very different motives and expectations which can be complementary or causing conflict. Identification and accommodation of these diverse motivations is critical to the success of these local (as well as international) partnerships.

This raises the big question of the role of internationalisation in nourishing the development of the Helsinki region of south-east Finland. There is no doubt that the EU funded activities associated with research, including TACIS, PHARE, EURATOM, the Fourth Framework, the Cohesion Fund, etc., have played a significant part in stimulating research based technological enterprises, and the university clearly needs to ensure its continuation with the Fifth Framework, whose priority areas accord with many local needs.

The international dimension of continuing education – especially in fields like executive development, postgraduate programmes for existing professionals, the preparation of people for international employment and contacts – seems relatively untouched by the international effort permeating much of the rest of the university. The PRT would recommend early attention to this, and which organisations within or attached to the university, should make the main initiatives. This is an area of ambiguity to which we now turn.

The PRT was both intrigued and puzzled by the role that the university companies, such as Development Services Ltd, Knowledge Services Ltd, and the Lahti Research and Training Centre, played in the internationalisation of the University of Helsinki. During the PRT meetings with both administrators and academics, any questions about these units usually yielded responses that they knew very little about these companies except that they were very separate from the university, that they worked internationally and that further information was desired and needed in order to assess whether co-operation was possible with these units. Without having met with representatives of these companies, the PRT does not have any concrete information with which to make any suggestions; therefore, the PRT comments are in the form of questions.

The questions the PRT raises are:

- What contribution, academically and economically, do these companies make and could they make to the internationalisation of research and teaching and to the overseas reputation of the university?
- Are there opportunities for closer co-operation with other institutes, centres and academic departments?
- Are there networks and contacts in foreign countries useful for other forms of international academic co-operation and the integration of an international dimension into the basic functions of the university?
- Are there missed opportunities for cost-effective internationalisation initiatives by having these companies appear to be so separate and marginalised from academic units on campus?

The University of Helsinki should pay more attention to marketing its strengths in teaching and research to the international academic community. In the opinion of the PRT, too much attention is given to study and teaching abroad opportunities for its own students and scholars. The success of the University of Helsinki in EU research programmes is an indication of its strength in the area of research, as is its active participation in ERASMUS of its strength in teaching. The university should make that a much more central feature of the promotion of its internationalisation policy.

The elements here to be emphasising in a market strategy would include: *i*) information on excellent research groups in general; *ii*) niche research areas (epidemiology); *iii*) unique resources (the Russian Library); *iv*) IT based international co-operative network; and *v*) excellent research conditions and traditions.

Research

The University of Helsinki has a strong research orientation. This is reflected in the set of goals and priorities for the 1990s, where the promotion of high quality research is listed as the top priority for the institution. The international research contacts of the university are extensive, and the departments and individual faculty members have a clear sense of international contacts in research as a basis for quality in research and teaching.

The university places emphasis on the internationalisation of research, and takes as much as possible advantage of international research funds. The most important source of these funds are the EU research programmes. Since the appointment of a Research Liaison Officer in 1994, the University of Helsinki has been extremely successful in attracting EU funding for research, with a very impressive strike-rate percentage of bids submitted. The support services for applying for the funds work well, including a person in the financial administration that assists in the preparation of budgets for EU research fund applications.

131

The critical successful factors here which should be commended, include the following:

- Excellent on-line information networks which facilitate the speedy transmission of intelligence for bids.
- Good intellectual property arrangements.
- Regular seminars.
- Quick processing and compilation of project bids by staff who understand the academic mind, who can screen projects sensitively from financial and scientific perspectives.
- Good networking.

However, there does seem to be scope for the further development of the Research Office services in:

- More exploitation of internationally funded research for local enterprise development.
- Diversified research funding from international foundations, multinational industry, contract research.
- New parts of the world – South-East Asia, Latin America and Japan (with better intellectual property arrangements).
- Ph.D. training – where very few international students exist, and where existing institutional consortia should be more heavily exploited.

As a result, an increasing proportion of the research conducted by the university is being funded from outside sources, primarily from the EU IV Framework Programme. The goal set by the institution for attracting EU funds is clearly being met. This may be a double-edged knife: the institution is able to create large research projects in those areas prioritised by the European Commission. However, this policy may be perceived as not very diversified, and, there is a potential danger that the institution in the long run will lose some of its control over its research policy. In the discussions with deans and rectors, it was clear that the university is aware of these potential dangers and takes them in consideration in its research strategies.

The EU funds concentrate mainly on certain areas, that correlate in several cases with those that have been defined by the university or by the ministry as Centres of Excellence, and therefore are eligible for additional institutional or national funds. In areas as social sciences and humanities, with less tradition of working in large research groups and with a more indirect relevance to competitiveness, opportunities for external funds, particularly EU funds, are more scarce. More external funds require a large financial input from the institutional or other outside source. It is easier to obtain these for research by the Centres of Excellence in the aforementioned areas. If the pace of development continues to be equally rapid, it may result in the gradual channelling and concentration of funds to fields that fit better into the EU priorities. Certain special measures should be taken to guarantee the long-term funding from both institutional and national sources for fundamental research and research in areas that are not priority for the European Commission.

As the pressures for the university to fund an increasingly large proportion of its activities from outside sources grow, the issue of sustainability needs to be addressed. The external funds for research, again the EU funds being a good example, are short-term funds, often of the matching kind. They do not provide for a long-term funding of basic research and, in the case of EU also cost money. The university is starting to address this issue by, for example, placing emphasis on creating wide-ranging contacts with the business and industrial sectors, but in the departments the awareness of the implications of the shifting funding mechanisms for research may still be low. The faculties and departments are for the most part responsible for funding their research, but a certain level of buffer funding to ensure the continuation of excellent research projects after the external money has dried up might be one possibility for ensuring sustainability. This would need to be addressed at a strategic level in the institution.

As the amount of international funding has increased, the institution has improved its monitoring of the financial health of its international operations. However, it is still relatively difficult for the institution to conduct true cost-benefit analysis of its international research activities, and to calculate the actual costs of the externally funded research projects. The current accounting systems provide little possibility for a clear overview about the international income. Again, as the proportion of external funds increases, the institution should be able to create a greater awareness of cost-effectiveness.

In a research university like the University of Helsinki, the choice of partners for international co-operation is of fundamental importance. At best, the partners in the various research projects can also form the core for interaction in education. The institution would be wise to consider benefits of a more proactive linking of the international educational and research activities, so that they would benefit each other mutually. In this case, the possibility of merging the research office with the international office could be beneficial, as a "one-stop-shop".

Academic programmes

At a general level, it is difficult to give any precise feed back on the internationalisation of academic programmes at the University of Helsinki. As a result of the nature and structuring of the IQRP checklist and of the time pressure under which the self-evaluation had to be conducted, little evidence could be collected on the international dimension of curricula. Consequently, the comments given below are rather based on general impressions of the role of curriculum development in the wider internationalisation process, than on a systemic analysis of the institution's provisions in this area.

Motives to more explicitly involve the curriculum in the process of internationalisation could be threefold:

- The rectorate's emphasis on strengthening the teaching functions of the university; internationalisation is an important means for achieving quality improvement in teaching and learning.

- The emphasis of the European Union's educational programmes has currently shifted towards developing an international (European) dimension in the study programmes for the (95%) non-mobile students.
- The successful actions of the University of Helsinki in the area of student and staff mobility and in research could be more effectively linked by integration into the curriculum.

Potential sources for further internationalisation of curricula seem to exist in three areas:

- The presence of foreign students. Both exchange and degree students could be considered more explicitly as sources for internationalisation of the teaching and learning process. Highly interactive (*e.g.* group work, collaborative projects and case studies, etc.) course designs increase the benefit of their presence for domestic students.
- The institution's distinguished international research projects seem to represent an important source for internationalisation of the curriculum at, in particular, the postgraduate level. Spin-offs of efforts and investments could be optimised by channelling the results into the curriculum.
- An important condition for further internationalisation of the curriculum rests in the area of staff development. The existing opportunities for internationalisation of teaching staff should be continued and reward of staff performance in international education could be created.

Another important condition, or concern, is of a more conceptual nature. Internationalised curricula should not be too narrowly defined as courses taught in English. An international dimension in both content and learning processes is implied. Although teaching in English is of course a prerequisite for attracting foreign students, it may as well work as a separating mechanism (Finnish and foreign students being taught separately in different languages), detrimental to the above described spin-off effects. Also for reasons of cost-effectiveness a sufficient number of foreign students should be ensured by, for instance, clustering of courses or groups. The PRT has taken notice of the intention of the university to move into a situation, where there is no duplication of courses for Finnish and foreign students.

From an international marketing point of view internationalised curricula are important. Experiences in other countries show that these curricula attract more international students than traditional curricula do. Students are generally motivated to choose them as they are interested to study together with students from different countries.

It seems appropriate and challenging to encourage faculty level debates and analyses of the concept(s) of internationalised curricula, of the present provision in this area and of opportunities for further development. As for the last point, the institution's high quality and well-established contacts with foreign partner institutions may very well represent interesting options for joint curriculum development.

Students

Domestic exchange students

The number of outgoing domestic students in the framework of exchange programmes has been going up rapidly from 79 in 1989-90 to 451 in 1995-96. The target of 500 outgoing exchange students for 1998, will be most likely reached. But the mobility, both outgoing and incoming, is still too much taking place in the framework of ERASMUS (65%), followed by NORDPLUS (20%). Exchanges in the framework of bilateral agreements and ISEP, although growing in numbers as well, are still too much a minority. This can create an overdependence on external programmes and on inner-European mobility.

According to the PRT, the University of Helsinki in its student exchange policy is still too much reactive to external targets and programmes and too much inner-European Union oriented, and lacks a clear autonomous policy to reach the ambitious aim, stated in the internationalisation plan, "that by the year 2005 every graduate will have had the opportunity to spend some time abroad". Although there are clear signals by the central administration that expansion outside the European Union is seriously considered, they seem to be based more on national policies (expanding the relationship with South-East Asia) and European programme opportunities (Latin America, through the so-called Alfa programme), rather than on institutionally determinated priorities. Setting clear targets and budgets, taking autonomous institutional initiatives and stimulating departmental initiatives for student exchange, independent of the European Union and outside of the European Union, are necessary instruments to reach that goal in the coming ten years.

The PRT was surprised by the fact that neither faculty nor students give much importance to credits in studying abroad. There is, in the system, a feeling that study abroad is more of an added value, rather than an integral part of the curriculum; the prolonged study time tends to be considered as a real problem. Neither national nor institutional regulations have, until now, contributed much to really deflecting students from this feeling. However, new measures by the government, such as the financing of the universities based on the number of degrees, may change that soon. More attention to credit transfer and integration of study abroad into the curriculum, is recommended. The decision of the University Senate in 1993 to apply the European Credit Transfer System (ECTS) as extensively as possible, is an important factor in stimulating the transfer of credits.

Foreign exchange students

The PRT noted a strong feeling of uncertainty about the attractiveness of the University of Helsinki as a place of study for exchange students. Asked what is the biggest concern in the internationalisation strategy of the university, the answer, both of the central authorities, the Student Union and the faculties, is: "How to attract students and academics to come to Finland." At the same time, it is observed that the University of Helsinki makes itself extremely dependent on recruiting exchange students for the creation of placements for their own exchange students abroad. For that purpose the university even has

135

allocated bonuses to the faculties on the basis of the number of foreign exchange students. This does not give justice to the role foreign exchange students and scholars can play in the teaching and research environment of the university, and to the potential attractiveness of the quality of education and research at the University of Helsinki.

The PRT recommends that the university begin to move away from the present focus on the danger of imbalance as the main motivator for attracting foreign students and scholars, and instead stresses more the importance, in the own words of the SAT, that "foreign students [and scholars] make the academic community more international and they are seen as an enriching element as such".

The PRT is positive about the measures taken by the University of Helsinki to reduce the barriers for foreign exchange students to study at the university. The decision to create opportunities for courses taught in English, in addition to the existing instruction in Finnish and Swedish, is an important mechanism to create interaction in the classroom between Finnish students, foreign students and the teacher. An important requirement in this context is that opportunities are stimulated for Finnish students to take part in English taught courses. The knowledge of English among Finnish faculty and students makes that possible.

The services for the foreign students are organised in a excellent way: orientation programmes, providing accommodation, and so on. The active role of the University of Helsinki's Student Union, and in particular the ERASMUS Student Network in the provision of services and orientation to the foreign exchange students, is seen as positive. Furthermore, it is important to note that the PRT was positive on the offer of introductory courses in Finnish language and culture.

Foreign degree students

The PRT has observed a dualism in the policy of the University of Helsinki with respect to foreign students. Everything is done to recruit foreign exchange students, yet, the PRT also gets the impression, that foreign degree students are considered more as a burden than as an asset of the university. At the faculty level, a more positive attitude to foreign degree students is evident, but concern is expressed on the problems of language preparation, entrance levels of preliminary training and cultural integration.

In line with the internationalisation document of the university, the PRT recommends that more attention is paid to the selection and preparation of the foreign degree student (the creation of a preparatory year has in that respect been mentioned in the university) and to mechanisms of improving their active cultural integration.

The PRT applauds the efforts of the ERASMUS Student Network to assist both the foreign exchange and the foreign degree students in their introduction to the university. This is an excellent example for the rest of the university, to consider both categories of students as of equal importance for the internationalisation of the university. Indeed, the

PRT would wish to commend the Student Union organisation as a whole for its comprehensive range of services to overseas students and for the way in which it relates positively to university and other authorities, which also seemed client-oriented.

Organisational issues

After this review of the main activities and outcomes of the university's international policy, the PRT should comment on other most important elements in the delivery of the international portfolio, namely sustainability, centre-faculty relationships, planning and general quality arrangements, which, of course are very interrelated.

As universities develop their international work, it is useful to conceive of their internationalisation along two dimensions. The first is along a spectrum where at one end, the international effort is really marginal and peripheral, to the other end where it is of very high priority and centrality, and permeates the work of the university at all levels and in all domains. Helsinki is clearly moving towards the latter position very rapidly.

The other dimension is where the university stands in terms of the degree of systematisation of its efforts – from the *ad hoc* to the very systematic. Helsinki again is moving in the latter direction. The question for the university to consider is: are arrangements as systematic as they should be, without weakening that entrepreneurial urge which is essential to operate effectively in the international arena, in research grants or student marketing?

The PRT recommends attention be given to the following important organisational issues:

- Personnel policies: the attraction of high quality overseas academics on competitive salaries and a permanent basis; the better integration of visiting overseas teachers; an adequate budget for staff travel and international sabbaticals; broadening promotional criteria to include high quality teaching and overseas work. Staff development: country briefings, EU briefings, language skills, teaching multi-national classes; development of distance learning materials; contractual issues relating to overseas work.
- Financial management: visibility of income and expenditure flows for all aspects of international business; developmental/pump priming funds; accurate costing and pricing of international services – and optimum fee recovery; financial incentives to faculties and schools to operate internationally; stability, sustainability and diversification of international income sources; liability and risk cover for international projects; adequacy of intellectual property arrangements.
- Convergence and compatibility of university and faculty/schools plans, and the extent to which faculty priorities include university policy imperatives. Attention might profitably be given to: the ways which some unconvinced departments may be activated to perform adequately on the international scene; the closer articulation of goals and budget priorities; and how performance indicators for international

137

work may be sensibly and sensitively used to monitor strategic goals and act as an incentive for changing patterns of behaviour. These issues might be given attention in the annual planning agreements between the departments and the deans, and between the deans of the faculties and the rector.

- Curriculum review from an international prospective: here the role of interdisciplinary area studies may have some attraction, and in this context, the evolution of library provision, internet arrangements, etc., is relevant.
- Consistent quality assurance processes across the whole domain of international work. At present, arrangements for research (of conventional standing) clearly work reasonably well because of the primacy of external peer groups. The same cannot be said of teaching, administrative operations or students services. The latter group may well be excellent, but the PRT was not aware of specific quality assurance arrangements.

Finally, there is the question of centre-faculty-department relations, on which the PRT was able to develop partial insights, and which usually represents an area of some tension in most universities. The main issues here seem to be:

- Articulating central policy priorities with those of the faculties, and below then the departments. We have already referred to the rector-dean discussions. There is a case for extending this practice to departmental briefings also, so that departments prepare their priorities clearly aware of university wide goals and how they should respond.
- The roles of central units. The university should consider how a service/client oriented attitude may be extended, with the resultant pushing back of more traditional bureaucratic cultures. This may be accompanied by a version of service-level agreements; explicit and visible incentive structures to departments to operate constructively in the international arena; and designated link persons in departments and faculties for international business.
- A close integration of effort between the International Relations Office and other central units, so that a cohesive set of views and support mechanisms is provided for departments. From what has been already observed on aspects of personnel and financial management, this is not always the case at present.
- The continuing proactive role of central units, and the senior academic officers of the university, but in an entrepreneurial rather than a bureaucratic spirit. This may have to go beyond the facilitating to the promotional dimensions in the context of teaching, if not so much in research.

7

Integrating the IQRP in the Strategic Plan Monash University, Australia

by

Grant McBurnie

The university setting

The Australian higher education system consists of 36 government funded universities and two private universities. In addition, there are eight government funded higher education institutions which are not called universities. Monash University, a government university, was established in 1958, and began taking students in 1961. The university is now Australia's largest, with more than 45 000 students spread across six Australian campuses and one Malaysian campus, or enrolled in Monash transnational programmes in the Asian region. In Australia, academic staff total some 2 500 and general staff number more than 2 700. Monash has ten faculties/schools including: Art and Design; Arts (Humanities and Social Science); Business and Economics; Information Technology; Education; Engineering; Law; Medicine; Science; and Pharmacy. Qualifications offered range from bachelor through to Ph.D., with master by coursework and/or research and postgraduate diploma available in a number of fields.

The university is headed by the Vice-Chancellor, who is also President. There are three Deputy Vice-Chancellors: International and Public Affairs; Academic and Planning; Research and Development. Financial and administrative operations are under the General Manager. Together these constitute the Vice-Chancellor's Group, or senior executive management of Monash. The basic academic organisational unit is the department, and these are grouped by discipline into faculties. Each faculty is headed by a Dean, and has three Associate Deans, representing the faculty regarding variously teaching, research and international matters.

OECD 1999

Nature and extent of international dimension

Monash has a strong profile across all of the dimensions of institutional internationalisation identified by Back and Davis (1995, pp. 121-122) in their study of "the scope of internationalisation in Australia": staff and student mobility, internationalised curricula, international links. Indeed, the authors of the independent *Good Universities Guide* judged Monash the Australian University of the Year in 1994 when internationalisation was the key criterion of the award (Ashenden and Milligan, 1994).

Back and Davis (1995) describe the trend from "aid" (assistance for developing countries) to "trade" (attracting fee paying international students) to "process" (seeking to integrate an international dimension into the core functions of the institution) which broadly characterises the international focus of Australian higher education in recent decades. Monash (along with the University of New South Wales) was one of the universities at the forefront of these movements. Its history also shows that these phases overlapped and combined in many ways. From its commencement, the university integrated area studies into its teaching and research programmes through the Centre for Southeast Asian Studies and similar specialised operations. At the same time that Monash welcomed students from Asia under the Colombo Plan aid scheme in the 1960s and 1970s, it also attracted significant numbers of private students. Interestingly, at Monash the highest percentages of international students (18%) were present on campus in the early to mid-1980s, before fees were made chargeable at the end of that decade. As the university pursued fee paying international students from the late 1980s, it made a commitment that the key Asian countries from which students were drawn – including Malaysia, Indonesia, Hong Kong, China, and Singapore – would be part of the academic research and teaching profile as well as the "market" of the institution. In 1991, Monash was the first Australian university to appoint a Pro Vice-Chancellor to deal exclusively with international programmes and development.

In parallel with taking its own initiatives, Monash – sometimes in consortia with other institutions – has participated with enthusiasm in the many Australian government programmes promoting international education links, such as the "Targeted Institutional Links Programme", the "University Mobility in Asia and the Pacific" scheme, and country specific co-operation arrangements.

The university's approach to internationalisation has been threefold:

- To internationalise the composition of the student body.
- To internationalise the educational experience of students and faculty.
- To establish and enhance a Monash presence overseas.

The international composition of the Monash student body is readily quantifiable. There are more than 5 500 international students from 70 countries enrolled at the Australian campuses of Monash, more than 600 enrolled at the Malaysian campus (planned to grow to 5 500 by the year 2003), and over 2 500 undertaking Monash courses transnationally in Hong Kong, China, Singapore, Indonesia and Malaysia. Australia is a multicultural nation, and this is closely reflected in the mix of national origins of Australian citizens and permanent residents enrolled at Monash. For some 20% English is not the main language spoken at home, and more than 20 languages are represented.

Success in internationalising the educational experience of students and faculty is, of course, not as easy to measure, and is an ongoing process. The university has fostered an academic culture encouraging the internationalisation of the curriculum. This has broadly taken four forms: degrees with an international focus such as bachelor of arts (Asian studies) and bachelor of business (international marketing); area and language studies; subjects with an international focus, such as Indonesian politics or French history; the use, wherever possible, of international examples within a subject, such as water purification in Thailand as a case study within environmental science. There are a wide variety of such options for Monash students.

Over the years, numerous Memoranda of Understanding have been signed with foreign universities, institutions and government departments. Flowing from this are ample opportunities for student and staff mobility, supported by bursaries for students and funded sabbaticals and Outside Studies Programmes for tenured faculty. Numerous research centres at the university specialise in international, regional or country focused studies. These include the Monash Asia Institute, the Centre for Southeast Asian Studies, and the recently established Monash Centre for Research in International Education. The physical presence of Monash overseas includes a full campus in Malaysia, and various partnership arrangements providing teaching sites in Malaysia, Hong Kong, China, Singapore and Indonesia. Monash academic centres for Australian studies have been established in partnership with other universities in the United States, England and Germany. Plans are well advanced for a campus in South Africa.

Why IQRP was introduced

To understand the context of the study at Monash, it is important to note that the IQRP took place in advance of (and, to some extent, in anticipation of) major planned changes in the overall organisational structure and senior leadership of the university. The review of internationalisation at Monash was one part of a broad internal review encompassing all aspects of the institution.

While Monash has a strong profile in international education, its achievements in the field could be seen by the critical eye as a mixture of careful central planning, individual initiative, historical trends, happy circumstance and ad hoc developments. Monash wished to take stock, build on successes, identify and address problems. The overall goal was to reassess the university's objectives, articulate them as explicit university policy, and build strategies for internationalisation into the new institutional plan.

It should also be noted that the Australian university system does not have a strong history of external review. Government universities are self-accrediting, in line with rigorous procedures supervised by each university's Council or Senate. National reviews of education quality have been ad hoc, and systematically examining the internationalisation of the student experience has not been a government priority.

In looking at the internationalisation of education, Monash was and is keen to use external quality measures, especially those internationally based, as a method of examining its profile in the context of the world. Like institutions around the world, Monash acknowledges that "quality" has many meanings (fitness for purpose, world's best practice, value for money, client satisfaction and so on) which must be negotiated and discussed in relation to education. The university continues to promote debate about these issues.

The IQRP is an international, external quality instrument. In a climate where external review is not a regular expectation, the connection of IQRP with the highly-respected OECD would likely win the respect and confidence of the Monash community which would be involved in the process. The opportunity to undertake the IQRP was very attractive to Monash for all of these reasons.

Implementation of the IQRP

The self-assessment analysis and report

Monash carried out the IQRP in a different order to that suggested by the model. Given the size of the university, and the ongoing nature of planning, it was more practical to consult the wider university community *after* distributing the self-assessment report and the peer review report as a basis for discussion and analysis.

The preparation of the SAT report was co-ordinated by the International Office, headed by the Pro Vice-Chancellor, International Programmes and Development.

There were three aspects to completing the SAT report.

Assembling existing information held by the International Office

A range of internal and external material relevant to the IQRP was already held in the International Office. Most readily available was information about the international matters for which the office was responsible, such as student mobility, staff exchange, inter-university relations, international student recruitment and support. Existing reports and studies were utilised, including documents prepared for the visit by the *Good Universities Guide* panel; internal Monash reviews (on Language and Learning Support Services, the Monash Asia Institute, Asian Language Provision); and structured surveys of international student satisfaction. Other sources included university strategic planning and policy documents, public relations and marketing material, course catalogues, statistical reports, staffing regulations, and staff development course material.

The office also put together historical and contextual information relevant to the internationalisation of higher education in Australia. This included material by the Australian Vice-Chancellors' Committee (AVCC) and federal government departments such as the Department of Employment, Education and Training (DEET) and the Department of Foreign Affairs and Trade (DFAT). In some cases it was necessary to clarify for the PRT that certain staffing and student policies (regarding employment restrictions and student visa regulations) were a result of compliance with government legislation rather than university strategy.

Obtaining information from appropriate sections of the university community

An explanation of the background and purpose of the IQRP, together with specific questions for completion was sent to relevant sections of the university. These were the same people scheduled to be interviewed by the PRT. Those well-acquainted with international issues welcomed the invitation to elaborate on the role of their area. For those who dealt primarily with domestic issues, this was a fresh opportunity to reflect upon the international dimension of their activities.

Carrying out additional institutional research

Once the collected material was combined into a coherent whole by the Pro Vice-Chancellor and his staff, further research was carried out to fill in any identified gaps and to update information. For example, at the request of the International Office, the Human Resources Branch systematically examined Outside Studies Programme (sabbatical leave) reports to draw a profile of countries where academic staff carried out sabbatical activities. The Research Branch updated material on Monash publications in international scholarly journals, and collaborative research with international colleagues.

A first full draft was sent out to those who had contributed information, affording them the opportunity to revise their section in the light of the overall document. The revised draft was then given to the PRT and those scheduled to be interviewed.

143

The Monash SAT report, while detailed and thoroughgoing, is something of an interim document, which was later integrated into the larger Monash planning process.

The peer review team visit and report

Following the preparation of the self-assessment report, the second phase was the visit by the peer review team. The PRT was aware of the order in which Monash intended to carry out the IQRP. The PRT report noted that "the university's self-assessment report and this account of the external review will be used by the university in an on-going institution-wide evaluation of the internationalisation activities and planning" (p. 1).

Over two days, the PRT interviewed some forty Monash faculty, staff and students according to an agreed schedule. Members of the Monash community interviewed included:

- Senior management involved in university planning, governance and organisational systems.
- Area and language studies faculty.
- Faculty teaching internationalised curricula (in arts, business, information technology, and medicine).
- Student services administrative staff.
- External relations staff.
- Faculty and management dealing with international research and scholarly collaboration.
- Human resources management, including those dealing with appointments, professional development and the outside studies programme (sabbatical leave).
- Language and learning services staff (providing academic support for students with learning difficulties).
- Study abroad and student exchange students, faculty and administrative staff.
- International students.

As the third phase, the PRT provided a written report to Monash, addressing each of the categories covered both by the IQRP and the self-assessment report. The PRT report acknowledged areas of strength, and provided constructive criticism regarding areas it suggested needed attention.

Benefits of the IQRP

Immediately following the IQRP, Monash underwent the GATE review of the off-shore courses. Lessons learned from IQRP and GATE, each serving different but complementary functions, were then incorporated in the Monash planning system. GATE now has an ongoing role in Monash off-shore quality review, and the university anticipates carrying out an IQRP (or similar) exercise at its international campus(es).

In light of these developments, the sections below look at the use of quality instruments in relation to internationalisation across three dimensions:

- Institutional planning for internationalisation: IQRP and the Monash Plan.
- Quality assurance in transnational education: GATE certification of Monash programmes offered in Hong Kong, China, Malaysia and Singapore.
- International campuses: the Monash Global Programme in Malaysia.

The IQRP and institutional planning: the Monash Plan

Strategic planning

The impact of the IQRP is most apparent in its contribution to the strategic planning of the university. As part of an ongoing process of planning and development, the university in 1997 published *Leading the Way: The Monash Plan 1998-2002* which includes clear goals and performance targets. The internationalisation of the university is a key element of the plan, expressed in the section entitled "Becoming Global" and throughout the document.

Following the IQRP, the SAT report, the PRT report and explanatory contextual information were packaged together and forwarded to all faculty Deans and senior management, who were asked to provide feedback. The combined information was used as a resource in the broader task of producing the Monash Plan. One of many resources, the IQRP was particularly valued because of its comprehensive, systematic framework, and the external, international perspective it provided.

The peer review team report observes that Monash "is among the premier institutions in the world to have internationalised to the breadth" (p. 5), and commends the university on a number of strengths. At the same time, it makes several incisive criticisms and suggestions, always in a constructive spirit and for the purpose of facilitating the shared goal of improvement.

Rather than list the actions taken by Monash in response to each of the matters raised in the PRT report and the self-assessment process, it can be noted that each has been taken up, together with many other matters, in the context of the Monash Plan and its associated activities. To illustrate, one key aspect, internationalisation of the curriculum, will be highlighted and discussed.

Internationalisation of the curriculum

At the time Monash underwent the IQRP, the strategy for internationalising the curriculum of the university operated chiefly by encouraging individual academics and schools to incorporate an international dimension into the subjects they taught, and providing students with many options for combined degrees. The other key aspect was the provision of a suite of options for students to carry out part of their study overseas.

In judging Monash the Australian university of the year for 1994-95 when the theme was internationalisation, the authors of the *Good Universities Guide* commented particularly on the efforts of the university to enhance the experiences of students:

> "Monash has been among the first to see that there is more to being an international university than selling places to international students. It wants to change the way young Australians see themselves and their working futures. Pushing this ambition further and faster than others, it is among the first to find that some internationalising is easy to do, and some is not. Opening doors to students from around the region, around the world, can be done relatively quickly and relatively easily. Lifting the quality of educational and other services to these students is harder, and takes longer. Opening windows on to worlds for Australian students (...) is hardest of all." (Ashenden and Milligan, 1994, p. 83)

Internationalisation strategies proved very successful for some faculties (particularly Arts, Business and Economics, Law and Medicine), but internationalisation was less evident for other disciplines.

The PRT report noted the successes of the university in this respect, but observed that in their view "it remains unclear if there is a deliberate institutional policy for internationalising the curriculum, currently carried out by individual teaching staff or departments" (p. 3).

Under the Monash Plan, the goal of internationalising the curriculum is now explicitly stated as university policy:

> "Consistent with one of its three key themes, Monash will ensure that all its students have the opportunity to gain an international education. Within two years, all Monash award programmes will demonstrate within their curriculum a commitment to key internationalisation outcomes." (Monash University, 1997, p. 8)

To assist with realising this goal, the international dimension has been integrated as a standard part of the university's course approval procedure. Each new course routinely undergoes a peer review process in accord with specified criteria (concerning matters such as elements of content, assessment methods, mode of delivery and so on). One of the requirements is to demonstrate how the course contributes to the student's international perspective on the discipline (Monash University, 1998, pp. 8-9). A similar requirement will be implemented for existing courses from 1999. The success of this strategy will need to be examined further down the track.

Study abroad

Studying abroad is another key means of internationalising the educational experience. While Monash can point to several of its student mobility programmes which have had a strong impact, the university acknowledges it has not attracted as many participants as it would like. Through the IQRP, the SAT and PRT together identified a number of matters which needed to be addressed to raise the international mobility of Monash students:

- Integrating study abroad into the curriculum wherever possible.
- Developing a consistent policy on academic credit for international study.
- Streamlining the processes for students to avail themselves of study abroad opportunities offered by the university.
- Drawing together the central administrative and faculty-based resources for better service to students.
- Improving and linking the predeparture (including visa, accommodation arrangements and academic programme information) and post return services (including debriefing and granting of academic credit) to students.

In *Leading the Way* (Monash University, 1997), the university has taken three steps to deal with these issues: setting a measurable target; putting a process into place which involves close collaboration between academic and administrative staff; devoting a substantial and increasing budget line to the task. The Monash Plan sets the goal of 10% of commencing students to complete part of their studies overseas for credit toward their Monash degree. In the first year of operation, more than A$1 million has been budgeted for this purpose, and it is anticipated that the figure will rise as the number of students participating in the programme increases.

A Monash Abroad Office has been established to administer programmes, and to liaise with each faculty/school to devise discipline-appropriate strategies for enhancing student mobility. A range of programmes is offered, including:

- Student exchanges.
- Language study.
- Internships.
- Business tours.
- Art and culture tours.
- Community service projects.

The success of this new mobility scheme will be measured by a number of performance indicators, including: number of participants, spread across disciplines, academic progress, and student feedback. The Monash Abroad Programme,

147

as it relies on various means of accessing overseas study opportunities, has underlined the need to carefully evaluate the nature and vigour of the university's international relationships.

International institutional agreements

Over time, the university has signed Memoranda of Understanding (MOU) with 168 institutions from 30 countries, for the purposes of student and staff exchange, and collaborative research. One of the issues raised in the IQRP was the level of activity of these agreements. As one might expect, the answers ranged across the spectrum from high to sporadic to moribund.

The Vice-Chancellor, Professor Robinson, has noted that:

> "Formal co-operation is the most rapidly growing aspect of the internationalisation of inter-institutional relations. Co-operation in this sense is much more than paper agreements. Too many university vice-chancellors and rectors have inherited too many such agreements, filling too many rarely opened filing cabinets." (Robinson, 1998, p. 5)

In an earlier phase of internationalisation, increasing the number of institutional relationships was a priority. In line with the Monash Plan, the university is reviewing its inter-institutional agreements "in order to identify a smaller set of key relationships which are fully active and important" (Monash University, 1997, p. 17). One approach is to clarify the nature of the relationship with each institution. The categories include:

- University level relationships (where three or more faculties/schools are involved on each side).
- Faculty level relationships (where one or sometimes two faculties are involved on each side).
- Relationships functioning across the range of activities: student exchange, staff exchange, exchange of academic materials, collaborative teaching, collaborative research.
- Relationships focusing on one activity, such as student exchange, or joint consultation on a community service project.

A number of organisational actions have been taken to address these issues, and to deal with the ongoing implementation of the Monash Plan. Under the Deputy Vice-Chancellor, International and Public Affairs, three core consultative and advisory groups have been established to promote cross-university interaction on internationalisation. The "Monash University Global Group", which includes Associate Deans International from each faculty/school, deals primarily with academic and discipline oriented internationalisation. The "International Working Group" is a small "think tank" addressing institutional level international issues. "Country

Focus Groups" comprise faculty and staff interested in interactions with a particular country.

Quality assurance in transnational education: GATE certification of Monash University

The university's concern to review the quality of internationalisation within its Australian campuses was naturally mirrored by a desire to formally examine and ensure the quality of its programmes operating overseas. To this end Monash in late 1996 invited the Global Alliance for Transnational Education to pilot the GATE quality assessment principles by reviewing Monash off-shore courses. The university simultaneously piloted its own internal "Off-shore Quality Assurance" review procedures. This undertaking was foreshadowed in the SAT report, and welcomed by the peer review team, which noted (p. 3):

> "The extensive off-shore offerings of Monash are generally well accepted throughout the university and in the countries where they are provided. Although the university is careful to assure general quality through a combination of centralised and decentralised means, the recent instituting of a quality assurance process for these programmes is both accepted and necessary. The result is the adoption of an integrated quality assurance system combining ongoing internal review and regular external certification."

The GATE review process and the IQRP serve quite different purposes. IQRP is concerned with helping a university assess its success in, and devise strategies for, achieving its own goals regarding internationalisation – in this case the internationalisation of the education experience for Monash students and faculty. GATE focuses on the quality of the delivery and support of education programmes offered outside their country of origin. In the experience of Monash, the two quality instruments complement each other well, and carry synergistic benefits for the institution concerned with various aspects of the quality of internationalisation.

Transnational education

GATE focuses on the growing transnational dimension of the internationalisation of education (refer to Chapter 11 for further discussion on GATE and the certification approach). Some background on both transnational education and GATE will help clarify these phenomena.

GATE offers a succinct definition of transnational education in the introduction to its Certification Manual:

> "Transnational Education denotes any teaching or learning activity in which the students are in a different country (the host country) to that in

which the institution providing the education is based (the home country). This situation requires that national boundaries be crossed by information about the education, and by staff and/or educational materials." (GATE, 1997a, p. 1)

There are a variety of ways in which education is conducted transnationally, including via: distance education (with or without local support); twinning programmes; articulation programmes; branch campuses; and franchising arrangements (McBurnie and Pollock, 1998).

Transnational education has been growing in popularity for some years. In 1998, for example, 34 out of 38 Australian universities reported offering courses off-shore, to an estimated total of more than 20 000 students (AVCC, 1998). Acknowledging the importance of transnational education, the Australian Vice-Chancellors' Committee has published a voluntary code of ethics for the provision of off-shore courses (AVCC, 1995).

Transnational education is attractive to students seeking to gain a foreign qualification without moving from their country of residence. It can also be attractive to employers and governments looking at options for human resource development (including multinational or global corporations with a geographically dispersed workforce). Education providers seeking ways to expand their export markets are also attracted to the possibilities opened up by transnational education. The devaluation of Asian currencies is likely to increase the demand for transnational offerings in the region, as students find it more difficult to afford the cost of living as well as tuition fees in foreign countries.

At the same time that it presents possibilities for students, governments, employers and providers, transnational education underlines the need for review systems to address the quality of the education available. The operation of bogus or substandard providers is of course an important "consumer protection" concern. However, even where a qualification is provided transnationally by a reputable university, recognised or accredited by its home country, a number of questions arise, including:

- Is the course content the same as that provided at the home institution (and should it be)?
- Is there appropriate cultural sensitivity to the local requirements in terms of content (including appropriate use of local examples, and explanation of foreign terms or context)?
- Are the methods of teaching appropriate for achieving the objectives of the course (i.e. teaching styles may not always translate well from country to country)?
- Are the physical, administrative, communication and other resources adequate to support successful learning?

Monash has pursued these quality issues regarding its transnational offerings using its own internal guidelines and the GATE principles.

GATE certification

GATE gives the following reasons as to why an institution or government may find GATE certification of value:

> "To demonstrate commitment to quality education; certification is required by a country to permit a foreign institution to offer a programme; certification is accepted by a country for the purpose of recognising the institution's graduates; to ensure or enhance the employability of graduates; to provide international comparability; to provide international mobility; to permit transportability of qualifications and partial qualifications; to permit international credit accumulation; to attract students; (...) as a check on the quality of education being exported by or imported into the country." (GATE, 1997*b*, p. 3)

Several of these reasons were applicable to Monash. The university is concerned with assuring – and being seen to assure – the quality of its transnational programmes. Motivations included showing a commitment to quality, demonstrating the university's quality in a competitive international market, concern for the consumer rights of students and, overall, maintaining the reputation and image of Monash. Another motivation was the desire to take the initiative in an age where it is likely that governments, employers and students will increasingly demand education providers quality.

Review of Monash off-shore courses

With the mandate of the University Council, in late 1996 a small team (including two GATE board members, and members of the Monash Off-shore Quality Assurance Committee) simultaneously piloted the GATE principles and Monash's internal Off-shore Quality Assurance guidelines.

The review team examined 18 bachelor level and masters level courses across Malaysia, Singapore and Hong Kong, China. The disciplines included business, computing, nursing and arts. These were either fully taught in classrooms by a combination of local academics and visiting Monash staff, or undertaken by distance education supported by local staff. In all cases, Monash curriculum material was used, and students had access to staff support, computer and library facilities. The partners were variously: local universities operating through their professional and continuing education arm; local institutions or professional bodies authorised by their government to offer foreign qualifications in partnership with registered foreign universities; or licensed private education companies.

The team requested written reports from the Monash academic faculties running the courses. These were normally prepared in co-operation with the overseas partner. In accord with the prescribed guidelines, detailed descriptions and documentary evidence were provided for matters including:

- Provision of curriculum material.
- Appropriate use of local examples and context for material foreign to the local culture.
- Admission standards.
- Assessment of students.
- Staff selection.
- Channels of communication.
- Teaching facilities.
- Notification of student results.
- Appropriate marketing of courses.
- Contractual arrangements.
- Local professional accreditation requirements.
- Legal requirements of the host country.
- Ongoing evaluation procedures.

After digesting the reports the team visited the off-shore operations, meeting with academic and administrative staff and students, and inspecting physical facilities including classrooms, libraries, and computer equipment. For each course, the Monash Off-shore Quality Assurance (OQA) team wrote an item by item report which was submitted to Monash University Council, the relevant Monash faculty/school and the off-shore partner. Each report contained recommendations concerning any conditions the continuation of the course should be subject to, and suggestions for improving the course. The faculty was then required to report to council on how it has/will implement any changes recommended. Among the issues raised in the OQA reports and acted upon by the university were, in some cases:

- The need to ensure appropriate local content and explanation of context for foreign material.
- Upgrading and substitution of library materials (in some instances the textbook prescribed in Australia was not readily available in the host country).
- Enhancement of channels of communication between the host and the provider, including specifying protocols and turnaround times.
- Resolution of contractual issues with partners.

For each course the GATE members of the team prepared an itemised report addressing each of the GATE principles. These reports were then considered by the 12 member GATE board which awarded certification to those Monash courses which had been reviewed and satisfied the requirements. While the outcome of the certification was a Yes or No result, it was important that Monash received detailed evaluative comments for the enhancement of courses, and comments anticipating possible future problems or issues requiring attention.

Following the pilot phase, both the Off-shore Quality Assurance system and GATE certification have now been formalised and integrated into the overall Monash academic, budgetary and strategic planning programme. The curriculum content and academic standards of Monash courses operating off-shore are subject to the same processes of approval applied to all Monash offerings. Initially they are carefully scrutinised by the faculty, the Education Committee, and Academic Board in accord with published regulations.

Off-shore courses undergo two additional processes to ensure that their standards are maintained when they "cross the border": *internal review* in line with the Monash Off-shore Quality Assurance Committee, and *external certification* by GATE. Under the terms of the Off-shore Quality Assurance Committee, course proposals are scrutinised twice-yearly, and courses are reviewed on a rolling three-year cycle. The GATE certification is due for renewal in late 1999, when Monash courses will again be subject to this independent review process.

The use of such quality instruments is a strategic part of the Monash Global Programme.

The Monash Global Programme

As part of its internationalisation strategy, Monash has embarked on what it calls the "Monash Global Programme". The goal is to establish a significant Monash presence in up to seven key international locations by the year 2002. Perhaps the most innovative aspect of the programme will be the establishment of a number of Monash campuses overseas.

The terms "branch campus", "foreign campus", "international campus" and "overseas campus" are ambiguous. In the North American context, these frequently refer to an arrangement whereby the host institution – perhaps as part of a study abroad programme – has licensed a site in a foreign country where its own (American) students can study for a semester or summer school for credit towards their degree. In the Australian context, branch campus is sometimes used synonymously with "twinning programme" or with overseas support sites for distance education programmes (as discussed above).

In the context of the Monash Global Programme, three criteria define the international campus:

- It offers complete programmes from commencement through graduation, culminating in a regular qualification of the provider institution.
- It is part of the education system of the host country.

- It is a full campus of the provider institution, integrated as seamlessly as possible into its mainstream academic, administrative and resource systems.

Monash has established the first such campus in Malaysia in 1998, at the invitation of the Malaysian government. Plans are well advanced to establish a campus in South Africa, with the close involvement of that country's government.

The Monash University Malaysian Campus

The Monash Malaysian campus is the first of its kind in Southeast Asia, and is an example of what may become a new phenomenon in international education: a sovereign government asks a foreign university to establish a campus, to offer programmes in line with the national strategy, and to be integrated into the local education system including reporting lines to the government.

This development offers interesting possibilities in internationalisation. It also raises a number of important issues, and the need for appropriate quality instruments. GATE is part of the process. In due course, the university anticipates the need to carry out an IQRP (or IQRP related) review of the international education experience of students in relation to the Malaysian campus. In that case the goals to be explored would be those formulated collaboratively by the national government of Malaysia and the university. Monash University has been involved with Malaysia since shortly after the university's foundation. From 1963, Monash welcomed large numbers of Malaysian students under the Colombo Plan and other aid mechanisms. As fee paying international students became part of the Australian education environment from the late 1980s, Malaysia continued as a major source of Monash students. The university also established twinning programmes in Malaysia, whereby students carried out part of a degree in their home country and completed their studies in Australia. There are some 9 000 Monash alumni in Malaysia, many of them playing key influential roles in society. One consequence of this close and continuing relationship, is that Monash enjoys a strong profile with the Malaysian government, professions, employers and students.

The Malaysian government, as part of its "Vision 2020" national plan, declared its goal to strengthen the educational infrastructure of the country. Addressing a conference on "Reforms in Education: The Next Stage" shortly before the announcement of Monash Malaysia, the Malaysian Minister of Education outlined the approach:

"The introduction [of six pieces of education legislation was] intended to bring about a quantum leap to the education system which will bring about sweeping change to the country's learning institutions ... This is in line with our mission: to develop a world class quality education which is flexible and innovative ... [and] will make Malaysia a regional education hub and a centre for education excellence as we approach the next millennium... Inherent in the policy, is the need to decentralise and liberalise the system. It also became abundantly clear to us that education based solely upon the public sector will restrict and inhibit growth. No government has unlimited resources on education. The writings on the wall have clearly pointed to the fact that we now require the private sector to be involved in education, in particular, at the tertiary level. This has led us to encourage the setting up of private universities... [within a] proper legal framework." (Razak, 1998)

The "Private Higher Educational Institutions Act" of 1996 and other legislation opened the way for foreign universities, upon government invitation, to found campuses in Malaysia.

The present Monash Malaysia campus has developed from its successful twinning programme run since 1990 in partnership with Sunway College, a private Malaysian educational institution. The operation at Sunway was reviewed as part of the GATE certification discussed above. The ministry has made it clear that government funded institutions are well able to meet the nation's requirements in the fields of arts, humanities and social sciences. Monash Malaysia will concentrate particularly on disciplines which clearly relate to the government focus on improving the industrialised science-technology profile of Malaysia: engineering, science, information technology, commerce. The campus will also offer programmes by distance education. The government of Malaysia has been negotiating with a number of universities from various countries concerning the establishment of foreign campuses. It is possible that such arrangements may be made involving several universities and countries. While these are early days, it is worth reflecting upon some of the issues involved in what may become a new dimension in the internationalisation of education.

There are a number of benefits to the host country, in this case Malaysia:

- At no cost to the Malaysian taxpayer, a well-regarded foreign institution is integrated as part of the Malaysian system to provide programmes in line with goals of national development.
- Programmes are introduced with the consultation and approval of the government.
- The educational infrastructure of the country is expanded particularly with respect to science and technology programmes (or whichever fields are priorities for the nation).
- Students can fully carry out a foreign degree at home, thereby saving costs in terms of travel and overseas living expenses.
- The campus can assist Malaysia in its goal of becoming a net exporter of education, by attracting students outside the country to study on campus or by distance education.

There are two key differences between this relationship and the other off-shore components of the university: it is a full (seventh) campus of the university; it is a part of the education system of the country, with Monash having a direct line of responsibility to the Malaysian government.

A number of issues in the internationalisation of the university arise from these two factors. There will be additional opportunities for international and intercultural cross-fertilisation in the fields of teaching, research and administration:

- Strategies for internationalising the curriculum will be able to incorporate perspectives from the international campuses, including case studies and subjects devised in response to specific country needs.
- The international profile of research programmes can be broadened as staff at campuses in different countries collaborate. Research undertaken in response to the needs of other countries where Monash is represented will also have an international focus not necessarily present in Australian based projects.
- The staff and student profiles of the university will be increasingly internationalised.
- Administrative structures and procedures will have opportunity to take on international components, as the regulations and requirements of different countries must be met within the overall Monash system.
- The Monash Abroad mobility programme will be extended to include Monash students regardless of the country they are based in.
- Monash will need to develop some new programmes which would not otherwise have existed within the university. For example, Monash will offer students in Malaysia subjects in line with ethics and culture components of the government's plan: "Islamic Studies" for Malay students; "Moral Studies" for non-Malay students from Malaysia; "Malaysian Studies" for foreign students. Monash faculty in Australia and Malaysia will collaborate in the design and teaching of these courses. Naturally, there will be opportunity for such studies to inform cultural and other studies at the Australian campuses, and for cross-cultural perspectives to be an integral part of the courses.

Allowing for national differences, Monash is developing a model for implementing this kind of arrangement in several countries.

A number of critical concerns and potential problems must be kept in mind. These include:

- Appropriate handling of Western values.
- Sensitivity to local requirements.
- Ensuring the full programme is provided to students in the branch campus.
- Appropriate pedagogical styles.

- The danger of academic matters being driven by financial considerations ahead of educational values.
- Industrial issues for faculty and staff.
- Political, cultural and equity issues relating to the language of instruction.

These issues are topics of energetic discussion at Monash and elsewhere, and must be addressed in the planning mechanism. In addition to systems applied internally by Monash, there are at least two external quality instruments Monash has found important, and which it intends incorporating into the Global Programme.

The Malaysian campus (and future campuses in the planned Global Programme) will be reviewed by GATE to provide an external quality assurance mechanism, as well as by internal Monash Off-shore Quality Assurance procedures. Indeed, certification by the independent, internationally based GATE was one of the components considered by the Malaysian government in its invitation for Monash to establish a full campus in that country.

The university anticipates that, in due course, an IQRP oriented review will be needed to help rigorously gauge progress in realising the possibilities of the Global Programme in terms of further internationalising the educational experience for staff and students of Monash University, regardless of country.

Conclusion: what is the impact of IQRP

The IQRP benefited Monash in at least four ways:

- It brought together a diverse cross-section of the Monash community to focus, in a rigorous and structured manner, on international matters.
- It provided an impetus to take a detailed snapshot of internationalisation at Monash. The range of information had not previously been put together into one package (rather it had been spread across filing cabinets and minds around the university).
- The university received feedback and suggestions that were internal, external, local and international.
- It helped to identify areas of strength, and areas needing attention. This had of course been done before, but the external/international aspect of the process added extra weight to the observations.

The IQRP material fed ideally into the planning process Monash embarked on in 1997, and is redeveloping annually.

If the internationalisation of education is to provide real benefits for the university community, there is an ongoing need to define goals and objectives, to implement strategies for their achievement, and to gauge the quality of the outcomes. In this light, the key impact of IQRP at Monash has been at the level of

157

university planning. Together with quality instruments such as GATE it has played, and will continue to play, a vital role in energising the internationalist axons of the institutional mind.

Bibliography

ASHENDEN, D. and MILLIGAN, S. (1994),
"Monash: A Window on to Worlds", *The Independent Monthly*, August, p. 85.

AUSTRALIAN VICE-CHANCELLORS' COMMITTEE (AVCC) (1995),
"The Code of Ethical Practice in the Provision Offshore of Education and Educational Services by Australian Higher Education Institutions", Canberra.

AUSTRALIAN VICE-CHANCELLORS' COMMITTEE (AVCC) (1998),
"Offshore Programmes conducted under Formal Agreements between Australian Universities and overseas Higher Education Institutions and Organisations", Canberra (available at http://www.aarnet.edu.au/avcc/internat/offshor.htm).

BACK, K.J. and DAVIS, D.M. (1995),
"Internationalisation of Education in Australia", in H. de Wit (ed.), *Strategies for Internationalisation of Higher Education: A Comparative Study of Australia, Canada, Europe, and the United States of America*, EAIE, Amsterdam.

DEPARTMENT OF EMPLOYMENT, EDUCATION AND TRAINING (DEET), HIGHER EDUCATION DIVISION (1993),
National Report on Australia's Higher Education Sector, Australian Government Publishing Service, Canberra.

DEPARTMENT OF EMPLOYMENT, EDUCATION, TRAINING AND YOUTH AFFAIRS (DEETYA) (1998),
Learning for Life: Final Report, Review of Higher Education Financing and Policy, Australian Government Publishing Service, Canberra.

GLOBAL ALLIANCE FOR TRANSNATIONAL EDUCATION (GATE) (1997a),
Certification Manual, Washington DC.

GLOBAL ALLIANCE FOR TRANSNATIONAL EDUCATION (GATE) (1997b),
GATE, Vol. 3, No. 3.

MCBURNIE, G. and POLLOCK, A. (1998),
"Transnational Education: An Australian Example", *International Higher Education*, No. 10, Winter (available at http://www.bc.edu/bc_org/avp/soe/cihe/direct1/News10/text7.html).

MONASH UNIVERSITY (1997),
Leading the Way: The Monash Plan 1998-2002, Clayton.

MONASH UNIVERSITY (1998),
Learning and Teaching Operational Plan, Clayton

RAZAK, YB. Dato' Sri Mohd Najib Tun Haji Abdul (1998),
"Reforms in Education: the Next Stage", Keynote Address by Minister of Education at the National Education Conference, Selangor, 26 February (available at http://www.moe.gov.my/ucap7.htm).

ROBINSON, D. (1998),
"From International Relationships to a Global Presence: With Monash as the Case Example", unpublished paper presented at conference "Higher Education Reform in Germany and Australia: Challenges for the 21st Century", Potsdam, 20-22 January.

RUBIN, A.M. (1997),
"Certification Process Created to Insure Quality of College Programmes Offered Abroad", *The Chronicle of Higher Education*, 24 October, p. A65.

8

IQRP as a First Step
Moi University, Kenya

by

Joseph Koech and Peter Opakas

Introduction

The Internationalisation Quality Review Process (IORP) of Moi University, Eldoret, Kenya, took place with different objectives from the other case studies in the pilot phase of the IQRP project. At Moi University, IQRP has been used as an instrument to prepare a self-assessment report of the international activities of the university as the first step towards preparing a strategic planning seminar on internationalisation.

The Seminar on Internationalisation of Higher Education took place in Moi University from 21 June to 29 June 1998. It was organised under the auspices of the MHO Central Services Project, the objective of which is the improvement of the central services, both academic and administrative, at the university. The project is part of a broader institution building project, run by NUFFIC, in which Dutch universities co-operate over a long period with faculties and schools of Moi University, in the field of environmental studies, health sciences, technology, agriculture and tourism.

The seminar was facilitated by two external experts in the field of internationalisation of higher education: Jane Knight, Ryerson Polytechnic University, Toronto (Canada), and Hans de Wit, University of Amsterdam (the Netherlands), who are also the project leaders for the IMHE/OECD internationalisation project and the IQRP pilot project. Peter Opakas and Joseph Koech, principal administrative officers at Moi University, were assigned as project leaders for Moi University MHO Central Services Project.

161

The university

Moi University was established as the second public university in Kenya on the 8 June 1984 by an Act of Parliament. The decision to establish a second university was necessitated by the increasing demand for higher education, and the consequent pressure that this demand was exerting on the University of Nairobi which was the only public university in the country at that time. The proposed university was to introduce new areas of learning which would help to meet the high level manpower requirements of a modern and increasingly technological society. In this connection, Moi University was established as a technologically oriented university, focusing on problems of rural development in its training and research programmes.

The first group of 83 students were admitted in October 1984 and all were in the Department of Forestry on transfer from the University of Nairobi. Since then the university has grown from strength to strength and currently has a student population of 5 594 and 2 748 members of staff.

The university has three campuses. At the moment, the university is composed of the following faculties, schools and institutes: at the Main Campus: the Faculty of Education, the Faculty of Information Sciences, the Faculty of Technology, the Faculty of Law, the School of Graduate Studies, the School of Environmental Studies, the School of Social, Cultural and Development Studies, and the Institute of Human Resource Development; at the Chepkoilel Campus: the Faculty of Agriculture, the Faculty of Forest Resources and Wildlife Management and the Faculty of Science; at the Town Campus: the Faculty of Health Sciences.

Nature and extent of the international dimension

Since its establishment, Moi University has had key defining international characteristics. The Report of the Presidential Working Party which recommended the establishment of the second university in Kenya in 1981 (eventually Moi University), was Chaired by a Canadian, Dr. Collin B. MacKay, President, Emeritus University of New Brunswick, Canada. As part of the inauguration of the university in December 1985, an international conference was organised to map out the vision of the university and the faculties and departments that were to be established. The theme of the conference was "The Role of a New University in a Developing Country". Since its establishment, the university has continued to experience growth of the international dimension in its functions and programmes. However, despite this growth the international dimension is still marginal and rather implicit instead of a recognised, explicit strategy of the university.

For that reason and in preparation for the Seminar on Internationalisation of Higher Education, an institutional self-assessment on the status of internationalisation at Moi University was carried out. The Internationalisation

Quality Review Process questionnaire was distributed to all the deans of faculties and the staff of the central administration. The deans in consultation with members of their departments completed the questionnaires which were then used to compile the self-assessment report on the state of internationalisation at Moi University. The self-assessment report in turn served as a starting point for the seminar and the planning of an internationalisation strategy for Moi University. A summary of the findings of the self-assessment exercise follows.

Academic programmes

Area and language studies

The School of Social, Cultural and Development Studies offers courses in area studies. The Department of Linguistics and Foreign Languages offers studies in a variety of languages such as English, Arabic, Kiswahili and French. There are also plans to introduce Spanish. Anthropology and other aspects of cultural studies do focus on specific areas of interest. Other degree programmes also include an international component such as studies on international co-operation and peace which train students to co-operate in international contexts.

Students who go through Kenya institutions where English is the language of instruction usually have good command of the language. It is, therefore, not mandatory that students have to learn other foreign languages but they can undertake that at their own will. All courses are taught in English except in cases where other languages are being learnt.

Research and scholarly co-operation

One area in which the university has a fairly strong international dimension is in research and scholarly co-operation. Moi University scholars are able to attend international conferences in their respective areas of specialisation funded by the Dean's Committee of Moi University Senate. On the other hand, faculties/departments invite international scholars to the university to share their knowledge and experiences and explore joint initiatives. University researchers publish articles in international, refereed journals and present papers at international conferences.

Relatively few research projects in Moi University are funded by the private sector. Most of the research undertakings are sponsored by international funding and development organisations, at both bilateral and multilateral levels.

Moi University has organised, hosted and continues to participate in many international conferences and workshops. In 1997, the university hosted the International Medical Students Workshop which attracted participants from 30 countries. More recently there was a regional workshop on Information, Education Communication and Behavioural Changes in the Prevention of HIV/AIDS organised in

163

conjunction with the Royal Tropical Institute of Amsterdam in the Netherlands (KIT). A number of workshops and seminars are being held at faculty level addressing critical issues in teaching and research taking into consideration the rapid technological advancements.

Moi University has a successful research co-operation project between the School of Environmental Studies and the Faculty of Environmental Sciences of the University of Amsterdam supported by the MHO programme. The Faculty of Health Sciences has established linkages with Linköping University, Sweden; Indiana University, United States; McMaster University, Canada; and Limburg University in the Netherlands. The Faculty of Information Sciences has links with Thames Valley University in the United Kingdom. The Faculty of Technology of Moi University has links with Delft University of Technology, the Netherlands. The Faculty of Forest Resources and Wildlife Management has links with Toronto University, Oxford University, Memorial University of Newfoundland and Wageningen University, the Netherlands.

Faculty and staff

International activities and mobility of staff

Moi University encourages and provides opportunities for interaction and exchange of ideas for its staff with other local, regional and international scholars. Staff are therefore involved in international seminars, conferences and workshops. Faculty staff have a lot of direct intellectual contacts. The recent development of modern communication technologies and especially e-mail services, provided with the support of the World Bank and the MHO project, will facilitate and speed up the creation of new contacts and enrich existing ones.

The university's terms of service allows and encourages staff to utilise their sabbatical leave for research and teaching in foreign universities. A significant number of Moi University staff have taken advantage of this opportunity. Funding problems and difficulties in arranging for substitute teachers have been the most common obstacles to teacher exchanges. The university is trying to create close links with donor organisations like the British Council, NUFFIC, DAAD and USAID to help in expanding staff exchange projects.

Although exact figures are not available, it is clear that a large proportion of the faculty of Moi University has received its master's and Ph.D. training abroad, mainly in the United States of America, Canada, the United Kingdom, neighbouring countries in Africa and more recently in the European continent, China, India and Japan. Given this large number of staff with overseas training, it is imperative that their experiences be used in the development of international linkages and activities.

Foreign staff

As at March 1998, Moi University had 52 foreign members of staff. The majority originate (29) from other African countries, 12 from the European, seven from India and four from North America. Foreign members are accorded full opportunities to teach, carry out research and interact with both students and other members of staff.

Visiting foreign members of staff are limited in number. Those who come and wish to teach are usually incorporated in the running schedule of academic programmes in their host department. They also have opportunities for classroom interaction and research.

Students

Domestic students abroad

The university tries to send a number of its students to undertake studies abroad, but mainly for Ph.D. training. During the period of their study, the university keeps close contact with the foreign host university in order to monitor the performance of the students. These students are usually attached to supervisors who send regular reports to Moi University on the student's progress. Every foreign study assignment has a specific time period which the students must honour. Graduate students are encouraged to participate in international research projects, networks and exchanges.

Due to inadequate funding only a few students get such opportunities. The university is seeking for financial support and other sources of funding to alleviate this dismal rate of international opportunities for students. Departments, in liaison with the office of the Chief Academic Officer, contact students about international opportunities. Information is provided by the office of the Educational Planner and that of the Public Relations Officer. The office of the Students Counsellor is responsible for the social counselling of the students while the office of the Chief Academic Officer advises students on their academic programme.

Study abroad and student exchange programme

The university has not been involved in exchange programmes which involve a large number of Kenyan students going abroad to foreign universities. Any exchanges that have taken place, have been through individual faculty/departmental arrangements. The level of exchanges is higher in some faculties than others. For instance the Faculty of Health Sciences has active exchanges with Indiana University in the United States, Linköping University in Sweden and Limburg University in the Netherlands. The bottleneck in these exchanges has been the lack of funding. The university is therefore seeking funds to expand these exchange programmes.

Foreign students on campus

There are few foreign students at Moi University. Some have come in the framework of development co-operation projects, such as the MHO programme between the University of Amsterdam and the School of Environmental Studies. Medical students from Linköping University undertake part of their training at the Faculty of Health Sciences, but these students are at Moi only for part of their studies. However, full time degree students mainly come from the region. In the academic year 1997/98, there were nineteen foreign students most of whom are in the Faculty of Forest Resources and Wildlife Management. The distribution by nationality is as follows: seven Sudanese, eight Malawians and four Rwandese students.

As part of the university's strategy to increase the number of foreign students, the Senate has passed a resolution to admit from the 1998/99 academic year on, above the number of new Kenyan students set by the national government, an additional 20% of foreign students. Income generation has been the main motive for this policy. The implications of such a steep increase in the number of foreign students have important implications for language, academic, social, accommodation and other support services.

Linkages

Since 1985, Moi University has continued to establish links with foreign universities. Most of these links consist of staff development for Moi University staff, provision of state of the art equipment for the university, staff exchange between the two partner institutions and joint research projects. Most of these links have focused mainly on institution building.

Moi University has for instance had collaborative links with five different universities/research centres on the European Continent, three in the United Kingdom and four in North America.

Services

Moi University has a modern and computerised library, the Margaret Thatcher Library donated by the British Government. The library is the biggest and most modern in East and Central Africa. The library serves the Moi University community and the entire Western Part of Kenya. The community therefore has access to requisite reading and research material from the library. Due to its communication network the library also enhances communication in the region and beyond.

The university recently hosted a Regional Informatics Network for Africa (RINAF) workshop for Internet systems administrators. This is to link all the countries in the region and be a centre for storage and retrieval of all research materials conducted within the region.

The creation of an International Liaison Office and the appointment of an International Liaison Officer by the university in 1998, is intended to support the departments and the central administration in strengthening the facilities for international students. In addition, plans to establish a project co-ordination office for international activities, programmes and linkages are at an advanced stage. This office will help both staff and students with information and fund-raising and can play an active role in the marketing of the university and its projects in the international arena.

Summary of the self-assessment

From the self-assessment it is evident that Moi University has certain strengths and opportunities for internationalisation. To build on these strengths and expand the scope of internationalisation, there is a pressing need for a more strategic, systematic and co-ordinated approach to planning and monitoring the fragmented and isolated international activities which already exist. International activities and linkages have silently existed for several years without policies or any strategic direction.

Most of the linkages have a strong development nature, dependent on donor funding. In some of the faculties, as Faculty of Health Sciences, Forest Resources and Wildlife Management, Agriculture, interesting examples of international activities take place. Most staff of Moi University have in general had some international training and exposure, and the university has a relatively high presence of foreign faculty, but these experiences appear underused. The university needs to create increased awareness of the importance and dimensions of internationalisation to its staff and students and to develop more dynamic policies and structures. The Seminar on Internationalisation of Higher Education was designed to be the starting point for a debate within the university on the development of an international strategic plan including the appropriate policies and organisational structures.

The Seminar on Internationalisation of Higher Education

Seminar objectives

The seminar was expected to:

* Bring awareness and an appreciation of the fact that Moi University should be part of the wider world-wide effort in advocating planning, implementing, reviewing and improving the university's international strategy.

167

- Enhance internationalisation in Moi University. It was necessary first for the complex term of internationalisation to be fully understood to avoid confusion and so that it could be provided with a clear working definition.
- To assess Moi University's perception of internationalisation. The seminar had to look into the self-assessment of the international dimension of Moi University and see to what extent the university has internationalised already, by way of the successes achieved; the failures encountered and the university's strengths and weaknesses.
- To look into how and why Moi University wants to internationalise. The rationale, reasons and objectives for internationalisation need to be defined.
- To assess the role internationalisation plays in the academic, economic, social, cultural and political sectors of the country and the institution.
- Increase awareness among the staff of Moi University on the need for quality assessment and assurance on the internationalisation of higher education and set up guidelines/framework to assess and enhance the quality of internationalisation strategies in accordance with the mission and objectives of Moi University.
- Provide feedback and complementary analysis from a different external and international perspective through the external peer reviewers/seminar facilitators.

At the end of the seminar the participants were expected to:

- Appreciate that an international dimension is part of the university's mission and major functions.
- Come up with specific internationalisation policies, procedures and programmes at Moi University.
- Acknowledge that quality assurance and related procedures benefit from an international input and approach.
- Be able as an institution to assess and enhance the quality of international efforts according to the university's stated mission and objectives by:
  - developing stated goals and objectives for internationalisation;
  - integrating an international dimension into the teaching and research priorities of the university;
  - including internationalisation as a key element in the university quality assessment system.

On the basis of responses enlisted from the self-assessment questionnaires, a list of participants was constituted. The list was composed of the deans of faculties and senior administrators of the university.

Seminar programme

The Seminar on Internationalisation of Higher Education was held at the university. The seminar itself was divided into three parts.

First part: opening session

The first afternoon session started with a welcome address by the Vice-Chancellor of Moi University, who stressed the importance of linking Moi University to the rest of the world; a presentation by the two external facilitators on "The Meaning and Rationales for Internationalisation"; a presentation by the internal facilitators of their self-assessment report of Moi University; and an introduction of the participants, their units and their expectations of the seminar.

Second part: visits to faculties and administrative units

After this first session, the four facilitators visited over two days the different faculties, centres and schools of the university. They discussed with the deans of faculties and their staff, as well as senior university administrators, the issues and challenges related to the development and implementation of international activities and strategies in their respective faculties and departments. The purpose of the visits and discussion was to sensitise seminar participants and the university community to the importance and dimension of internationalisation and to get an idea of the issues and concerns with respect to international activities within the university.

The facilitators were in particular keen to learn:

- What the objectives and priorities for internationalisation at Moi University are and whether they are clearly formulated.
- Whether or not the university is providing the necessary support and infrastructure for successful internationalisation.
- Whether or not the university is aware of its present international dimensions, what kind of operational framework it has to enhance its international activities and if so, what plans are there to improve the internationalisation strategies.

From the discussions during these visits, the following key issues emerged.

a) Need for mechanisms

The university has fragmented and isolated international activities without adequate policies and there was a need to develop a more strategic, systematic and co-ordinated programme of activities for internationalisation.

The recent establishment of an International Liaison Office is a step in the right direction and the university community needs to understand the mandate and work of this unit.

169

There is a clear need for the development of policies to guide and monitor the internationalisation activities of the university.

b) International experience and expertise of staff

It is evident that a good number of both academic and administrative staff at the university had been trained abroad. It is felt therefore that their international experience and their linkage with their foreign host university should be used for greater advantage in the internationalisation of Moi University.

c) Staff training and development

Most faculties/departments see internationalisation as one avenue for staff training and development overseas.

d) Uniqueness of centres for teaching and research

It is noted that the university has some unique centres or areas in its programmes which could be used to enhance international work. These include the Faculties of Information Sciences, Wildlife Management, Refugee Studies, Tourism, Kiswahili and Cultural Studies, to name only a few.

e) Curriculum issues

It is agreed that curriculum is a fundamental area for the development and enhancement of internationalisation both for domestic and foreign students. It is noted, however, that the existing curriculum is inflexible as it does not accommo-date foreign students. It needed to be more flexible so as to provide for credit transfer to other universities and vice-versa.

f) Need for more linkages

Most faculties/departments are keen to develop more linkages to enhance teaching, research and service of the university. At the same time, it is necessary to look for ways to sustain these linkages so that they are active agreements not just paper ones. The development, sustaining, and evaluating of linkages requires the investment of resources.

g) Electronic access to information

An efficient and effective tool for faculty and students to stay in touch with the world is through electronic access to information. There is need to access journals, publications and colleagues at foreign universities. However, it was noted that the establishment of the infrastructure for electronic communication is an expensive

exercise and therefore it is necessary to strategically plan and invest more resources in this area.

h) International students

It is encouraging to note that the University Senate has adopted a policy which
provides that 20% students being admitted to a faculty are international students.
However, given this development, there is need to critically examine the implication of this policy in terms of the diverse support services needed for international students.

i) Income generation

The university should consider and plan for international activities that would
generate income which could be used to fund internationalisation activities and
other university's priority areas.

j) Need for means and funding

It is difficult to internationalise without some investment of human and financial resources. Concern was expressed about the overreliance on donors for international activities and this dependency could jeopardise the sustainability of some
initiatives. Internationalisation should be planned, budgeted and implemented
strategically and in phases.

Third part: strategy session

The final session lasted one and a half days. During the first part of the session,
the facilitators reviewed the key issues and challenges identified during their
meetings with the deans and central administrative units. After a full discussion of
these issues it was agreed that there was a need for international training of staff;
further promotion and utilisation of Moi University's unique strengths in academic
programmes and research interest and capacity; more extensive development of
linkages with universities abroad for research, teaching and student/staff exchange;
and a review, where appropriate, of the curriculum restructuring so as to make the
curriculum more flexible and responsive to international exchanges and foreign
students. It was emphasised that there is not "one way or a right way" to
internationalise a university. Moi University has to internationalise "in its own way"
responding to its own particular needs, priorities, strengths and resources.

The importance of a clear and explicit set of rationales and objectives for
internationalisation was stressed. Moi University identified its motives and purposes for internationalisation as the following: the need to be connected to the
rest of the world and not isolated; the desire to achieve international standards
for academic excellence; the importance of preparing all round graduates who are

able to function and contribute to Kenya, Africa and the world; the opportunity to generate additional and alternative sources of income from international initiative; and lastly, the promotion and development of Kenya. There was strong agreement that Moi University needs to market itself to neighbouring countries and the rest of the world.

The following were cited as important steps and components in the development of an internationalisation strategy for Moi University:

- Staff development and training.
- Publicity, information and awareness.
- Flexibility of the curriculum.
- Rewards and reinforcement to outstanding achievers in internationalisation.
- Planning, policies and budgetary provision for internationalisation.
- Income generating projects.
- Review of international activities in the university.

The second part of the strategy session, participants were divided in three subgroups. Group 1 was to design possible programmes and organisational strategies at the level of faculties, centres and schools; the task for Group 2 was to design programmes and organisational strategies at the central administrative level; and Group 3 was to concentrate on developing strategies for a particular internationalisation activity – the case of international students. This case study was chosen because of the recent Senate decision to substantially increase enrolment of foreign students.

In the final part of the strategy session, all the results of the seminar – the conceptual framework, the findings of the self-assessment exercise, the identified needs and key issues and the subgroup reports – were brought together in for conclusions and the development of an action plan.

Seminar conclusions

The main conclusions of the Seminar on Internationalisation of Higher Education were:

- Internationalisation is a timely, important and inevitable activity that Moi University has to endorse and adopt.
- It will enable Moi University to live up to its mission statement.
- Excellence in research and training needs an international dimension.
- Due to the global nature of issues, internationalisation is important for the development of Kenya as a modern society.
- Internationalisation is not a way to erode a people's culture but a way of strengthening people's indigenous cultures.

- Internationalisation does not lead to homogeneity but to acknowledgement of the valuable differences that exist amongst people.
- National identity and culture are the key to internationalisation and it respects and strengthens local, regional and national priorities and cultures.
- Moi University needs an action plan for sustaining and improving the quality of the international activities at the university. The university stands to benefit from a strong internationalisation strategy.

Action plan task forces

One of the deliberations of the seminar was the formation of four action plan task forces that will prepare and organise implementation strategies to help achieve internationalisation at the university. These task forces consist of between four to six members with the option of co-opting other members as and when necessary. The reports of these task forces were to be fully discussed at the Dean's Committee of Moi University Senate in the fall of 1998.

The task forces established were:

- International students committee.
- Linkages and partnership committee.
- Curriculum reviews and development committee.
- Electronic and communication committee.

Concluding remarks

The use of the Internationalisation Quality Review Process at Moi University has been a very interesting and useful case study both for Moi University and the IQRP pilot project. IQRP was designed to assist institutions of higher education in assessing *i*) the achievement of the institution's stated goals and objectives for internationalisation; *ii*) the integration of an international dimension into the primary functions and priorities of the institution; and *iii*) the inclusion of internationalisation as a key element in the institution's overall quality assurance system.

However, in the case of Moi University IQRP is used mainly as a self-assessment instrument to help the institution become aware of the opportunities and threats of internationalisation and its strengths and weaknesses in this area and secondly, based on an analysis of existing activities and programmes, to design possible goals and objectives for internationalisation of the university, and to develop new international priorities. IQRP in this case comes at the very beginning of a process of planning instead of in the course of an existing strategy. The role of the external facilitators was not one of peer review, but a supporting one, bringing in external expertise to the internal debate, more than as a review.

The use of IQRP for such a purpose requires adaptations. The self-assessment becomes more a kind of inventory of activities, events and statistics, than an assessment. The peer review becomes more a facilitating exercise to help the university in formulating objectives, goals and priorities as well as possible organisational structures. It might be useful to make a follow up to this endeavour after two years to see what has been the effect of the project.

In summary, the self-assessment and the seminar were a challenging, timely and worthy undertaking. The entire IQRP process received positive response at all levels within the university, as became clear from the evaluation of the seminar at its end, and out of an evaluation meeting with the Vice-Chancellor and senior administrators after the seminar. It has placed internationalisation on the agenda of Moi University. There is no doubt, that with time, the impetus created on the internationalisation initiatives of the university should bear fruit.

Bibliography

GOVERNMENT OF KENYA (1981),
Second University in Kenya: Report of the Presidential Working Party, Nairobi, Government Printers.

KNIGHT, J. and DE WIT, H. (1995),
"Strategies for Internationalisation of Higher Education: Historical and Conceptual Perspectives", in H. de Wit (ed.), Strategies for Internationalisation of Higher Education: A Comparative Study of Australia, Canada, Europe and the United States of America, EAIE, Amsterdam.

KNIGHT, J. and DE WIT, H. (1997),
Internationalisation of Higher Education in Asia Pacific Countries, EASI, Amsterdam.

MOI UNIVERSITY (1987),
Revised Six Year Development Plan, 1994/95-1999/2000.

MOI UNIVERSITY (1996/97),
Calendar.

9

The International Dimension under Review Warsaw School of Economics, Poland

by
Marian Geldner and Bernd Wächter

Introduction

In the spring of 1998 the Warsaw School of Economics (*Szkola Glówna Handlowa* – SGH) underwent the Internationalisation Quality Review Process (IQRP).

One of SGH's main features is its openness and its international orientation. Internationalisation as an SGH policy is clearly stated in the school's mission, and in its SOCRATES/ERASMUS "European Policy Statement". The academic leaders of SGH consider internationalisation as one of the school's strategic priorities, which result directly in quality improvement in both teaching and research.

After 1989, internationalisation of the school progressed rapidly, substantially impacting on the curriculum, and becoming visible in the implementation of numerous international programmes and in the intensification of internationally-oriented research. Thus, after several years of very dynamic transformation of the school, it was thought that IQRP could offer SGH an opportunity to assess and critically evaluate the quality and the outcomes of the internationalisation efforts of the last years. Therefore, SGH welcomed the possibility to take part in IQRP and considered it as a very timely and potentially rewarding exercise. In particular, after having already included internationalisation as a key component into its quality assurance system, IQRP was seen as an attractive tool to:

- (Self-)evaluate the present scope and level of internationalisation.
- Assess the extent to which the school achieves the aims and objectives it set itself in its mission and strategic plans.
- Benefit from the feedback and the opinions of the peer review team.
- Benefit from the discussions and exchange of opinions during the IQRP self-assessment and the peer review team visit.

177|

In this contribution we describe the context of Polish higher education, the institution itself, its international orientation, the self-assessment, the peer review and the impact of IQRP on SGH.

Context: higher education in Poland

The Polish higher education system has been subject to considerable transformation processes in the 1990s. At the beginning of systemic transformation, the economic, social and political life was centrally planned and regulated, and so was academic life. As early as 1989, the academic community, not waiting for system change, started to undertake the modernisation of the school's curricula through implementation of necessary changes. The Act on Higher Education of 12 September 1990 granted more autonomy to universities and their constituent units, resulting in a better adjustment of the graduates' profile to the needs of the emerging market economy.

Poland has 99 state higher education institutions: universities (*uniwersytet*), technical universities (*politechnika*), academies (*akademia*) and colleges called "higher schools" (*szkola wysza*). Some 770 000 domestic students were enrolled in state higher education institutions in the academic year 1996/97, plus some 5 000 foreign students. Full-time students constitute about 62% of the total student population, while part-time students in extra-mural (evening) or extension programmes make up the remaining 38%.

Until 1990, the Catholic University of Lublin was the only private university in Poland. Today, there are 134 non-state higher education institutions. They are usually smaller than state institutions, and their total enrolment is at 50 000. They offer programmes in those fields of study in most demand. The most popular disciplines are business and management, chosen by more than two thirds.

The rapid growth of the private higher education sector should be viewed as a generally positive phenomenon. At present, however, it also creates some organisational, ethical and legal problems and dilemmas, such as double or triple employment of staff resulting in conflicts of interest. To guarantee high academic standards in the private sector, the Ministry of Education and/or other accreditation bodies should introduce an accreditation system, which can be valid for many years to come.

In terms of enrolment, state higher education institutions in Poland can be ranked as follows: traditional universities (38%), technical schools (27%), teacher training colleges (11%), agricultural and economic academies (8% each), medical academies (4%), academies of physical education (3%), naval and art colleges, and theological academies (about 1% each).

Since 1991, non-state higher education institutions have offered programmes in fields of study with high demand from students. Most popular are the business and management academies, enrolling about 41% of all students in the private sector. They provide courses in management, marketing, banking and computer science. The other favoured fields of study are education (25%), theology (14%), and social sciences (13%).

The institution

Historical background

The Warsaw School of Economics is the oldest school of economics in Poland. Its history dates back to 1906. In 1919, the school obtained academic status, and it was granted the right to award master's and doctoral degrees in 1925. After World War II, SGH resumed its activities. Curricula remained very similar to those in force before the war. In 1949, the Communist authorities changed the name to that of the Central School of Planning and Statistics (SGPiS) and termed it the "first and prime socialist school of economics in Poland".

The Polish reforms of 1989 resulted in very favourable changes for SGH. It re-mained a state institution, but it gained much more independence in deciding over its study programmes. As reflected in the mission, the main objective of the school is to educate its students for the needs of a market economy and according to the highest academic standards. As part of the reforms, the school's organisational structure was changed, and so were the study programmes. Some of these changes were revolutionary in Polish higher education, such as the aboli-tion (and substitution) of faculties, freedom of the study programmes, the stu-dents' right to choose their lecturers, enhanced democracy in the management of the school, and broad internationalisation. The school has also re-adopted its original name: *Szkola Glówna Handlowa* (SGH) or Central School of Commerce. For international purposes it decided to use the name Warsaw School of Economics.

The abolition of the five former faculties meant that students are no longer enrolled in a specific faculty, which limited their choice of courses, but admitted to the school as a whole. The former faculties were replaced by the *collegia*, which are made up of a group of departments and institutes. The collegia are organisational units, responsible for research, course development, and profes-sional development of staff.

In its new and changed shape, the school has retained much of its heritage. It is still an institution concentrating on management and economics, together with a broad selection of offers in social sciences, mathematics, econometrics, statis-tics, demography, computer science, and foreign language teaching. In the cur-rent curriculum, problems of economics and management find their reflection in many subjects of a particularly practical character. In this sense, SGH continues the tradition of the pre-war School of Commerce and the Central School of Planning and Statistics. SGH students can choose from a wide range of course offerings, practically setting their own "path of study". Thus, the knowledge they gain is very similar to that offered at schools in Europe and the United States. The study programme is interdisciplinary in nature, giving students the opportunity to study problems in the fields of economic sciences, management and other social sciences.

Unlike the Central School of Planning and Statistics, SGH today is not a school which predominantly educates its students for positions in the state economy and administration. Instead, it has regained its pre-war mission of preparing highly-qualified professionals for Polish and foreign companies, who need a thorough knowledge of economics and management and who are capable of anticipating, identifying and solving problems.

Today, SGH has a total of 1 402 staff, including 803 academic staff, of whom 189 are full or associate professors. In the academic year 1997/98, the school has some 13 000 full-time and part-time students. The teacher-student ratio is 16.

Education and types of studies

SHG has introduced a teaching system, which ensures constant updating and improvement of the quality of content taught, and which enables students to make wide-ranging decisions concerning the selection of their teaching programme, and their resulting professional profile.

Responsibility for the school's programmes rests with the autonomous Senate. Degree courses are divided into an initial three-semester "basic studies" phase, with an obligatory curriculum, and an ensuing "diploma studies" period, with a high degree of freedom for students to select courses. A bachelor's degree (*licencjat*) can be earned after three and a half years, a master's degree after five years of study.

The SGH system of studies allows for significant flexibility in shaping an individual "study path", and particularly in the choice of specialisations. SGH awards bachelor's and master's degrees in the following specialisations: Economics, Finance and Banking, Quantitative Methods and Information Systems, Management and Marketing, Public Economy, and International Economic and Political Relations.

The Warsaw School of Economics offers four types of studies:

- Full-time studies: these are free of charge. Every year, approximately 1 300 students enrol in full-time studies.
- Part-time studies: these are fee-paying programmes, which run in parallel with full-time studies. Again, about 1 300 students enrol each year in this programme.

- Post-master studies: these studies address students who hold a degree and who wish to develop and update their professional qualifications. They are open to full-time and part-time graduates of SGH as well as other universities. SGH offers about fifty such fee-paying programmes per year. They take the form of part-time studies and usually last for two semesters.
- Doctoral studies: doctoral studies are available both full-time and part-time. Students can obtain a doctorate in economics, management and marketing. Full-time doctoral studies are free of charge, part-time students pay tuition fees.

Diploma studies are result-based. Within the limits of minimum requirements set by the Senate, students freely choose their courses from an extensive range of offerings listed in the school's course catalogue every year. The results of student achievement are expressed in a credit system which allows students to adjust the intensity of their studies to individual needs and abilities. It is also possible to obtain more than one degree during the five years of study. SGH introduced its credit-point system also with the aim of creating compatibility with higher education systems and institutions in other countries. Equally, it has been designed in a way which ensures compatibility with ECTS and which creates a basis for international student exchange.

The international character of studies at SGH finds expression in two ways: by basing the teaching programme on those quality standards applied in the leading academic centres of the world, and by creating the conditions for international student exchange. A part of SGH's courses are taught in a foreign language. Credits obtained at foreign universities are recognised for SGH degrees.

Nature and extent of international orientation

Internationalisation of the curriculum

SGH has recently radically changed its curricula and their modes of functioning. The changes have been inspired not only by SGH's experiences, but also from models practised in foreign countries. The most important ones are:

- Professional development of SGH's lecturers at foreign universities.
- Use of course books and teaching aids developed at foreign universities.
- A transfer of teaching methods and content originating from international programmes.
- The introduction of "international" disciplines (international business, international economics, European studies and international relations) into the curriculum.
- Delivery of part of SGH's courses in a number of foreign languages.

A high internationalisation effect has been achieved by a good foreign language provision at SGH. More credits are awarded trough a course taught in a foreign language than through the same course held in Polish. Similarly, incentives have been created for teaching staff teaching their classes in foreign languages, by counting these courses with a multiplier, thus reducing teaching load. At present, almost 100 members of the SGH teaching staff are able to conduct classes in foreign languages.

Foreign language studies (as distinct from delivery of normal courses in a foreign language) are an important part of the curriculum. The share of foreign language classes in an SGH master's degree amounts to 23%. It is compulsory for SGH students to study two foreign languages. Many additional foreign languages are available in SGH's Foreign Language Learning Centre, on a fee-paying basis. SGH's admission policy attaches considerable importance to foreign language command. In the very competitive entrance exams, besides tests in mathematics, geography or history, students sit for tests in two foreign languages of their choice. The aim of the high entrance requirements is to recruit as good students as possible to SGH.

International programmes and exchanges

International co-operation is an important element in the school's mission, having been one of the cornerstones of SGH's programme reform. The aims of the international orientation are in particular:

- To develop and dynamise the school's international links.
- To increase the qualification of SGH teaching staff and to introduce new teaching methods.
- To prepare teaching programmes of an international standard.
- To initiate international research, educational programmes, and joint publications.
- To increase SGH's activity in the central and eastern Europe region.

Funding for international co-operation comes from two sources: SGH's overall budget, on the one hand, and a number of external funding programmes of various agencies (USAID, CIDA, TEMPUS, SOCRATES, etc.), on the other.

The following administrative units are in charge of international co-operation: the International Co-operation Office, the International Programmes and Student Exchange Office, the Polish-American Centre for Economics and Management, the Polish-Canadian Programme Office, and the Polish-Japanese Management Centre.

The International Co-operation Office has the following duties:

- To provide administrative support in the framework of any international SGH activity and contact for which no separate administrative structure has been created.

- To provide information and advise to all parts of SGH on available forms of international co-operation and exchange.
- To service all foreign Ph.D. students and visiting scholars at SGH.
- To provide organisational and logistic support for activities in the framework of TEMPUS, SOCRATES and CEEPUS.
- To provide organisational service to all outgoing SGH staff (about 300 missions a year).
- To organise the programmes of official visitors to SGH.
- To provide information on SGH's Internet homepage.
- To provide organisational and administrative support to international conferences held at SGH.
- To administrate SGH's accounts for international co-operation.

The International Programmes and Student Exchange Office is responsible for a number of specific programmes, amongst which are the following:

- The postgraduate programme "Managing the European Economy", carried out in close co-operation with the HEC Group in Paris under the patronage of the *Fondation France-Pologne* and the French Embassy.
- The postgraduate programme *"Banques et marchés financiers"*, carried out in co-operation with the Université Paris Dauphine, likewise under the patronage of the *Fondation France-Pologne* and the French Embassy.
- The "School of Practical Management", an undergraduate programme run jointly with the French Institute of Management.
- The "Polish-German Academic Forum", an undergraduate scheme, funded by the German Academic Exchange Service (DAAD) and the Foundation for Polish-German Co-operation, and carried out in close co-operation with a group of leading German universities in Duisburg, Mainz, Jena and Cologne.

Among the responsibilities of the Polish-American Centre for Economics and Management (PACEM), the most important programme is the Executive MBA run in co-operation with the University of Minnesota. The centre also organises courses and training sessions for American students, such as a CIEE programme and the Penn Summer Abroad Programme implemented in co-operation with the University of Pennsylvania. It also organises round table seminars, academic workshops, and it conducts publishing activity and runs a library and a computer lab.

The Polish-Canadian Programme Office started an Executive MBA for Polish and foreign students taught in English together with the Canadian Consortium of Management Schools.

An interesting programme is also the master's degree in "European Integration and Public Relations" in co-operation with the IEP in Paris.

The Polish-Japanese Management Centre has only just started its operations.

SHG has a wide net of partner institutions in many parts of the world. In this context, the co-operation with the "Community of European Management Schools" (CEMS) is of particular importance with regard to the internationalisation of the school. Full membership in CEMS has been a priority target for SGH. Co-operation within the CEEPUS programme is also of great importance in the school's activities. This programme, which organises a short-term exchange of students and teachers, covers the region of central Europe, and in particular Slovakia, Hungary and Austria. Another specific regional SGH programme is the "Academic Initiative East", focusing on academic co-operation with the Baltic States, and on help for the Polish minorities there. Within this programme, the school accepts a number of students of Polish origin from the area of the former Soviet Union, in particular from Lithuania. In the framework of this programme, vocational training and academic co-operation are being conducted with Baltic States' partners. It should also be mentioned that SGH participates in various academic and non-academic international programmes, such as DIS in Copenhagen, and student exchanges with several French universities.

Co-operation within the TEMPUS programme, and – since its opening to Poland in 1998 – within the SOCRATES programme, is of particular relevance and opens many opportunities. Both programmes facilitate significantly SGH's international exchange and co-operation with foreign universities in Western Europe. For the year 1998, SGH has signed 52 co-operation agreements with European universities in the framework of SOCRATES.

In addition to organised mobility within structured programmes, a substantial number of SGH students spend a period of study abroad on a self-arranged basis. Annually, over 3% of all full-time students pass a semester or a year at a foreign university. In the reverse direction, a total of about 300 foreign students enrol at SGH in full-time, MBA or Ph.D. programmes, of whom 70% study at master's level. Many being of Polish origin, a majority of them take courses held in Polish. For non-Polish speakers, SGH offers its courses in foreign languages (mainly English). All foreign students have the opportunity to benefit from the Polish language instruction offered by SGH.

Internationalisation of research

International co-operation plays an important role in the school's research activities. In 1997, SGH's academic units undertook 76 joint research projects with foreign partners, mainly from Germany, the United Kingdom, the United States, Japan, France, Canada, Belgium, Italy, the Czech Republic, Hungary and the Netherlands. Also, a considerable increase of interest in joint research with institutions in central and eastern Europe could be observed. Apart from Hungary and the Czech Republic mentioned above, this concerned Lithuania, Latvia, Estonia, Ukraine, Russia, Slovakia and Slovenia. Due to financial constraints, the opportunities are obviously more limited than with Western countries. An attempt at a temporary solution to these constraints is the participation in international re-search conducted by Western institutions with an interest in Eastern problems.

SGH also conducts research and consultancy work for major international organisations, such as the European Union, the Council of Europe, the World Bank, the IMF, OECD, UNIDO, UNFPA, ILO and CECO. Research themes of the past year concerned in particular European integration, restructuring and privatisation of the state sector, transport and ecological policies, systemic transformation, banking, public finance, and demographic and sociological processes.

Results of SGH research have been presented in numerous publications, as well as at international conferences. Conference participation has been a source of the transfer of latest knowledge in the field of economic sciences to SGH academic staff, and it has naturally enriched their lectures, seminars, studies and publications. Participation in conferences, as well as faculty exchanges carried out within institutional partnership arrangements, have allowed the school's academic staff to establish, continue and renew academic and research contacts with many institutions, and to present to the international academic community SGH's work. On average, some 300 visits of SGH staff are undertaken to academic institutions abroad. Twenty per cent of those concern research collaboration, and 50% participation in conferences and seminars. SGH publishes an annual English language report entitled "Poland: International Economic Report".

The self-assessment analysis and report

The self-assessment team (SAT) set up by SGH had eight members, including both academic and administrative staff. The team was headed by the Vice-Rector for External Relations. Other members were the Chair of the Senate Committee on Curriculum Development, the Deputy Dean of the Diploma Study Programme, the Director of the International Programmes and Student Exchange Office, the Head of the International Co-operation Office, the Director and another member of the Centre for Economic Studies Development, and the CEMS Exchange Co-ordinator. The members of the SAT can be characterised by their key role in SGH's internationalisation process, of which they are promoters or "champions". The task of the SAT was to:

- Collect data necessary for the self-assessment report (SAR).
- Perform a critical analysis of the collected data and information.
- Prepare the SAR.

The SAT organised its work along the lines suggested by the self-assessment structure contained in the IQRP guidelines. The SAT worked for almost three months and produced the SAR (30 pages and annexes). The analysis resulted in the identification of certain weaknesses (or areas in need of improvement) and strengths of SGH in the field of internationalisation. The main weaknesses were thefollowing:

- An administrative and technical infrastructure not yet sufficiently developed for the purposes of international exchanges and co-operation, which includes a foreign language barrier among administrative staff.
- An imperfect division of responsibilities and flow of information inside SGH with regard to foreign co-operation.
- Too small a range of courses taught in foreign languages, which are only available in certain fields, with the consequence of mostly not being able to admit foreign students to SGH's full degree programmes.
- A small number of visiting faculty only, with effects on the internationalisation of teaching at SGH.
- The absence of a foreign language journal presenting the school's research results.
- Remaining shortages in the field of information technology and computerisation, despite constant and significant progress.
- An under-utilisation of the existing infrastructure with a view to new co-operation forms, such as an international summer school.
- An insufficient integration of student organisations into the process of internationalisation (such as an involvement in the preparation of student exchanges).

Regarding SGH's strengths, the following points were identified:

- The quality of academic staff, and the strong international orientation of a substantial part of the latter.
- The foreign language requirements, both for admission and as an obligatory component of the curriculum.
- Flexible programmes, which facilitate both student participation in foreign exchanges and the transfer of credits (*e.g.* through the use of ECTS).
- A large number of renowned academic institutions among SGH's foreign partners.
- A high appreciation of the quality of SGH students by their foreign host universities.
- A top position in the ranking of Polish universities.
- A high appreciation of SGH graduates by employers, inclusive of international companies.
- Impressive careers of SGH graduates on an international scale.

The peer review visit and report

The joint OECD/ACA peer review team visited Warsaw from February 22 through 24, 1998. It was composed of the following members:

- Bernd Wächter, DAAD/ACA, Bonn/Brussels (co-ordinator).
- Jan Karlsson, OECD/IMHE, Paris (rapporteur).
- Sr. Miriam Mikol, University of Western Sydney, Nepean, Australia.
- Professor Knud Erik Sabroe, University of Aarhus, Denmark.

The peer review team received the SGH SAR well ahead of the visit, thus enabling it to develop a joint approach and a set of questions already prior to meeting in Warsaw. On arrival, the team had a half-day meeting to fine-tune its strategy for the visit.

During the three-day visit the team had the opportunity to meet with all decision-makers of SGH, including the Vice-Rector Marian Geldner, who was in charge of organising the visit at SGH, and the Rector, Janina Józwiak.

The peer review report, which was drafted by the rapporteur and complemented by team members, was submitted to SGH a few weeks after conclusion of the visit. SGH accepted the report with a few corrections of factual errors.

It should be underlined that the peer review team decided to concentrate on the field of education, and did not look, in any systematic way, at SGH's research efforts.

Institutional aspects

The most eye-opening and instructive experience for the peer review team was the realisation that an approach which differentiates too rigidly between international activities of a university on the one hand and more "domestic" aspects relating to the "core areas" of a university, on the other, is less than adequate for institutions in countries of transformation. It might, incidentally, also be an outmoded concept for world regions such as Western Europe and North America. For SGH, such aspects as catching up with the global academic state of the art are intrinsically international in nature. This applies to all major reforms introduced since 1989, such as an overhaul of the degree structure, which makes for more compatibility with foreign models, the academic reorganisation with the result of abandoning the older type of faculty model and substituting it by collegia, the individualisation of degree content after the third semester, the organisation of a fee-based part-time and continuing education sector, and the general orientation towards competition, which finds expression in SGH's student admission policies. For SGH, institutional reforms are thus only partly domestic in nature. Rather, they also constitute the institution's forceful attempt to find answers to present-day globalisation and to catch up with international standards.

Given the difficult framework conditions, the SGH hopes that the speed and determination with which institutional reforms have been implemented would endorse SGH's claim to joining Europe's top international schools of economics very soon again.

Internationalisation of curricula

The above applies to the field of curricula in particular: the introduction of a system comparable to the bachelor – master model, the injection of "international" or comparative teaching content into the degrees, and the changes in teaching methods, have an intrinsically international dimension.

In a more traditional sense, the internationalisation of curricula has been implemented through the wide range of degree programmes offered in conjunction with high-profile universities in Western Europe and North America, leading either to foreign or international degrees (such as an MBA), or even to double degrees. These schemes, many of which encompass a study-abroad period, clearly constitute SGH's flagship programmes, and they bear witness to the institution's high aspirations in terms of quality and prestige. The peer review team acknowledged the model efforts made in this domain, and expressed its hope that these flagship schemes might positively reflect on the entirety of SGH's educational offers.

A most suitable measure in this regard is the introduction of a substantial foreign language requirement in all SGH degrees. Each SGH student needs to study a minimum of two foreign languages, amounting to nearly a quarter of the total study load over the full duration of a degree course. As already mentioned, the school's Foreign Language Learning Centre provides additional language offers on an optional basis. Other aspects of the institution's foreign language policy are the offer of a number of content-based courses taught in standard foreign languages, and the higher "weight" such courses carry in the SGH credit system. While such measures might not yet be sufficient to attract larger numbers of foreign students to a country with a less-widely-spoken language, the peer review team felt that they constituted a considerable achievement for SGH's Polish student body.

Another measure introduced with the obvious intention of creating compatibility with higher education systems and institutions abroad is SGH's credit system. It is a systemic instrument to facilitate student mobility with foreign countries by easing recognition procedures both for studies undertaken abroad and for credits earned at SGH. What is more, its main orientation along the lines of the European Union ECTS credit point system should provide the basis for a further growth in student exchanges in the framework of the SOCRATES programme, which Polish institutions now have access to.

Student exchange

Apart from internationalising study conditions at home, SGH attaches particular priority to an increase in student mobility, to and from the institution.

The broad array of SGH's partnership agreements with higher education institutions abroad, both in terms of numbers and target countries, is quite exceptional for an institution of its size, and should provide the basis for a future large-scale student exchange, even if some of the partnerships might not be active at present.

Outward mobility is high. Out of the roughly 5 600 full-time students enrolled at SGH in 1997, 180 studied abroad, making for an annual rate of 3.2% and a total rate of 16% (multiplied by five years). A high percentage, even if it cannot be ruled out that some stays of a rather short duration might be included in these data. If any improvement would be conceivable in this domain, it concerns the distribution of the mobile students, who, to a considerable extent, seem to concern the most performing ones. Likewise, the outward mobility appears to happen to a considerable degree within SGH's flagship programmes and partnership networks, such as CEMS. A future step would appear to consist in an opening up to the more average members of the student body.

SGH's statistics show inward mobility at a percentage of 3.9. Included in this figure is a fair number of Polish speakers from Lithuania or other countries in central and eastern Europe. While the present situation is by no means an underachievement given the language barrier that Polish constitutes for most foreigners, it is understandable that SGH is eager to increase numbers. In this respect, the strategy adopted, which combines tuition in foreign languages with a substantial offer of accompanying Polish language classes, should be continued and strengthened. A supplementary strategy proposed by the peer review team is to step up information about SGH's study opportunities abroad. One component of such a strategy would appear to publish an English language version of SGH's course catalogue on the institution's Internet homepage.

SGH makes use of a variety of programmes by national, foreign and international funding agencies in order to finance student mobility. Clearly, sufficient funds are of strategic importance to keep up and increase the present level of mobility. The peer review team encouraged SGH to actively look into the possibilities of the SOCRATES programme, for which the institution submitted a first proposal, in order to increase exchanges, but also to make use of the other components of the programme.

Academic staff mobility

Given the aim of acquainting teaching staff with modern teaching methods, and of increasing their foreign language expertise (for classes to be taught at SGH), it is understandable that SGH is set on increasing teaching staff mobility, particularly in the outgoing direction. Academic staff mobility statistics display a considerable extent of missions abroad of SGH staff. It appears, however, that these are very often of a rather short duration, and serve such purposes as attendance at conferences and meetings as well. Longer stays, for teaching or research, should indeed be stepped up.

Support structures

SGH's work in the field of international relations rests on many shoulders. Beyond those responsible in a political function (Vice-Rector, Senate, deans of the collegia), a broad range of individuals and administrative units are available to carry out the day-to-day tasks necessary to keep up the high level of activity. There are presently no less than five offices which look after SGH's international affairs. On the one hand, this a privilege which few institutions can boast of. The peer review team also learned that the existence of the variety of administrative units had a historical explanation and that, moreover, the continuation of the existence of some was explicitly required by the foreign partners in those programmes described above. On the other hand, it is clear that the wide distribution of functions necessitates an enhanced level of communication and co-ordination between the different actors. With the activity volume possibly still rising in the future, SGH might find this co-ordination task to become increasingly difficult to handle. This might be the stage where SGH would want to introduce more formal communication and co-operation procedures between theses units, in order to avoid double effort and ensure a minimum of a joint strategy.

In its self-assessment report, SGH stressed the perceived need to increase the professionalism of those administrative officers managing the international relations. While the peer review team found that SGH international staff was acting both with dedication and competence, it suggested that SGH might consider larger-scale staff exchanges with the international offices of the partner institutions to further improve the professionalism of its staff.

Strategy and quality assurance

International activities are an explicit part of SGH's mission. This applies in two ways: it becomes apparent in the *de facto* priorities of the school, as described above. But there is also explicit mention of international co-operation, and orientation at international standards, in the school's written mission. A more recent example of a spelled out mission is the SGH's "European Policy Statement", produced as part of the first ever SOCRATES application. In line with these documents, SGH's leadership attaches a high priority to the international character of the school, and it is clearly able to state its guiding principles. Yet, as in almost any university in Europe and beyond, actual activity, while in no way in contradiction to codified policy, seems to develop rather independently of it. To a degree, this is inevitable. Moreover, decentralisation and autonomy of the "collegia" is a stated policy of SGH as well.

Yet, it might be in keeping with SGH's ambition to be one of the motors of internationalisation in central and eastern Europe, to create, as one of the first institutions, a clearer interface between international policy and practice. Especially since the volume of activity can be expected to increase, and more formalised ways of communication, co-ordination and decision-making might be advisable, it would be worth the attempt to break down policy level orientations into activity targets, and to check on achievement at regular intervals. No doubt, this is a far-reaching expectation. No doubt, few institutions around the globe do today live up to such an expectation. But SGH, the peer review team felt, has the potential to introduce such self-evaluation measures which might further contribute to the quality of its international activities.

Conclusions on the case and its impact

Overall, SGH found its participation in the IQRP a most valuable exercise. The self-assessment component of the process created a useful opportunity to reflect on key issues and to perform a critical self-evaluation with regard to the strengths and weaknesses of the international activities of SGH. This was particularly valuable given that the recent years in SGH's development were characterised by a very dynamic "internationalisation drive", combined with radical reform of the institution as a whole and with fundamental systemic changes in the school's environment. The rapid pace of development and change over the last decade made it necessary to take stock in a structured way, to review and possibly rethink options, and to formulate future strategic and operational targets. IQRP proved to be an adequate instrument for this purpose. In this regard, the discussions with the peer review team in the course of the site visit, and the observations and comments contained in the peer review team report proved to be very valuable. Comments and observations concentrated on the areas specified by SGH as in particular need of scrutiny, thus answering to the self-identified needs of SGH, but they also brought to awareness other issues which had not been the object of reflection previously.

As to the further development of the IQRP instrument itself, the main conclusion is probably that the check list of aspects and activities so far contained in the methodology would need to be widened beyond international aspects *sui generis* towards more institutional matters. Certainly for higher education institutions and countries in transition, but probably also for institutions in a more stable environment, "core" matters of an institution such as the degree structure, the organisation of studies, and forms of governance and management, decidedly must have an international dimension, and must be taken into account alongside the more obvious international matters such as co-operation, exchange and curriculum development.

OECD 1999

PART III
QUALITY REVIEW:
APPROACHES AND ISSUES

10

Reflections on Using IQRP

by

Jane Knight and **Hans de Wit**

In the previous chapters, case studies on the use of Internationalisation Quality Review Process in six different institutions have been presented. These case studies and the other pilot cases of IQRP have provided valuable insights and information on using IQRP to assess and enhance the international dimension of higher education. This chapter discusses the experiences gained and lessons learned from the case studies and reflects on the application of IQRP to institutions which will use IQRP in the future.

Application of IQRP in different contexts

Use in different educational contexts

One of the most complex issues in the design of the guidelines for the Internationalisation Quality Review Process was to take into account the diversity of cultures and systems in higher education. As already stated, a guiding principle for the project was that "the review process be international in application... and that acknowledgement and recognition of differences among institutions and countries is essential." Therefore, a key factor in selecting the pilot institutions was diversity. The final selection included nine institutions in eight countries in five continents.

During the review of the lessons learned from the pilot case studies, there was consensus that IQRP was useful and effective in different types of institutions in different regions of the world. The pilot case studies have demonstrated that IQRP is relevant to and adaptable to the following differences in educational contexts:

- Differences between private and public institutions.
- Differences between the universities and the non-university sector.

- Differences between large, comprehensive universities and specialised institutions.
- Differences between undergraduate colleges, research universities and professional schools.

During the revision of the IQRP guidelines particular importance was given to ensuring that the guidelines were applicable and sensitive to different types of higher education institutions. Therefore, the revised IQRP guidelines (see p. 241), have been crafted so that they are flexible enough to recognise and accommodate the variety of higher education institutions which are interested in assessing and assuring the quality of their internationalisation efforts.

Use in different cultural contexts

A key challenge in developing the conceptual and operational frameworks for the IQRP was its application in different cultural contexts. Because IQRP is based on two fundamental principles, those of self-assessment and peer review, it was very important to be sensitive to different cultural orientations to these principles. The notion of "face" or "reputation" was of particular concern. Would the process of self-assessment result in a "promotional or public relations report" which would identify strengths and accomplishments only and gloss over areas needing improvement? Would the peer review report be credible and accepted if it focused on specific issues and activities which needed further development and enhancement? Would culturally based interpretations of the concepts of internationalisation or globalisation negatively influence the process of reviewing the international dimension? Would the need for an explicit rationale and clearly stated goals and objectives for an internationalisation strategy be problematic in different cultures and regions of the world? These were the types of questions which were being asked during the design and revision stages of IQRP.

The experiences of the pilot case studies have demonstrated that the flexibility of the IQRP makes it adaptable and useful in different cultural contexts. Of course, the most important principle is that the IQRP respect and adapt to the individuality and fundamental cultural value and beliefs. Therefore, the frameworks and guidelines of IQRP have intentionally been developed to respect and accommodate different contexts, and in particular the cultural context. The discussion on approaches to self-assessment later in this chapter illustrates the way different institutions in different contexts have adapted the self-assessment process to suit their situation.

Use in institutions at different stages of internationalisation

The IQRP project was originally based on the assumption that IQRP would be most useful to institutions where there were a variety of international activities and relationships already operational and that secondly a comprehensive internationalisation strategy was in place to ensure that there was a holistic and integrated approach to the international dimension. In fact, the experiences of IQRP at several institutions proved this assumption to be false. There were several institutions where an explicit internationalisation strategy was not developed in spite of the many international initiatives and where the IQRP was instrumental in developing such a strategy.

It is interesting to refer to the actual experiences of the pilot institutions to elaborate on this point. The discussion on the different development stages of internationalisation at the pilot institutions is used for illustrative purposes. There is no comparison inferred or intended among or between the institutions.

In institutions like the University of Helsinki, Bentley College, Monash University and Royal Melbourne Institute of Technology there was, as expected, a comprehensive internationalisation strategy developed and more or less operational.

The cases of the National University of Mexico and Moi University in Kenya demonstrated that IQRP can also be used as a planning instrument to help design the overall institution's strategy for internationalisation. This was done, by assessing the strengths and weaknesses, opportunities and threats for a strategic internationalisation plan and/or for the formulation of the international dimension in the overall strategic plan of the institution.

In the case of Moi University, the self-assessment exercise was used as an instrument to help create awareness of the international dimension of higher education and its possible contribution to the overall mandate and goals of the institution. IQRP was a catalyst and a tool to raise awareness about the importance of the international dimension and to collect and analyse the existing but fragmented international activities, contacts and projects. Through the IQRP, the strengths and weaknesses of the current state of international activities were analysed and priorities for an internationalisation strategy were identified. Thus the first steps towards developing and implementing an overall internationalisation plan were taken through the IQRP.

In the case of the National University of Mexico, one can speak of an *ad hoc* and marginal approach to internationalisation, but recognise at the same time, an impressive selection of international activities, linkages and projects. The institution needed the IQRP to place the selection of international activities into a more explicit and coherent perspective and look to the possibilities to make organisational and programmatic changes for the development of an internationalisation strategy and for the incorporation of the international dimension in the overall strategic plan of the institution.

197

In summary, the experiences with nine case studies have shown that IQRP can be used by educational institutions at different stages in the development and evolution of a comprehensive internationalisation strategy.

Practical issues in using IQRP

The commitment to undertake an IQRP

Implementing a quality review of the internationalisation strategy only makes sense under certain conditions. The institution must be clear about the rationale for undertaking a quality review of the international dimension. The different constituency groups, including the leadership and the academic and administrative staff as well as students of the institution must be committed to all stages of the process of review. This includes the decision to undergo the review, the self-assessment, the peer review and the implementation of conclusions and recommendations.

There must be a clear identification of the follow up procedures to the review and how to implement any recommendations. Finally, there must be awareness about the resource implications of the review itself and of potential resource implications of the recommendations of the review.

Description versus analysis in the self-assessment

One of the greatest challenges and perhaps striking aspects of the self-assessment exercise was the tendency for the SAT report to be more descriptive than analytical. This is easily understood and can happen for a variety of reasons. In some cases, preparing the SAT report was the first time that the institution was attempting to systematically collect information on all the international initiatives and policies which exist in the institution. Developing a comprehensive picture of the nature and extent of internationalisation activities can be both a very revealing and overwhelming undertaking. In situations where this type of inventory did not exist, the SAT tended to focus more on the collecting of the data than on the analysis of the findings. In other cases, the membership of the SAT was too focused (*i.e.* international office only). In another instance, the team members were not experienced enough in dealing with academic planning and governance issues at the macro level.

For the SAT report to be a useful document for the institution and the PRT, it is necessary for there to be a clear articulation of goals and objectives/targets for internationalising the institution. The importance of having an explicit rationale, as well as clearly stated goals and objectives cannot be overstated. It is the rationale, goals and objectives which will guide the SAT and PRT as the whole exercise is driven by the institutions' mission and aims. Given that the underlying principle of IQRP is to assess and assure the achievement of the aim and objective as identified by the institution itself, it is critical that they are clearly stated. They can also provide or drive the framework for the analysis. The analysis of the strengths, weaknesses, opportunities and threats (SWOT) of internationalisation strategies is at the heart of the IQRP. Therefore a SWOT analysis is critical to ensuring that the SAT report is more than a catalogue of internationalisation initiatives. The SWOT analysis helps to identify what works well, what can be improved and what are new opportunities.

A second factor in ensuring an analytical approach to the IQRP, is the selection of the chair and members of the SAT and the type of support that is available to the team. The next section will address the importance of selecting the right chair for the SAT and the composition of the team members.

Self-assessment team members

The pilot case studies have indicated how important it is to carefully select the members of the SAT. It is important to have a senior leader of the university who is directly involved in or responsible for the internationalisation to head the SAT. This is important for a number of reasons. First is the strong message given to the community about the importance of the international dimension and the IQRP. Second is the leader's familiarity with the internationalisation work in particular but also the more general policy and governance of the institution. The third relates to the benefit of having a senior person's insight and influence for the implementation of the final recommendations for improvement.

To ensure that different constituencies of the institution are involved and to avoid appearing that it is a top down process it is important to have representatives of teaching and administrative staff as well as students on the committee. Experience has shown that it is also worthwhile to have members who are involved in international activities as well as those who are not. If only champions and promoters are members of the SAT, one gets a skewed picture of the commitment and support for internationalisation. The non-involved and even the internationalisation "nay sayers" can make a very useful contribution. That being said, one has to be aware of the size of the SAT. Of course it will greatly differ according to the institution but a team of four/six is often most effective. Consultation with the wider community within the institution is critical and this can be done in a variety of ways to ensure that a broad cross-section of views are heard. The views and voices of both domestic and international student views play a central role in the self-assessment process. In some cases, it may also be appropriate for the SAT to have a member external to the institution.

Approaches to the self-assessment exercise

The experiences of the pilot case studies have demonstrated that the IQRP framework is flexible enough to be adapted to different needs and characteristics of institutions. This is illustrated by the different approaches used to complete the self-assessment exercise. The guidelines outlined a process whereby the appointed SAT would consult with the different stakeholder groups on campus, collect information, conduct a SWOT analysis, and be fully involved in the preparation of the SAT report with recommendations. This process was successfully adapted to particular situations at different institutions. For instance, in two institutions, the SAT acted as an advisory committee to the leaders responsible for internationalisation who undertook the preparation of the SAT report and then consulted widely in the community for reactions and additions to the report. In another case, both the SAT and the PRT reports were prepared and then shared with the university for feedback and support for the recommendations. In another institution, seminars were held with representatives of the different stakeholder groups and the process was explained and participants became engaged in the preparation of the SAT and the whole IQRP. It is impossible and ill-advised to indicate which is the best approach. The culture of each institution is different and must be respected. Therefore, the IQRP framework and guidelines are deliberately flexible and adaptable to enable them to be used in the most effective way according to the goals and characteristics of the institution. An important point, which bears repetition is the necessity of the university community to be involved and committed to the process of internationalisation. The Internationalisation Quality Review Process, including both the self-assessment and peer review, can be a constructive way to increase awareness, involvement and commitment to internationalisation. It is for this reason that special attention needs to be given to the composition of the SAT and the best approach for the self-assessment exercise.

Peer review team members

As with the SAT, the composition of the PRT is also crucial. There are a number of factors to take into consideration when selecting the members and building the best team. However, experience has shown that there are two or three factors which are key. First it is assumed that all members are external to the institution and do not have any vested interests or biases. It is important to have at least one member who knows the local context and culture *i.e.* national education policies, trends, issues and can brief the other team members if necessary on any critical local issues. This has been especially important and successful feature in the pilot case studies. It is equally important to have at least one team member who is external to the country or region and is knowledgeable about different education systems and policies. Expertise and practical experience in internationalising an academic institution is absolutely essential, theoretical understanding is not enough. Experience in a senior management position in academia is also advisable so that both the macro governance and policy issues as well as operational issues are understood.

While it is an advantage to have quality assessment expertise represented on the team, it is not an absolute necessity. In fact, knowledge of best practices of internationalisation in different types of institutions in various countries of the world is probably more useful to the peer review process. Experience has shown that diversity of backgrounds of the team makes for a perceptive and robust review.

Conclusions and recommendations

The process of undergoing a self-assessment exercise is at the heart of quality assessment and assurance and improvement. The PRT is the second step and acts as a mirror to the findings and conclusions of the SAT process and report. The conclusions and the recommendations are an essential part of the SAT report. In some pilot case studies there was some hesitation to draw any conclusions or make any recommendations before the PRT visit. On one hand, this is understandable as it is helpful to get feedback and external perspectives on the findings of the SAT exercise before recommended changes are put forth. On the other hand, because the PRT serves as a mirror and a feedback mechanism, it is important for the PRT to be aware of the suggested recommendations and discuss them with the SAT and senior leaders of the institution. It is therefore highly recommended that the SAT think through and articulate the conclusions and recommendations prior to the PRT visit; then review and revise them after the PRT report has been received and then finally make a report on the recommendations for quality improvement. As already stated, ownership and commitment to improvement is an important outcome of the IQRP and this is especially true for the conclusions and recommendations.

Timing of the IQRP

There are three major points to be made with respect to the timing of the IQRP exercise. The first one relates to the stage of development of the institution relative to internationalisation. The original expectation was that institutions which were well along the path of internationalisation would be most interested in undertaking an IQRP. However, as discussed in two of the case studies, one of the unexpected outcomes of the project has been the value of the IQRP guidelines as a tool for strategic planning for institutions which are in early stages of internationalisation. This has been one of the key lessons learned and has expanded the potential use and benefits of IQRP beyond the initial design and objectives of the project.

The second factor relates to the institutions' priority and preoccupation with quality reviews. In the past several years there has been increasing importance being given to quality reviews for both accountability and improvement reasons. While this is a positive sign, there is also a greater risk of the "quality review fatigue" syndrome being experienced at the institution. It is therefore important to be sensitive to the timing of IQRP with respect to other evaluation or audit exercises so that there is not undue pressure or expectation put on the institution. However, another unexpected outcome of the project has been that IQRP is compatible with other quality review systems and that there are potential benefits in combining IQRP with other review exercises. Therefore, while attention needs to be given to other institutional reviews, one can also consider the possibility of undertaking an IQRP in conjunction with other exercises. An institution considering an IQRP should consider all factors which may positively or negatively influence the ability to consult a cross-section of the institution and its commitment to the process and the eventual improvements.

The length of time it takes to complete an IQRP is obviously influenced by many factors which are usually institutionally based and therefore differ from institution to institution. Experience has shown that between three and six months is an appropriate time to complete the exercise. Taking more time can result in "review fatigue" and it may be hard to sustain a high level of commitment and participation. An extended SAT exercise may also be a sign of overemphasis on data collection rather than analysis. After completion and submission of the SAT report, it usually takes another three months at least before the PRT phase is finished and the final report is submitted. Therefore one should aim to have the entire the SAT and PRT finished within nine months and then the institution can focus on implementing the recommendation for improvements.

Follow-up phase

At the start of the project, IQRP was designed as a three step process: 1) SAT phase; 2) PRT phase and 3) Improvement phase. Several of the pilot studies have indicated that a fourth step, a follow-up PRT exercise approximately one to two years after would be very useful to assess the impact of the changes made and the evolution of the strategic planning and institutionalisation of the international dimension. To date, a follow-up exercise has not been undertaken as it is premature for most of the institutions in this pilot project. There have been some requests and therefore serious consideration will be given to undertaking follow-up PRT visits. It is for this reason that the idea of a follow-up phase has been introduced into the IQRP guidelines (see p. 241). It may not be necessary for all the members of the original PRT to participate in the follow-up but it would be important that at least one or two members of the original team guide the follow-up peer review process.

Conceptual issues in using IQRP

Concepts and terminology

At the beginning of the project careful consideration was given to the selection and use of terminology. The term "internationalisation" was deliberately chosen over the term "globalisation". As discussed in Chapter 1, the notions of nation and culture are key elements of internationalisation. It seems that the current use of the term globalisation implies a type of homogenisation and does not appear to acknowledge or respect the notion of an individual nation's culture/s and cultural diversity. Internationalisation is therefore a preferred term for this project. Quality, as discussed in Chapter 2 is a term that also has many different interpretations and innuendos. That being said, however, the project is committed to using the term quality and takes a "fitness of purpose" orientation to the definition. "Review" was intentionally used to denote the ideas of "evaluation and improvement" and to avoid the ideas of accreditation or certification. The notion of "process" was used to ensure compatibility with the process-based definition of internationalisation and to reinforce the approach of a cycle of planning, integration and review.

At the end of project review, the title and terminology were evaluated to ensure that they were still appropriate and relevant. It was decided that the title adequately describes and denotes the original intention of developing an approach and set of guidelines to assist institutions to assess and improve the quality of the internationalisation efforts. Therefore, the notions "internationalisation", "review" and "process" remain as the conceptual underpinnings of the quality assessment and assurance instrument.

Rationale

As already noted, it is important for an institution to have a clear view of the major reasons for internationalisation. The pilot case studies indicate that in the majority of cases, there is not a well articulated set of rationales. Instead, there is a well-developed sense of the need for internationalisation (usually attributed to the impact of globalisation) and that secondly, there is an inherent goodness in internationalisation (that international initiatives will contribute positively to the institution). This leads to the conclusion that internationalisation should be a priority. However, when one probes further into "why" internationalisation should be a priority, there are often general and insupportable statements about wanting to be a world class institution. Clarity on the rationale, not on the need for internationalisation is therefore the challenge; but in reality, one cannot really separate the rationale from the need.

On the whole once can say that there is confusion and even tension about why institutions are placing increasing importance on internationalisation. There are several reasons for this but one of the most notable is the necessity for institutions to find alternate sources of funding. In many countries this can be attributed to the decline in government support. Income from full fee paying international students both on shore and off-shore, and revenue generated from international technical, training and consulting projects are two major sources of alternative funds. Therefore, there is a strong impetus to search for international markets for education products and services. This market orientation is often described as an economic or commercial approach and rationale for internationalisation – if in fact, it can be called internationalisation at all. An important question to be asked is whether selling of educational products and services to international markets is a strategy or form of internationalisation. This of course depends on the working definition of internationalisation. Nevertheless, if the working definition of internationalisation is "the process of integrating an international/intercultural dimension into the teaching, research and service functions of a higher education institution" a pure commercial approach could be a form of internationalisation but not necessarily. This is an issue worthy of further examination and debate.

What seems to be more emerging is an espoused academic rationale *i.e.* being a "world class" institution and achieving international standards but an implicit economic or commercial motivation. These rationales are not necessary in conflict nor are they mutually exclusive. What is most interesting is the desire to be seen as striving for a world class reputation but in fact taking a business like approach to generating revenue. Clearly, this does not apply to all case studies in the project but a distinct trend in this direction is discernible.

Focused or comprehensive IQRP

It was clear from the pilot institutions in the project that there are different rationales for why a university or college is interested in doing an IQRP. This was anticipated and for that reason IQRP was designed to be flexible to adapt to different types of institutions and different motivations for an IQRP.

An interesting aspect of two of the case studies (UNAM, Mexico and USM, Malaysia) was their focus on only part of the institution not the whole organisation. In the focused approach, however, it is still important that both academic departments and central administrative or service units are included. In addition, it is essential that a wide selection of faculty members, senior administrators, students, researchers, etc., are consulted by the SAT and PRT. When only the international office and other support units are included in the review, there are significant limitations to understanding the strengths, weaknesses, opportunities and threats of integrating the international dimension into the teaching, research and service activities of the institution. Likewise when only administrators are consulted by the SAT or PRT one gets a very skewed view; the opinions and perceptions of faculty, staff and students are important and should not be excluded. Therefore for both a focused and a comprehensive IQRP, it is essential that a cross-section of both academic (teaching/research) and administrative/support units is reviewed; and secondly that there is broad consultation across the institution.

Ad hoc versus co-ordinated and integrated approach

An interesting and encouraging trend is the gradual shift towards a more strategic approach to internationalising an institution. The process approach to internationalisation has emphasised the concepts of integration and co-ordination and has de-emphasised the fragmented activities approach. The key point is that there is an awareness and a gradual but perceptible change in planning and managing the international dimension.

The fact that IQRP has been used as a planning tool as well as a review instrument illustrates that institutions are ready to think about internationalisation strategies, not just as a series of isolated activities. And furthermore, institutions are ready and trying to develop an overall institutional action plan to integrate an international dimension into the teaching, research and service activities. The movement towards strategic planning is helping to make internationalisation a central part of the university mission and mandate, not a marginal, *ad hoc*, optional group of activities.

IQRP guidelines and self-assessment outline

In the two phases of the IQRP pilot project, two different types of guidelines have been used. In the first phase, the team worked with an extensive checklist, addressing the following major areas: the (inter)national context; the institutional profile; governance and organisation systems; academic programmes; research and scholarly collaboration; students; faculty and staff; external relations and services; and conclusions (project document *The Development of an Internationalisation Quality Review Process at the Level of Higher Education Institutions* (ACA, IMHE/OECD, March 1996).

In the second phase, the team worked with a more global self-assessment structure, covering six major areas without a detailed checklist: summary of the higher education system and the institutional profile; analysis of the (inter)national context; analysis of the institution's policy and strategies for internationalisation; analysis of the implementation and effects of the internationalisation strategies; analysis of the organisational structure and procedures for internationalisation; and conclusions (project document *The Development of an Internationalisation Quality Review Process for Higher Education Institutions* (IMHE/OECD in consultation with ACA, March 1997).

The reason for this change was that when the first three pilot institutions used the checklist, there was a tendency for the self-assessment teams to follow too closely the checklist and to be too descriptive in answering the questions in the list. Also, the checklist created confusion in the terminology used. Some of the terminology was too culture and region bound, such as "off-shore programmes", a term more familiar to Australian higher education than to Finnish higher education.

In the second phase, it was clear that several institutions found the new self-assessment structure too general and vague and started to use the checklist of the first phase in helping them to do the self-assessment. This was in particular true for those institutions which used IQRP more as a planning instrument.

205

The experiences with the two methods, as described in the case studies chapters and summarised above, have resulted in the development of a third version of the IQRP guidelines which are at the end of the volume, p. 241. The guidelines include a detailed self-assessment outline which covers the following major categories: context; internationalisation policies and strategies; organisational and support structures; academic programmes and students; research and scholarly collaboration; human resources management; contracts and services; and conclusions and recommendations. Each category requires a Strengths, Weaknesses, Opportunities and Threats (SWOT) analysis and contains a list of possibly relevant questions on the what and how, the effectiveness and possibilities of improvement. The outline is designed in such a way that it is distinctive from and at the same time applicable in combination with other instruments of quality assessment and assurance; and that it can be used at different stages of development of internationalisation, as well as in different regional, cultural and educational contexts.

11

Quality Assurance Instruments and their Relationship to IQRP

by

Jane Knight in co-operation with **Tony Adams**
and **Marjorie Peace Lenn**

The purpose of this chapter is to identify and briefly describe several quality assessment instruments which are being applied to the international dimension of higher education and which can be used alone or in conjunction with IQRP. These include: codes of practice, ISO 9000 guidelines, and the GATE certification process. An examination of these instruments illustrates the evolution in the tools being developed to assess and assure the quality of international education. They also reflect the complexity and diversity of quality review processes. Other quality assessment tools, such as bench marking, performance indicators and total quality management are not elaborated on in this chapter. They are noted as further examples of quality review and enhancement instruments used in higher education.

Codes of practice

Codes of practice are one of the more traditional approaches used to address the issue of quality assurance of specific international activities. For the most part, these codes of practice are statements of principles and can be interpreted as moral imperatives in defined areas of internationalisation. Codes of practice are very common at the national level. For example, the United Kingdom Council for Overseas Student Affairs (UKCOSA) in conjunction with the British Council, educational institutions and professional organisations were among the first organisations to develop a "Code of practice for educational institutions and overseas students".

In the mid-eighties, UKCOSA recognised that institutions were more and more interested and successful in selling education and training as a commodity

207

to overseas students. Examples of good and bad practice were evident and it was recognised that "it is both good business practice and a requirement of business ethics that value for money be provided". To that end a set of guidelines for good practice were developed in 1989 by UKCOSA on key aspects of international student recruitment. The guidelines cover marketing, information and promotion materials, admissions, and the need for an institutional level policy on the recruitment of overseas students.

The UKCOSA code is an example of the kind of approach used in the mid-eighties to ensure ethical and responsible recruitment practices and support services for international students studying in the United Kingdom. As the size of the market for international students increased, codes of ethics took on more importance and were often broadened in scope. The "Code of Ethical Practice in International Education" developed by the Canadian Bureau for International Education (CBIE, 1996) is a good example of this. It is interesting to note that the term "international education" is used in this code (not "international students") and that it covers many different types of activities.

The goal of the CBIE code is to provide standards of integrity for all facets of international student programmes against which organisations can measure their own performance. The development and implementation of exchange agreements and international education contracts are also addressed in this code thereby covering mobility programmes for international fee paying students and exchange/ study abroad students. The code therefore is also applicable to local students who seek opportunities to study abroad.

The CBIE code is essentially a statement of principles which all members accept by virtue of their membership in CBIE. Protocols for the monitoring or enforcement of the code are not articulated. However, there is a clear statement which reinforces the institution's individual responsibility. The code is not to be used as a substitute for the mission statements, goals and objectives which each institution must develop to satisfy its own requirements and standards.

The set of principles recently revised by the Australian Vice-Chancellors' Committee (AVCC, 1998) is an example of how codes evolve to respond to the changes in the provision of international education. The AVCC revised two of its existing codes of practice and has combined them into a new "Code of Ethical Practice in the Provision of Education to International Students by Australian Universities". International fee paying students studying in Australia and in off-shore locations or by distance education are addressed in the code by the following statement: "the provision of education services to international students, both onshore and off-shore, by Australian universities brings with it the ethical commitment that quality education be provided and that value be given for the investment made by international students".

The first part of the revised code contains "Guidelines for universities providing courses to international students". The major points covered by these guidelines are the following: promotion and marketing; agents and partners; admission; pre-arrival information for international students studying in Australia; arrival and orientation for international students studying in Australia; information for students; university infrastructure; student support and off-shore students returning home.

The second set of guidelines included in the code addresses the issue of fee refunds for international students. There are eight major points: total refunds; partial refunds; grounds for refunds; no refunds; fee refunds related to international students who obtain permanent resident status in Australia; agreements between institutions and international students regarding fee charging and refunds; payment of refunds and appeals process related to fee refunds.

The code is framed as a set of guidelines rather than as policy, thereby allowing a measure of flexibility for both institutions and their students. The AVCC has established the International Standing Committee to monitor and review the content and the implementation of the code and guidelines. The committee also acts as an advisory group to the AVCC where cases of questionable ethical practice are brought to the attention of the AVCC.

While codes of practice have been developed and adopted by national organisations for many years now, they remain a generic type of quality assurance instrument. In general, there is no regulatory system in place to assess compliance. Instead such a code appeals to the ethics and conscience of the institutions and the staff who are involved in international student mobility programmes and it tries to develop a set of values and principles to guide the process.

A more recent development in the field of quality assessment and assurance for one aspect of internationalisation has been the creation of a new organisation called GATE (Global Alliance for Transnational Education) which developed a code of good practice and a certification process.

The Globalisation for Transnational Education (GATE) certification process[1]

The impact of the global marketplace and the growth of new information/communication technologies have been major contributors to the internationalisation of higher education. For instance, higher education is no longer provided solely within national borders. There has been substantial growth in the number, nature and type of education opportunities being offered abroad (external to host country). These opportunities are offered through a variety of means including: dis-

---

1. Parts of this section were taken from GATE (1997), GATE (1998) and Peace Lenn (1998).

OECD 1999

tance education courses through mail, broadcast or electronic means, twinning programmes, satellite campuses among others. The term which is currently being used to label this kind of education provision is transnational education.

Transnational education, as defined by GATE (1997) "denotes any teaching or learning activity in which the learners are in a different country (the host country) to that in which the institution providing the education is based (the home country)". This situation requires that national boundaries be crossed by information about the education, and by staff and/or educational materials.

The significant growth in transnational education provision by higher education institutions and the private sector, a growing preoccupation with issues related to the quality, purpose and responsibility in the new arena of transnational education, and rapid globalisation of the economy and the professions are three key factors which led to the founding of the Global Alliance for Transnational Education (GATE) in 1995. The need for an organisation such as GATE was identified and acted upon by an international consortium of representatives from business (including multi-national corporations), government (including national quality assurance bodies) and higher education (including institutions with both virtual and traditional forms of educational delivery). GATE's primary purpose is to address the assurance and improvement of higher education and training which cross national borders.

GATE has developed a set of "Principles for Transnational Education" (1997) to guide the provision of transnational education. The principles serve as a code for good practice which institutions should adhere to when offering transnational education. A process of certification has also been developed.

GATE certification is an international quality assurance process for higher education and training which crosses national borders. The process itself follows internationally acceptable practice related to third party review for educational quality in that it: a) defines the characteristics of quality; b) asks the educational entity to conduct a self-evaluation based on those characteristics of quality; c) conducts an external review of the programme on site (at the "home" institution for virtual offerings and at the foreign site for physically based offerings); and d) confers GATE certification or not, dependent on the outcome of the process.

Principles for transnational education

At the core of the GATE certification process are the "Principles for Transnational Education". These principles were derived from an in-depth study of characteristics of quality provided by a variety of organisations related to transnational education. An abridged version of the principles follows.

Goals and objectives

Transnational courses must be guided by goals and objectives that are understood by participants who enrol in them and must fit appropriately within the provider's mission and expertise.

Standards

Students receiving education and education(al) credentials through transnational courses must be assured by the provider that these courses have been approved by the provider and meet its criteria for educational quality, and that the same standards are applied, regardless of the place or manner in which the courses are provided.

Legal and ethical matters

Transnational courses must comply with all appropriate laws and approvals of the host country.

Student enrolment and admission

Participants in transnational courses must be treated equitably and ethically. In particular, all pertinent information must be disclosed to the participants and each participant must hold full student status or its equivalent with the provider organisation.

Human resources

The provider organisation must have a sufficient number of fully-qualified people engaged in providing the transnational courses, and their activities must be supervised and regularly evaluated as a normal activity of the provider.

Physical and financial resources

The provider organisation must assure an adequate learning environment and resources for the transnational courses, and must provide assurances that adequate resources will continue to be available until all obligations to enrolled participants are fulfilled.

Teaching and learning

Transnational courses must be pedagogically sound with respect to the methods of teaching and the nature and needs of the learners.

Student support

The provider organisation must ensure that students are provided with adequate support services to maximise the potential benefit they receive from the transnational courses.

Evaluation

Transnational courses must be regularly and appropriately evaluated as a normal part of the provider organisation's activities, with the results of the evaluations being used to improve these courses.

Third parties

Where third parties, such as agents or collaborating institutions are involved in the transnational education, there must be explicit written agreements covering their roles, expectations and obligations.

Symbiosis: GATE certification, the IQRP and other evaluation processes

The GATE Principles for Transnational Education are not confined to the GATE certification process alone. They can be self-applied by institutions to their off-shore offerings, whether physically based or virtually transmitted; or GATE certification can be used in conjunction with other forms of internal or external review.

It should be noted that with growing frequency, the transnational offering, often conferring the same degree/course as the parent institution, is serving larger numbers of learners than the parent institution. Further, the transnational offering is affecting a significant population elsewhere and should be reviewed not only with the educational integrity of the parent institution in mind but with the quality of the offering within a different cultural context. Too often, "out of sight" means "out of mind" but as the global economy and new technologies accelerate the globalisation of higher education, "out of mind" is a risk one cannot afford to take.

Internal quality review

The most important component of all external review processes is the self-evaluation required of and by the institution or programme within an institution. Any educational entity can create its own set of standards/principles/performance indicators or use others already prepared and evaluate themselves against said. The GATE Principles for Transnational Education just like the self-assessment exercise of the IQRP, can be used separately from the external peer review process which each provides. Self-evaluation for the purpose of making regional or global comparison is a healthy process for higher education institutions and programmes. However, third party testimony (*i.e.* external review), if free of potential conflict of interest, assures a more objective evaluative process and renders the institution or programme with a "seal of approval" that comes from outside the institution and protects the institution from self-professed excellence.

External quality review

The GATE certification process has been used by institutions in combination with national accreditation, ISO 9000 and the IQRP. In each case, GATE certification addresses the transnational programmes which typically the other processes do not cover in depth.

National accreditation

GATE certification is the only external review process which specifically evaluates off-shore (*i.e.* transnational) offerings of institutions or educational programmes. Only two countries are known to follow and evaluate the cross-border educational activity of their institutions of higher education (the United States and the United Kingdom). GATE certification recognises this national accreditation process which goes a long way toward achieving GATE certification itself.

ISO 9000

ISO is a "process-driven" exercise (*i.e.* certain internal processes need to be present in order to have a framework for assuring quality), originally designed for industry. Accordingly, it is a generic exercise, applicable to a number of administrative settings, educational or not. Where ISO is process driven, GATE certification is both process and outcomes driven as specifically related to educational objectives of a transnational offering.

IQRP

The IQRP and GATE certification offer institutions a healthy symbiosis in educational review in both physical and virtual settings (although there has not yet been an IQRP process applied to a virtual institution). As currently envisioned, the IQRP is designed to ask information of an institution about the breadth and depth of its international activity, including but not limited to what offerings it may have outside its own national borders. However, as with most higher education evaluative process globally, the IQRP allows the institution to report the nature and quality of its transnational offerings but does not always conduct visits to each site to provide third party confirmation of this self-declared quality. As with most evaluative processes, this is predominantly a product of expense.

The ISO set of standards[2]

ISO 9000 is a generic term for the ISO family of standards and guidelines relating to quality assurance of management systems. In short, the standards specify requirements for what the organisation should do to manage processes which influence quality.

The ISO group of standards originated in the manufacturing industry and has been embraced and adopted by the service industry. The relevance to the education sector is seen to be growing as increasingly education is being seen as a service industry. The current emphasis on the quality of education services is leading governments to demand from colleges and universities to publicly demonstrate that they not only could state they were quality institutions but could provide evidence for it. As a result institutions are searching for concrete and coherent quality assurance systems which provide evidence in ways acceptable to an external audit process. The ISO 9000 family of standards has thus entered the education sector as one of these standardised external audit procedures. ISO 9000 standards are seen as a reliable means of providing quality assurance over the broad range of institutional processes and in some cases the design of the educational product itself.

ISO is not a certifying authority. It publishes agreed standards but does not certify the outcome. This is the responsibility of organisations which choose to implement ISO and they must approach the agency which is licensed to provide certification.

There are several sets of standards, each one having a specific purpose. For example, ISO 9001 is a standard that incorporates all facets of design, production and servicing of a product or service. ISO 9002 incorporates all facts of 9001, but not the design component. Two new ISO standards are under development. The first is ISO 9001:2000 which addresses Quality Management Systems Requirements for Quality Assurance and the second is ISO 9004:2000 which focuses on Quality Guidelines for Management of Organisations. This section will focus primarily on ISO 9002.

Institutions compete for government funding, for students, for research grants and training opportunities. Government funded institutions compete with private institutions and providers. Clients of a university will typically include students, parents, government departments, prospective students, current and future employers of graduates, community groups, companies or government departments requiring training, research sponsors, aid organisations, professional associations, and national accrediting authorities. The competition among higher educa-

---

2. Parts of this section are excerpts from unpublished paper by Adams (1998).

tion institutions, the increasing market approach and the breadth of the institution client base are reasons often cited for the importance and relevance for quality review and monitoring.

Universities in many countries are subject to national or regional quality assurance processes over their "educational product". Highly regulated accreditation processes both by government and professional associations have meant tight control by the community over standards of course design and delivery. Examples of this type of accreditation include the engineering or any other professional education programme. However, the standard of the educational product is only one aspect of quality assurance within a higher education institution. Another key aspect of quality assessment and assurance is the process or in other words the management system. This is where ISO is applicable. ISO 9002 addresses management processes. Basically, there are four primary aspects the ISO 9002 focuses on: documentation of systems, compliance with systems, audits, incremental improvement.

In an education setting, some of the management processes amenable to ISO 9002 application include student admissions, staff selection and development, strategic planning, teaching and learning, research and project administration, international activities, financial planning and accounting, etc.

A process for ISO 9002 implementation in a university environment

The following section examines the application of ISO to the international dimension of university activities. By extension it can be developed to relate to other university activities. It needs to be noted that the steps outlined below are key for the implementation of the ISO process of quality assessment and assurance. These steps may or may not lead to an ISO certification. It is the institution's decision as to whether it wishes to be certified. If so, only then is the last step, "external certification", undertaken.

Management commitment

Ensure that there is senior management commitment for the project and that it links to the institution's quality policy (if such a policy exists) and to the strategic plan.

Project responsibility

Appoint a person with delegated responsibility for the project and its administration. This person should report to a high level steering group. This could be a university wide international committee, and is intended to ensure that the project remains closely linked to the institutions' International strategy and objectives.

215

Management team

Establish a management team made up of representatives of work groups to review the current systems, provide advice on areas to be covered by certification and on the current status of systems, and develop an action plan. Undertake training of staff in TQM principles and ISO requirements.

Contact with auditing authority

Discuss with the auditing authority the proposal and timelines for an audit.

Quality system manual

Develop the quality manual. This document describes system processes, and the procedures within those processes. Checklists and flow charts show the connection of procedures and guidelines to be used where judgement is required. The manual also shows the responsibility for each process, external references to other documents and procedures, and the assessment and feedback procedures in place. It may also include the service contracts that the group has with clients, such as incoming international students, partner universities, etc.

The preparation of such a manual as a single unified document is a huge commitment. Where the international unit has in place a range of existing procedures in the form of individual documents such as student exchange handbooks, procedures for approving off-shore projects, etc., a more manageable approach is to develop a quality table that contains external pointers to the specific documents. Thus depending on the extent of existing documentation, the manual may be at one extreme a table to existing documents and procedures. At the other extreme, it may be a single document describing the quality system. The preparation of such a table in any case serves to highlight the gaps in existing systems.

Development and implementation of new procedures

An outcome of the review of the system is likely to be the requirement to develop new systems and to modify existing ones. This is an opportunity to open up the process to ensure staff undertaking work roles are deeply involved in the activity.

Internal audit of quality system

Undertake an internal quality audit to test compliance and to recommend improvement measures to be carried out.

External certification

This is optional and is the sole decision of the institution. The external audit is always carried out by the audit authority, followed by corrective action arising from it. The process should then be cyclic with a focus on incremental improvement of systems and remedying deficiencies in the system.

ISO and the international dimension

Quality assurance processes provide a means of demonstrating the institution's commitment to its clients both domestic and international. As a way to illustrate how ISO standards are equally important and appropriate for international initiatives several key areas of internationalisation activities which lend themselves to an ISO 9000 review are listed below. In each of the categories, examples of the management processes which could be documented and then monitored for quality compliance are given.

Development of appropriate missions, strategies and values

- Relationship of internationalisation strategy to institutional strategy.
- Mission and values.
- Explicit articulation of rationale, goals and objectives for internationalisation.
- Policy statements to enable and monitor internationalisation activities.
- Relationship of international initiatives and programmes undertaken to the international strategy.

Provision for international experience as part of academic course credit for 10% of students

- Promotion and access to study abroad opportunities.
- Criteria for selection of participants.
- Admission procedures.
- Academic, cultural, logistical support for incoming/outgoing students.
- Student satisfaction.
- Cross-cultural briefing and support.
- Articulation arrangements.
- Appropriate partner or host institutions.
- Relationship to internationalisation of the curriculum strategy.
- Relationship to internationalisation strategy.
- Programme evaluation.

217

Development of off-shore (transnational) degree programmes

This includes a range of delivery modes and direct teaching that provide opportunities for students to study and obtain a foreign degree completely or partially in their own country:

- Contract development and maintenance.
- Selection of partners and representatives.
- Project approval and review.
- Student admission standards compared to degree granting country.
- Processes for transfer of off-shore students to degree granting country.
- Relationship of courses taught transnationally with domestic courses.
- In-country cultural and ethical standards.
- In-country regulatory and tax advice.
- Local teaching standards compared to degree granting country.
- Marketing, recruiting and admissions.
- Evaluation of programmes.
- Relationship to strategy.
- Student support.

Recruitment of international fee paying students

- Marketing and recruiting strategy for international students.
- Publications strategy.
- International student admissions.
- International student support.
- Cross-cultural teaching and learning strategies.
- Cross-cultural training for teaching and administrative staff.
- English language standards of entry and support.
- Acceptance of overseas qualifications for entry and advanced standing.
- Relationship between domestic and international standards of entry.
- Selection and support of recruiting agents.
- International student performance and graduation rate.

Explicit and implicit internationalisation of the curriculum

- Cross-cultural teaching and support.
- Staff development.
- Courses internationalised.
- Relationship to student and staff mobility.
- Resources available for project development.
- Evaluation of projects.
- International internship and co-operative education openings for students.
- External funding performance.
- Use of best international professional practice case studies.

- Relationship of language teaching to student and staff mobility and international strategy.

There are other key areas of internationalisation where the management procedures can be documented, monitored and improved. These could include the development of strong collaborative arrangements with overseas institutions in the areas of student/staff mobility, best practice bench marking, collaborative research, joint teaching activities, international training and consulting both commercially and through aid funded projects.

In summary, ISO 9002 attempts to provide a coherent means of assuring the quality of international education by requiring a strategic framework and processes for detailed implementation and auditing of the strategies. Where appropriate ISO 9001 can go one step further and address the actual design of the product, or in other words assess and ensure the quality of the design of education or training programmes.

The relationship between ISO 9000 and IQRP

A discussion of the relationship between ISO 9000 and IQRP shows that there are some fundamental differences but areas of similarity as well. ISO is an approach that provides a measure of compliance against an external standard. Even though there is a great deal of flexibility and interpretation built into the process the outcome is likely to be primarily aimed at seeking a business reference with external clients. It is thus externally oriented even though an objective is to provide the organisation with confidence in its systems. It is this internal objective that may easily be lost if the organisation focuses too much on the external advantages of certification. On the other hand, IQRP is a process that is directed at the organisation understanding how its systems relate to its strategy. The self-assessment and peer review are reflective processes only. They are designed to ensure the organisation is on track and that there is an alignment between strategy and reality.

ISO 9000 is interested in the detailed implementation of processes and the evidence of their documentation and implementation. IQRP seeks only macro evidence of the system documentation and performance. It seeks assurance that such processes exist and are documented but is not interested in the fine detail. However, both ISO 9000 and IQRP are interested in strategic objectives, missions and goals. The primary focus of IQRP is how the strategy is borne out in practice.

The integration of ISO 9000 and IQRP can provide the opportunity to ensure that the self-assessment and peer review processes provide assurance that the organisation is reflecting properly on its strategy and implementation and is not over focused on external certification issues. ISO 9000 also provides the evidence to the IQRP process that detailed processes and procedures are "in control" and that incremental improvement processes are in place.

The IQRP self-assessment and peer review provide evidence to the ISO external auditors that the organisation is reflecting on its own systems in a real desire for improvement and not only on external certification.

Conclusions

This chapter has focused on three different quality assurance mechanisms which are all being used to review and improve the internationalisation of higher education institutions. Codes of practice are usually established by a national level organisation and individual institutions endorse and adopt these statements of principles. Codes of practice related to the international dimension are clearly different from but completely compatible with IQRP.

The GATE certification process has been described as both conceptually and operationally complementary to IQRP. The case study of Monash University, Australia, demonstrates how these two different instruments can effectively work in conjunction with each other by addressing different aspects and processes of internationalisation.

In a similar way, the recent experience of the Royal Melbourne Institute of Technology, Australia, has shown that it is possible to successfully combine IQRP and ISO 9002. Through IQRP the goals, objectives, strategies for internationalisation are addressed and through ISO 9002 the quality of the management systems and processes are addressed.

There are several other quality assurance instruments which are being used for improvement and accountability purposes in higher education institutions. Performance indicators, benchmarks, TQM, institutional reviews, programme accreditations are examples of more generic quality instruments which are being applied to the international dimension. This is an important stage in the evolution of the internationalisation of higher education.

It is recognised that the international aspects of education and research have historically been an important feature of higher education institutions. However, current issues such as globalisation, decreased government support for education, the knowledge economy, the rapid growth of information technologies are all directly influencing higher education. It is resulting in major shifts in the rationales and motivations for internationalisation. There are increasing tensions between academic and commercial based motives. One can also see the development of a more strategic, integrated and comprehensive approach to internationalisation. It is therefore very important that attention is given to developing new quality review instruments and that existing instruments are adapted and applied to internationalisation. It is equally important and an ultimate goal that the international dimension becomes a regularised part of all institutional audits or programme accreditation.

OECD 1999

Bibliography

ADAMS, T. (1998),
"ISO and the International Dimension of Higher Education", unpublished paper.

AUSTRALIAN VICE-CHANCELLORS' COMMITTEE (AVCC) (1998),
"Code of Ethical Practice in the Provision of Education to International Students by Australian Universities", Australian Vice-Chancellors' Committee, Canberra (draft revision).

BOUNDS, G., DOBBINS, G.H. and FOWLER, O. (1995),
Management: A Total Quality Perspective, South-Western College Publishing, Cincinnati, Ohio.

CANADIAN BUREAU FOR INTERNATIONAL EDUCATION (CBIE) (1996),
"Code of Ethical Practice in International Education", Ottawa.

COMMITTEE FOR QUALITY ASSURANCE IN HIGHER EDUCATION (1994),
"Quality Assurance Programme Guidelines", Canberra.

GATE (1997),
"Certification Manual", Global Alliance for Transnational Education, Washington, DC and Wellington.

GATE (1998),
"Global Alliance for Transnational Education Newsletter", Vol. 4.

HIGHER EDUCATION QUALITY COUNCIL (1996),
"Code of Practice for Overseas Collaborative Provision in Higher Education", London.

MIKOL, M. (1998),
"IQRP – Quo Vadis", unpublished paper.

PEACE LENN, M. (1998),
"The New Technologies and Borderless Higher Education: The Quality Imperative", *Higher Education in Europe*, CEPES/UNESCO.

SAYLOR, J. (1992),
"TQM: Field Manual", McGraw-Hill, New York.

SHERR, L. and TEETER, D. (1992),
"Total Quality Management in Higher Education", Jossey-Bass Inc., San Francisco.

TSUI, C. (1998),
"Internationalisation of Higher Education Institutions. A Total Quality Management Approach", unpublished paper.

WOODHOUSE, D. and CRAFT, A. (1993),
"Educational Export: From the Importer's View in Higher Education Management", IMHE/OECD, Paris, Vol. 5, No. 3, pp. 333-337.

12

Quality Assurance of Internationalisation and Internationalisation of Quality Assurance

by

Marijk van der Wende

Introduction

While quality and internationalisation of higher education are closely linked concepts, the internationalisation of higher education is challenging current quality assurance systems and practices, which are generally national in scope. This chapter reviews both the relationship between internationalisation and quality in higher education, and the tensions and incoherence between the two areas. Several approaches and models for ensuring the quality of internationalisation and for internationalising quality assurance are discussed. The conclusions emphasise the importance and relevance of developing the Internationalisation Quality Review Process.

Quality and internationalisation: a problematic definition

The internationalisation of higher education seems closely related to improving educational quality; many policy documents consider it to be a means to enhancing quality rather than an end in itself. In the 1980s, OECD publications examined quality, particularly in relation to the expected impact of the presence of foreign students on teaching and learning processes, curriculum and services (Ebuchi, 1989). The Maastricht Treaty (1992) articles that provide the basis for Community action in higher education reflect the aim of improving the quality of education through co-operation among the European Union member states. National and institutional policies for internationalising higher education generally also target quality (Kälvermark and van der Wende, 1997).

Statements concerning internationalisation and quality usually assume that international co-operation and student, faculty or research exchanges add to the critical mass, allow for mutual learning, for a comparison and synthesis of best approaches and practices, for cross-cultural understanding, and for foreign language acquisition, etc. International co-operation and exchange are expected to contribute to the quality of processes and outcomes at the individual, project, institutional, and even the system levels.

These are, however, just assumptions. There is considerable personal observation of positive and negative examples of the impact of internationalisation on quality, but this often simply reconfirms predetermined positions. There is little evidence on what the relationship between internationalisation and quality really means, partly because there is little empirical research. Moreover, there is generally very little systematic monitoring of internationalisation and existing quality assurance systems rarely address internationalisation adequately. Therefore, while higher education is internationalising, it continues to be assessed almost solely by nationally-oriented quality assurance systems.

Emphasising quality as an important goal of internationalisation without systematically monitoring and evaluating its impact is paradoxical and contrasts with the harmonious relationship between internationalisation and quality in research where tradition is different. In most academic fields, not only is it firmly believed that international co-operation contributes to research quality, but also research has a higher status and is truly assessed and recognised in an international arena through international competition for funding (*e.g.* European R&D funds). Moreover, major scientific bodies, organisations and journals are international in breadth and reach. Consequently, international activities and appraisal are taken into account in national assessments of research. Therefore, both the link between the concepts of internationalisation and quality, and the integration of practices, are more consistent in research than they are in education.

Furthermore, the internationalisation of higher education may also have other aims. It may target economic goals which play an increasingly important role in higher education (Kälvermark and van der Wende, 1997). Economic goals may be short term (increasing institutional fee income) or long term (investment in international trade relationships). In the former, there is a higher education export perspective which raises new questions concerning quality: is there, for instance, an "export quality" of education? And is that better or worse than "home quality"?

Therefore, although higher education may still be nationally based, it can no longer be considered as nationally bound. Consequently, systems for quality assurance which are nationally limited in breadth and reach are no longer satisfying. In general, historically the domestic process for quality assurance was not intended to serve an international purpose. But the internationalisation of higher education is forcing it at least to consider matters beyond its borders. Furthermore, as Peace Lenn (1994) and others have emphasised, there tends to be little co-ordination between those bodies formally involved in assuring quality in higher education and those which promote internationalisation. The question now is how to resolve this disparity. Should national quality assurance systems pay more and better attention to internationalisation, should quality assurance systems themselves be internationalised, or should they be replaced by completely different mechanisms? And who is to take the initiative and to have the responsibility? Is it the national or the supranational government, the institutions, independent organisations or "the market"?

Quality assurance and internationalisation: approaches and models

Scott (1996) identifies five different models, for the quality assurance of internationalisation:

- To concede that national quality rules imposed in the domestic context need not apply internationally. This is not to say that lower standards should be accepted; merely that, outside national jurisdiction, the laws of the market must apply. He adds that "although few European countries, or universities, would admit such an approach, it is still perhaps the most common" (p. 30).
- To extend existing quality assurance systems designed for the domestic environment to the internationalisation of higher education. The attempt of the Higher Education Quality Council to audit collaborative arrangements entered into by British institutions, including franchising arrangements, is one example of this type of effort.
- To adapt quality assurance systems to take better account of the special issues raised by internationalisation such as "codes of practice" on overseas marketing and recruitment of international students. Quality assurance systems could also be used to encourage institutions to improve services for international students, to internationalise academic programmes, and to develop systematic policies for internationalisation.
- To attempt to create a common currency for quality assurance, thus enabling supra-national systems to develop. Although this would probably enable cross-national comparisons, it would not necessarily encourage institutions to internationalise their staff, students, or programmes. Moreover, the difficulty of establishing such a currency would most likely limit it geographically.
- To treat the internationalisation of higher education as a political project to be encouraged. This goes beyond the competence of quality assurance in the narrow sense. All actors should be engaged in the evolution of higher education, its purposes, missions, and role in the global knowledge economy. In this context, self-evaluation instruments will be crucial to the ownership of internationalisation and its links to innovation and improvement.

This overview shows that there are various dimensions in the relation between internationalisation and quality assurance. One concerns the quality assurance of international activities and whether this should be included in existing quality assurance systems. Another refers to the internationalisation of quality assurance systems themselves. In many discussions and documents these two dimensions are mixed or confused. While exploring these two dimensions we will illustrate some of the models described by Scott.

Internationalisation of quality assurance

With respect to internationalisation of quality assurance, various approaches can be observed. In addition to initiatives on international co-operation and information-sharing between associations, agencies, and institutions responsible for quality assurance such as the International Network of Quality Assurance Agencies in Higher Education (INQAAHE), several interesting projects have been undertaken in recent years. In general, these concern initiatives aimed at widening the national basis for quality assurance, although they do not necessarily address the internationalisation of higher education *per se*.

The first example concerns the EU pilot project on quality assurance. Undertaken between 1995 and 1997 at the initiative of the European Commission, this project sought to increase awareness of the need for quality assessment in higher education, to give it a European dimension, to enrich existing national level quality assessment procedures, and to help improve the recognition of diplomas and study periods by promoting institutional co-operation and improving mutual understanding about programmes taught in different countries (Commission of the European Communities, 1995). The main European quality assurance systems share several features: the role of an independent (metalevel) managing agent, self-evaluation, peer review, and process outcomes reporting (van Vught and Westerheijden, 1993). This pilot project consisted of subject-based self-assessments by all participating institutions according to a set of common guidelines, and followed up with an evaluation visit of a group of peers (including experts from other European countries) and a published report. This process provided experience in developing a European dimension in quality assurance; the European dimension of the institutions and their study programmes were given only limited attention, however.

A second example concerns the Programme of Institutional Quality Audits of the Association of European Universities (CRE). Here also the process is based on self-assessment and a peer review conducted by a team of European experts. The focus is on the management of the institution as a whole rather than on a specific subject area or discipline. Consequently, a wider, but more general range of issues is considered. Additionally, the development of thematic audits to address specific areas, such as financial management, human resources policies, and internationalisation is being planned.

Other "bottom up" initiatives can be observed in Europe. Networks of European institutions, in some cases established in the context of European co-operation programmes, are developing their own models and mechanisms for quality assurance. For instance, the Community of European Management Schools (CEMS) offers a common master's degree in Economics and Business Administration. It has taken the initiative to develop a quality review process of all aspects of the CEMS programme aimed at quality control, the transfer of good practice, co-operation on quality improvement of the CEMS curriculum, developing a common CEMS policy and approach to quality improvement, and designing a tool that can help CEMS evaluate potential partners. The first step of a pilot project begun in 1997 involved collecting information about the institutions' experience with and traditions for internal quality assurance. The assessment phase of the project combines information gathered through questionnaires for student evaluation of the exchange term at another CEMS institution with peer review (Kristensen and Plannthin, 1997).

It is important in this context to elaborate on the development of common (European) degrees and standards and, in particular, on the role played by professional organisations. Initiatives such as the European Association of Biologists and the European Federation of National Engineering Associations (FEANI) demonstrate that an agreement on quality standards can be reached and that a specific designation ("European Engineer") can be awarded on that basis.

Professional organisations are actively involved because professional recognition of foreign credentials and qualifications is becoming important for increased professional mobility. This, in turn, is facilitated by regional (*e.g.* EU, NAFTA, APEC) and global trade agreements (*e.g.* the World Trade Organisation's General Agreement on Trade in Services, 1994). These indirectly affect higher education by calling upon the member countries to develop mutually acceptable standards and to provide recommendations on mutual recognition. Furthermore, professional organisations and their respective accrediting bodies are being pressured to consider mutually acceptable standards for co-operation with other countries; they will also have to accept international application. These organisations are facing a new situation in which higher education institutions may seek multiple, regional, or global accreditation (Peace Lenn and Campos, 1997).

The Accreditation Board for Engineering and Technology (ABET), a federation of the United States professional engineering societies, and its international activities, is an important example. As, in recent years, the global economy has expanded and the demand for engineering mobility has increased, the assessment of the quality of education in engineering programmes at institutions outside the United States has become increasingly important. To meet these needs, ABET has become involved internationally through mutual recognition agreements, programme evaluations, educational consultancy visits, assistance in developing accreditation systems in other countries, and, only very recently, in the accreditation of engineering programmes outside the United States (Aberle, Paris and Peterson, 1997).

The question now is how these initiatives and developments are to be understood and interpreted and what the possible future directions in internationalisation of quality assurance in higher education will be. In an attempt to answer this question, we will draw comparisons between authors who emphasise the differences between national quality assurance systems and others who stress their common features.

Kells (1997) claims that although some general patterns can be identified in the existing quality assurance systems, they tend to travel poorly because of cultural differences and preferences regarding purpose. These include tendencies towards elitism versus egalitarianism, positions concerning church-state relations, the extent of differentiation and the range of quality permitted in the system, the willingness to compare and rank, openness about weaknesses, the relationship between higher education and the state, the extent of accountability, etc. For Kells, these cultural forces may produce very different systems.

The CEMS project illustrates the influence of cultural differences. Kristensen and Plannthin (1997) reported that in a multi-institutional and multi-national assessment process, the cultural element becomes crucial in several ways, related to different academic traditions. Different views of the concept of quality constituted the first main obstacle to terminological clarity. Harvey and Green (1993) analysed different meanings of quality and noted that it can be viewed as *exceptional*, as *perfection* (or consistency), as *fitness for purpose*, as *value for money* and as *transformation*. In the Humboldtian tradition, quality is largely related to the reputation of professors (quality as exceptional), whereas in the Nordic tradition, the teaching and learning processes and interaction (quality as transformation) are more important. No general understanding on the concept of quality could be reached. Nor could the question of who the stakeholders of the process are be easily resolved. Are students products, clients, customers, consumers, users, or participants? Furthermore, participant institutions emphasised improvement and accountability differently as functions of quality assurance. Differences of opinion and tradition occurred in several other areas as well (Kristensen and Plannthin, 1997). "Those who believe that higher education is being homogenised and becoming very similar across the world – because of the existence of similar problems and some similar initiatives which are attempted by leaders who are communicating in a global community – should consider the vastly different inclinations on the cultural dimensions and concerning why, what and how to evaluate in higher education" (Kells, 1997, p. 4).

Quality assurance systems also share many elements. Van Vught (1994) suggests designing a general framework of a system of multiple accreditation in higher education based on common elements of systems in the United States, Canada, and Western Europe (involvement of a management agent, the self-evaluation and peer review processes, reporting results and the relationship with funding). Here, a number of accrediting organisations would each offer accreditation to institutions or programmes, using pre-stated standards and a review process combining self-study and peer review. Furthermore, many accrediting organisations already exist, each with its own set of clearly defined standards attuned to the needs of their constituencies: employers, students, professions, etc. Higher education institutions would seek accreditation for their programmes on a voluntary basis from one or more accrediting organisations, and together they would form a "market" and quality networks (networks of institutions or programmes with related missions, and accredited by the same accrediting bodies and thus with the same status). Regional level (*e.g.* the United States, the European Union) could offer a sufficient scale for this type of multiple accreditation. However, no international or supra-national decision-making is required for a multiple accreditation system to develop. The "third round" quality assessment procedure in the Netherlands, for example, contains the possibility to replace the "normal" assessment by an ABET accreditation. This is a first step towards a multiple accreditation system.

Peace Lenn claims that multiple accreditation activity will eventually be replaced by global accreditation motivated by trade agreements. She argues that the globalisation of the professions and the need to provide common professional preparation have accelerated the movement to set global standards and accreditation (Peace Lenn and Campos, 1997).

Quality assurance of internationalisation

Many countries have become aware, over the past few years, of the importance of quality assurance of internationalisation strategies and activities and have attempted to evaluate and assure it. Several approaches have been taken.

Codes of practice. These generally apply to student exchanges and overseas recruitment or delivery of educational programmes and services overseas. They usually concern a set of minimum requirements to be respected in certain practices but may also refer to situations or actions to be avoided. These codes are descriptive, objective, and can be used ex-ante or ex-post. They are generally used independently of broader quality assurance or accreditation processes in institutions or programmes. These codes lead to no external judgement, funding decision, or particular status (accreditation or licensing). Examples include: the Code of Ethical Practice in the Provision of Education to International Students by Australian Universities (Australian Vice-Chancellors' Committee); the NAFSA Ethics Programme – Ethical Practice in International Exchange; Recruitment and Support of International Students in the United Kingdom Higher Education (Committee of Vice-Chancellors and Principals of the Universities of the United Kingdom); the Code of Practice for Overseas Collaborative Provision in Higher Education (Higher Education Quality Council).[1]

---

1. The HEQC has been subsumed by the Quality Assurance Agency for Higher Education (QAA), which is currently developing a new code of practice on collaborative provision in higher education.

Self-evaluation instruments for internationalisation strategies and activities offer a framework that allows an institution to evaluate its internationalisation efforts and achievements against its objectives, including student and staff exchanges, internationalisation of the curriculum, teaching and learning processes, joint degrees, organisation and services. These instruments are analytical and subjective and used ex-post. They may be part of a wider quality assurance process involving outside evaluation of self-evaluation outcomes through peer review and leading to recommendations. The Centre for International Mobility, Finland (Snellman, 1995) developed *Goals, Prerequisites and Quality Assurance for International Education*; the Netherlands Organisation for International Co-operation in Higher Education (NUFFIC) and the Association of Dutch Colleges and Polytechnics (van der Wende, 1995) developed *Quality in Internationalisation – Guidelines for the Assessment of the Quality of Internationalisation in Higher Professional Education*. The Dutch example was designed especially to fit into the wider quality assurance process for higher professional education, by applying the methodology and structure of the national system to the evaluation of the quality of internationalisation. The general manual for quality assurance recommends its use, but on a voluntary basis for self-evaluation and peer review. This integrative approach was made possible by the co-operation between an internationalisation and a quality assurance agency during the development stages.

Certification practices were developed by the Global Alliance for Transnational Education (GATE). This organisation represents a partnership of the multi-national corporate community, national associations, and governments and higher education institutions, primarily to address the assurance and improvement of education crossing national borders. Transnational education is defined as: "any teaching or learning activity in which the students are in a different country (the host country) to that in which the institution providing the education is based (the home country). This situation requires that national boundaries be crossed by information about the education, and by staff and/or educational materials (whether the information and the materials travel by mail, computer network, radio or television broadcast or other means)". Examples of such transnational education include: branch campuses, franchised programmes, twinning arrangements, corporate programmes, distance education programmes, etc. GATE has developed a set of "Principles for Transnational Education" that can be used as a code of practice. Furthermore, through a process of self-evaluation and external review, GATE can *certify* an institution that provides transnational education, primarily for consumer protection. And although certification concerns a yes/no decision, recommendations for improvement are normally also made. Compared to the others, this approach seems to address a wider range of initiatives, including corporate and distance and virtual programmes.

Situations exist where internationalisation is being assessed as an integrated part of a broader or general quality assurance or accreditation procedure at either the institutional or programme level. In Europe, this fourth type of practice is emerging in some countries, Sweden, the Netherlands, and France for example. However, this part of the evaluation process is not always clearly defined or sufficiently explicit. Appropriate evaluation criteria may be lacking along with a clear understanding of the issues or their context. These approaches often take a very narrow look at internationalisation, focusing almost exclusively on student mobility and exchange.

As the examples above show, higher education institutions, individually or in groups, or associations, have undertaken many initiatives, some of which interest national agencies. Besides the Dutch example (above), in Australia, the Australian Committee for Quality Assurance in Higher Education regularly comments on internationalisation. Its 1994 report expressed particular concern about integrating international content into the general curriculum. In the United Kingdom in 1996-97, the Higher Education Quality Council undertook some audits on collaborative programmes of British institutions overseas. The Dutch Inspectorate for Higher Education has regularly expressed concern about institutional internationalisation activities and has recommended that those undertaken in European programmes and in foreign partner institutions be subject to regular quality assurance (Inspectie van het Onderwijs, 1995).

Despite these expressions of concern and some related initiatives, national governments or agencies have difficulty defining their position and role towards quality assurance of international(ised) higher education. This may well be related to the fact that internationalisation is affecting the relationship between higher education and the national government, as the next section illustrates.

The influence of internationalisation on the relationship between higher education and the nation state and on the functions of quality assurance systems

National systems assess higher education generally but pay little attention to its international dimension, for several reasons: the close relationship between higher education and the central government, the importance of public funding for higher education, and the emphasis on public accountability as an important function of quality assurance systems. However, these factors are changing rapidly creating tensions between internationalisation and quality assurance.

As a (logical) result of the internationalisation process, higher education is outgrowing its national context, including its quality assurance system. This process is taking place in various ways and to various extents, as will be described below:

- *Internationalisation* as a policy outcome aimed at integrating international elements into teaching, research and service, introduces co-operation, exchange and an internationalised curriculum into higher education. In addition to bi-lateral co-operation and mobility schemes, multi-lateral initiatives such as the European Union's SOCRATES and LEONARDO programmes and the EC-United States, EC-Canada, EC-China programmes, provide an important basis for developing this type of activity. These initiatives are based on agreements among countries but respect the national basis of the education system and national sovereignty in governance. International elements introduced by this type of internationalisation are generally expected to contribute to the quality and competitiveness of the system and its outcomes at different levels, as described above. Furthermore, these elements are becoming structural characteristics of the higher education systems in many countries. However, quality assurance systems and procedures, generally do not include or address them adequately, and thus become incomplete or insufficient.

- De-*nationalisation* of higher education refers to several processes causing or facilitating the expansion of higher education systems across national borders. The balance in the control of higher education systems is changing. As introduced by Clark (1983) in his triangle of co-ordination in higher education, the forces of academic oligarchy, state authority and market demand interact with each other to give shape and direction to academic work in national systems of higher education. Many governments have introduced deregulation policies and concepts like "steering at a distance" in favour of more institutional autonomy and stronger market influences (Dill and Sporn, 1995, Goedegebuure *et al.*, 1994). Furthermore, increasing competition, globalisation, and decreasing public funds motivate higher education institutions to expand their activities across national borders: the United States, Canada, the United Kingdom, Australia and New Zealand all have examples of internationally enterpreneurial universities. These not only attract many fee-paying foreign students, but also operate actively overseas through branch campuses, franchised programmes, etc. Finally, information and communication technology (ICT) facilitates transnational delivery through a new type of distance learning programme making it easier to export higher education on a large scale to a virtual, borderless world.

  International strategies and activities resulting from the de-nationalisation of higher education usually exceed the restrictions of existing quality assurance systems. Consequently, a proper assessment of international programmes and overseas activities must be separately organised. Furthermore, these developments may affect the functions of quality assurance systems (*e.g.* accountability in relation to new money flows from international income and funding) and raise questions about responsibility and other legal issues (*e.g.* in the case of virtual universities).

- Race (1997) describes the *regionalisation* of higher education, or cross-border co-operation between neighbouring states, as "large scale sub-continental co-operation between economically comparable regions". Such co-operation exists in the Nordic countries, between the Netherlands and adjacent Belgium (Flanders) and Germany (Bremen, Lower Saxony and Rhineland Westphalia) (see Race, 1997 for other types and definitions of regional co-operation in higher education). This is a new type of international co-operation that emphasises structural educational and administrative co-operation to make both systems more responsive to the needs of regional labour markets and to enhance mutual access and complementarity. Joint programmes and degrees are being developed and human resources shared. The future may include cross-border co-ordination of educational provision and ultimately even institutional mergers. Initiatives would then face different quality assurance systems, if and as they exist in the co-operating countries, and mutual recognition and trust in each other's quality and systems would be required. This would mean adjusting, mixing, choosing from among national quality assurance systems, or developing entirely new systems.

These various forms of internationalisation have shown how the relationship between higher education institutions and the national government is affected. Furthermore, as described above, globalisation trends through the role of professional organisations and the practice of international accreditation influence higher education directly (*i.e.* without any direct involvement of the government) in the development of internationally acceptable standards for professions.

Finally, internationalisation also seems to influence the functions performed by a quality assurance system: *accountability, improvement, transparency* and *accreditation* (Weusthof and Frederiks, 1997). Especially when internationalisation represents foreign sources of income, the government cannot require the same degree or type of accountability for spending as it does for national or public funding. Furthermore, internationalisation increases requirements for the transparency of quality assurance systems. Consumer protection emphasises this by requiring adequate information on institutions, their courses of study, programmes, quality and differences. This is particularly important for students interested in taking study programmes from or at foreign institutions and for employers recruiting internationally and who must be able to evaluate foreign courses and degrees.

Conclusions

In this chapter, the *relationship* between the concepts of quality and of internationalisation of higher education has been discussed. Quality improvement may be a major aim of internationalisation but the process of internationalisation of higher education puts *pressure* on the current systems of quality assurance, which are generally national based and do not adequately address the international dimension of higher education. There is generally *little co-ordination* or co-operation among those organisations involved in quality assurance of higher education and those promoting internationalisation. A number of initiatives have been described.

Internationalising quality assurance systems and methods. In addition to one project initiated at the supranational (EU) level, *"bottom up"* initiatives have been identified. They originate from international networks of quality assurance agencies,

235

and from international associations, consortia or networks of higher education institutions. The role of *professional organisations* is important here because of the increasing international mobility of professionals that is facilitated by regional and global trade agreements on international trade in professional services. They have initiated far-reaching agreements on mutual recognition of professional qualifications and on international quality standards, and actively support the development of *international accreditation* practices. Arguing from the similarities between various quality assurance systems, multiple accreditation on a regional and eventually global accreditation is forecast for the near future. However, *different cultural and academic traditions* will also prove to be stumbling blocks. This may imply that areas and disciplines strongly influenced by the *professional* field may internationalise quality assurance (*e.g.* international accreditation) more rapidly and easily than in disciplines where cultural factors and different academic traditions and concepts of quality may be less easy to overcome.

Quality assurance of internationalisation. Many of these initiatives have a *"bottom up"* character and have been undertaken by institutions or by groups of institutions. Although national governments and agencies are concerned about the international activities of higher education institutions, their initiatives are generally quite limited, both in number and scope. This may well be related to the *blurring effect* of the internationalisation process on the role of national governments and agencies and their relationship with higher education institutions, and on the accountability function of quality assurance systems. At the same time, the *transparency* function of quality assurance systems has become more important because employers and students need to be able to evaluate the quality of foreign courses and qualifications. This introduces the concept of *consumer protection* as an important new consideration and responsibility for governments regarding the quality of internationalised higher education.

It is to be hoped that progress in the quality assurance of internationalisation and in the internationalisation of quality assurance will converge where both the scope and the methodology of quality assurance will be international. This would mean an approach that takes the international dimension and elements of higher education explicitly into account, is internationally applicable, and which gives outcomes that can be internationally recognised. In order to achieve this, at least two important conditions have to be met. First, as Scott (1996) states, institutions should make internationalisation explicit, and develop clear institutional strategies in order to internalise it and to create a sense of ownership. Only in this way can a shared responsibility for quality assurance and improvement be achieved. Secondly, co-ordination among those organisations involved in quality assurance of higher education and those promoting internationalisation should be encouraged and enhanced.

The project on the Internationalisation Quality Review Process (IQRP) is therefore a major step forward. It encourages institutions to make their internationalisation strategies explicit, to review them in their own right and to search for improvement. Moreover, it is the first international level project combining the perspectives of quality assurance of internationalisation and internationalisation of quality assurance. Finally, it has been undertaken by two organisations – the IMHE programme of the OECD and the Academic Co-operation Association – which bring together extensive expertise in the fields of quality assurance and internationalisation of higher education.

Bibliography

ABERLE, K.B., PARIS, D.T. and PETERSON, G.D. (1997),
"Quality Assurance in International Engineering Education: A summary of ABET Activities", in M. Peace Lenn and L. Campos (eds.), *Globalization of the Professions and the Quality Imperative. Professional Accreditation, Certification and Licensure*, Magna Publications, Madison.

CLARK, B.R. (1983),
The Higher Education System, University of California Press, Berkeley.

COMMISSION OF THE EUROPEAN COMMUNITIES (1995),
European Pilot Projects for Evaluating Quality in Higher Education. Guidelines for Participating Institutions, Commission of the European Communities, Brussels.

DILL, D.D. and SPORN, B. (1995),
Emerging Patterns of Social Demand and University Reform: Through a Glass Darkly, Pergamon Press, Oxford.

EBUCHI, K. (1989),
Foreign Students and Internationalisation of Higher Education, Research Institute for Higher Education, Hiroshima University.

GOEDEGEBUURE, L., KAISER, F., MAASSEN, P., MEEK, L., VAN VUGHT, F. and DE WEERT, E. (1994),
Higher Education Policy: An International Comparative Perspective, Pergamon Press, Oxford.

HARVEY, L. and GREEN, D. (1993),
"Defining Quality", *Assessment and Evaluation in Higher Education*, Vol. 18, pp. 9–34.

INSPECTIE VAN HET ONDERWIJS (1995),
Over Internationalisering: studenten en kwaliteitszorg [about internationalisation, students and quality assurance], De Meern.

KÄLVERMARK, T. and VAN DER WENDE, M.C. (1997),
National Policies for Internationalisation of Higher Education in Europe, National Agency for Higher Education, Stockholm.

KELLS, H.R. (1997),
"The Higher Education Quality: Evaluation and Accreditation Movement: An International Retrospective Analysis", Paper presented at the staff workshop of the World Bank, March, Washington DC, United States.

KRISTENSEN, B. and PLANNTHIN, M. (1997),
"Quality Assessment at a Multi-national Level", Paper presented at the 19th Annual EAIR Forum, August, Warwick, United Kingdom.

PEACE LENN, M. (1994),
"International Linkages and Quality Assurance: A Shifting Paradigm", in A. Craft (ed.), *International Developments in Assuring Quality in Higher Education*, Falmer Press, London and Washington.

PEACE LENN, M. and CAMPOS, L. (1997),
Globalization of the Professions and the Quality Imperative. Professional Accreditation, Certification and Licensure, Magna Publications, Madison.

RACE, J. (1997),
"Regional Co-operation in Higher Education. A Background and Overview", Paper for the Joint Conference on Regional Co-operation in Higher Education, Council of Europe – Nordic Council of Ministers, Council of Europe, Strasbourg.

SCOTT, P. (1996),
"Internationalisation and Quality Assurance", in U. De Winter (ed.), *Internationalisation and Quality Assurance: Goals, Strategies and Instruments*, EAIE Occasional Paper No. 10, EAIE, Amsterdam.

SNELLMAN, O. (1995),
International Education in Finnish Universities: Goals, Prerequisites and Evaluation, CIMO Occasional Paper 1, University of Lapland, Centre for International Mobility (CIMO), Helsinki.

VAN VUGHT, F. (1994),
"Intrinsic and Extrinsic Aspects of Quality Assessment in Higher Education", in D. Westerheijden, J. Brennan and P.A.M. Maassen (eds.), *Changing Contexts of Quality Assessment. Recent Trends in West European Higher Education*, Lemma, Utrecht.

VAN VUGHT, F. and WESTERHEIJDEN, D. (1993),
Quality Management and Quality Assurance in European Higher Education. Methods and Mechanisms, Commission of the European Community, Brussels.

239

VAN DER WENDE, M.C. (1995),

Guidelines for the Assessment of the Quality of Internationalisation in Higher Professional Education (HBO) in the Netherlands, Netherlands Organisation for International Co-operation in Higher Education (NUFFIC), Association of Dutch Colleges and Polytechnics, the Hague.

VAN DER WENDE, M.C. (1996),

"Quality Assurance in Internationalisation", in U. De Winter (ed.), Internationalisation and Quality Assurance: Goals, Strategies and Instruments, EAIE Occasional Paper No. 10, EAIE, Amsterdam.

WEUSTHOF, P.J.M. and FREDERIKS, M.M.H. (1997),

"De functies van het stelsel van kwaliteitszorg heroverwogen" [the functions of the quality assurance system reconsidered], Tijdschrift voor Hoger Onderwijs, Jaargang 15, No. 4, pp. 318-338.

Guidelines for the Internationalisation Quality Review Process (IQRP) for Institutions of Higher Education

The key role of internationalisation and its contribution to higher education are gaining recognition around the world, in both developed and developing countries. Internationalisation of higher education is understood as the process of integrating an international dimension into the teaching, research and service function of the institution. As internationalisation matures, both as a concept and process, it is important that institutions of higher education address the issue of the quality assessment and assurance of their international dimension. For those institutions that want to implement an internationalisation strategy, it is important to have a framework that assists them in the design and evaluation of such a strategy.

The Internationalisation Quality Review Process (IQRP) is a process whereby individual institutions of higher education assess and enhance the quality of their international dimension according to their own stated aims and objectives. The review process includes procedures, guidelines and tools to be adapted and used in both a self-assessment exercise and an external peer review. The purpose of IQRP is to assist institutions to improve their internationalisation work; it is not a certification or accreditation process.

The IQRP is a process developed by the Programme on Institutional Management of Higher Education (IMHE) of the Organisation for Economic Co-operation and Development (OECD) in collaboration with the Academic Co-operation Association (ACA) in Brussels. IMHE/OECD together with ACA owns the intellectual property of the guidelines.

1. Background of the IQRP project

The IQRP project was designed with the following objectives in mind: to increase awareness of the need for quality assessment and assurance in the internationalisation of higher education; to develop a review process whereby individual institutions can adapt and use a set of guidelines to assess and enhance the quality of their internationalisation strategies according to their own aims and objectives; and to strengthen the contribution that internationalisation makes to the quality of higher education.

OECD 1999

There have been two phases to the IQRP project. In phase one, 1995-97, draft guidelines were developed and piloted in three institutions: University of Helsinki, Finland; Bentley College in Massachusetts, the United States, and Monash University, Melbourne, Australia. In 1997-98, a second group of six institutions used the IQRP and assisted in testing and further refining the process: National University of Mexico, Mexico; Warsaw School of Economics, Poland; Tartu University, Estonia; Moi University, Kenya; Universiti Sains Malaysia, Penang; and Royal Melbourne Institute of Technology, Australia.

The testing of the IQRP in eight countries in five different parts of the world, provided valuable information for the design of the final guidelines. Three comprehensive institutions (Helsinki, Monash and Tartu) and two specialised institutions (Bentley and Warsaw) with well developed strategies for internationalisation used the IQRP to assess their strategies. Two comprehensive universities (Mexico and Moi) used the IQRP to assist in moving from a marginal and implicit international dimension to a central and explicit internationalisation strategy. One comprehensive university (Sains Malaysia) used IQRP to create awareness of the importance of an internationalisation strategy by assessing certain parts of the institution. The Royal Melbourne Institute of Technology used IQRP to further the integration of the international dimension into all functions of the university.

As part of the project, presentations and seminars were given on the IQRP in many countries in different parts of the world. The feedback and comments gained from these sessions were extremely valuable in helping the IQRP recognise and be sensitive to the intercultural and international influences on quality assurance of the international dimension.

The preparation of the IQRP guidelines was done by a team of international experts, who were also involved in the peer reviews. After consultation with the experts and the Academic Co-operation Association, the present guidelines were approved by the Directing Group of the Programme on Institutional Management of Higher Education (IMHE) of the OECD for use in the field of higher education.

Based on the results of the IQRP project, IMHE and ACA are exploring with the Association of European Universities (CRE) how to offer an Internationalisation Quality Review (IQR) as an option to European institutions of higher education. In the near future, it is expected that similar services (using the IQRP guidelines) will be created to provide assistance to institutions of higher education in other parts of the world to implement a quality review of their international dimension.

2. Purpose of the IQRP

The purpose of the IQRP is to assist institutions of higher education to assess and improve the quality of their international dimension by focusing on the identification of:

- The achievement of the institution's stated policy (goals and objectives) for internationalisation, and its implementation strategy.

- The integration of an international dimension into the primary functions and priorities of the institution.
- The inclusion of internationalisation as a key theme area in the institution's overall quality assurance system.

3. Guiding principles of the IQRP

The starting point for the review is the institution's own stated aims and objectives. The review process assesses the extent to which institutions actually achieve the aims and objectives which they set for themselves. The assessment of the relationship between objectives and actual achievement is the core of the quality issue.

The purpose of the self-assessment process is to provide a critical self-evaluation of a variety of aspects related to the quality of the international dimension of the institution. The more emphasis given to self-assessment, the more self-assessment will function as a means of training and assisting the institution to take responsibility for its own quality improvement. Self-assessment should not be seen as an exercise to produce information for the external peer review team, but rather as an opportunity to conduct an analysis of the extent and quality of internationalisation initiatives.

The purpose of the external peer review is to mirror the self-assessment process and to provide feedback and a complementary analysis to the self-assessment by the institution, from a different, external and international perspective.

Whilst the review process is intended to be international in application, acknowledgement and recognition of differences among institutions and countries is essential.

The self-assessment and external peer review reports are for the use of the evaluated institution only. The reports are owned by the institution and can only be published by the evaluated institution or with its explicit approval.

The review process is not intended to prescribe practices or advocate uniformity or standardisation of internationalisation approaches or procedures. There is no explicit or implicit comparison with other institutions involved, it is an exercise for self-improvement. This does not exclude the possibility for an institution to combine the IQRP with other quality assurance procedures such as bench marking, ISO 9000, Global Alliance for Transnational Education (GATE) certification or Total Quality Management.

The review process is seen as part of an ongoing cycle process of advocating, planning, implementing, rewarding, reviewing and improving the internationalisation strategy of the institution.

243

4. Who should conduct an IQRP?

The IQRP guidelines and framework are designed in such a way that they are applicable in a great variety of circumstances. Experience of the use of IQRP has indicated that the IQRP can be used in:

- The university and the non-university sectors of higher education.
- Small and large institutions.
- Comprehensive and specialised institutions.
- Private and public institutions.
- Institutions wishing to assess an existing strategy for internationalisation but also institutions wishing to initiate such a strategy.
- Institutions in both developed and developing countries.

The specific circumstances of the institution and of the objectives have to be taken into consideration in the implementation of the IQRP. This implies a flexible use of the guidelines. Whilst the IQRP is guided by the institution's own goals and objectives for internationalisation, there are major areas which are common to many institutions and which the review process will address.

5. The operational framework of IQRP

The emphasis and orientation of the self-assessment exercise is on the analysis of the quality of the international dimension of the institution. It should not merely be a description of the various internationalisation initiatives. At the same time, it is recognised that, in particular for those institutions that intend to use the IQRP to initiate an internationalisation strategy, a qualitative and quantitative inventory of international activities will be an important basis for the assessment.

5.1. Self-assessment

5.1.1. Role and structure of the self-assessment team

A self-assessment team (SAT) is formed at the institutional level and is given the mandate to:

- Collect the necessary information.
- Undertake a critical analysis of the provision for and the quality of internationalisation, as well of the contribution of internationalisation to higher education.
- Prepare the self-assessment report.
- Engage the commitment of various parties inside and outside the institution to the whole process.

The institution chooses the members of the team to reflect the internal organisation and aims of the institution. Ideally, the SAT should consist of (central and departmental level) representatives of both the administrative and the academic staff as well as international and domestic students. In order for the team to be functional and accomplish its task in a relatively short period of time the group should be relatively small and the members should be administratively supported to undertake the work.

The full endorsement and active involvement of the institutional leadership is essential for the success of the self-assessment team.

The SAT has a chairperson and a secretary. It is recommended that the key person in the institution responsible for internationalisation strategy and policy be the chair of the SAT. The secretary will be responsible for organising the work of the SAT and for co-ordinating the preparation of its report.

The SAT will exchange comments with the PRT on the self-assessment report prior to its visit, will prepare the programme of the visit in conjunction with the PRT and will discuss the draft peer review report with the PRT. The secretary of the SAT plays an important role in the liaison with the secretary of the PRT.

5.1.2. The design of the self-assessment process

It is important to emphasise that the whole purpose of the self-assessment is to analyse the international dimension, not merely to describe it. Collecting data to build a profile of all the different activities, programmes, policies and procedures related to the international dimension of the institution is only a first step. It certainly is an important and rather time-consuming step, in particular for those institutions that use the IQRP as an instrument to assist in the preparation of an internationalisation strategy and that do not yet have mechanisms in place to make a quantitative and qualitative description of these activities, programmes, procedures and policies. But the analysis of an institution's performance and achievements according to their articulated aims and objectives for internationalisation is critical to assess and eventually assure the quality of the international dimension and the contribution internationalisation makes to the primary functions of the institution. The process must indicate directions for improvement and change of the internationalisation strategy of the institution, which follows from the diagnosis itself.

The self-assessment outline is designed as a template for the process of analysing the aims and objectives, the performance and achievements, the strengths and the weaknesses, and the opportunities and threats regarding the international dimension of the institution. It needs to be emphasised that it is the international dimension which is being reviewed and analysed. For instance in the case of curriculum activities and research initiatives, it is how the international dimension is addressed and integrated which is under review, not the curriculum or research itself.

The outline is a starting point and a guide for the institution to undertake the preparation of their self-assessment. It is not intended to be a coercive structure. There may be questions and issues included in the outline which are not relevant or appropriate to the

245

mandate of the specific institution. In other instances, there may be important items which have not been included in the outline which the SAT wants to address and therefore these should be added.

The self-assessment report should give an adequate profile of the institution, reflecting its particular directions, priorities and effectiveness of its operations, and is aimed at giving directions for improvement and change. The self-assessment should recognise and reflect the potential diversity of rationales and strategies between faculties and schools.

This self-assessment should not primarily be regarded as a descriptive exercise, but rather as a critical analysis of the institution's performance and achievements in the field of internationalisation. Besides providing the necessary information, an analysis should be made of strong and weak points, indicating how well the various internationalisation efforts are being realised, and formulating potential avenues to improvement.

Terminology often differs from country to country and from institution to institution. Institutions should use the terminology which they find appropriate for their situation. It would be helpful to add a note of explanation so that the peer review team understands the use of terms in their institutional context.

5.1.3. Outline for the self-assessment process

A. Context

a) Summary of the higher education system

Provide a brief description of the higher education system in the country and indicate the position of the institution in the system.

b) Summary of the institutional profile

Provide information on:

- Age of the institution.
- Student enrolment (undergraduate/graduate).
- Number of faculty and staff.
- Faculties and departments.
- The mission of the institution.
- The history of internationalisation efforts in your institution.

c) Analysis of the (inter)national context

Undertake a Strengths, Weaknesses, Opportunities and Threats (SWOT) analysis of the (inter)national context for internationalisation of the institution. Make reference to national and regional policies and programmes of relevance for the institution's international dimension.

B. Internationalisation policies and strategies

(Address those issues which are relevant to your institution and undertake a SWOT analysis on the internationalisation policies and strategies of the institution.)

Why is internationalisation important to your institution (rationales)?

What is the institution's stated policy (goals and objectives) and implementation strategy for internationalisation? Attach existing policy documents, if available.

What is the relationship between the internationalisation strategy and the institution's overall strategic plan, and what links exist with other relevant policy areas?

How is internationalisation valued with respect to the institution's overall strategic plan by the different actors in the institution: administration, faculty, students?

How has the decision-making process for internationalisation policy been structured?

What is recommended to improve the policies and strategies for internationalisation?

How can the support and involvement be improved of both leadership, administration, faculty and students to the internationalisation policies and strategies of the institution?

C. Organisational and support structures

(Address those issues which are relevant to your institution and undertake a SWOT analysis on the organisational and support structures for internationalisation of the institution.)

a) Organisation and structures

What office/unit/position has the overall and ultimate policy-level responsibility for the internationalisation of the institution?

Which unit(s) have direct operational responsibility for international activities?

What is the reporting structure, liaison and communication system (both formally and informally) between the various offices/units/persons involved in internationalisation? Provide an organigram, if possible.

How effective are the existing support structures in relation to the strategic plan for internationalisation?

What improvements are recommended to make the organisation and support structures more effective in relation to the existing strategies and policies?

b) Planning and evaluation

How is internationalisation integrated into institution-wide and department level planning processes and is it effective?

What system is in place for the evaluation of internationalisation efforts? What impact does it have on these efforts?

Does the overall quality assurance system (internal/external) include reference to internationalisation? If so, what is its impact?

What proposals for improvement in the planning and evaluation processes for internationalisation are recommended?

c) Financial support and resource allocation

What internal and external sources of support exist for internationalisation? How effective are these funds for the realisation of the objectives and goals for internationalisation?

What is the mechanism for the allocation of resources (at both central and departmental level) for internationalisation? How effective are these mechanisms?

What is the institution's process for seeking, securing and maintaining internal and external funding for internationalisation? Are these processes effective?

What proposals for improvement in the fund allocation and fund-raising for the realisation of the internationalisation of the institution are made?

d) Support services and facilities

What specific services and infrastructure exist to support and develop international activities and how effective are they?

What level of support is available from institution-wide service departments? What is their impact?

To what degree do the facilities (*e.g.* libraries) and the extra-curricular activities on campus include an international or cross-cultural dimension? What is their impact?

What recommendations are made to improve the support services and facilities to bring them in line with the internationalisation strategies and policies of the institution?

D. Academic programmes and students

(Address those issues which are relevant to your institution and undertake a SWOT analysis on the international dimension of the academic programmes and student policies of the institution.)

a) Internationalisation of the curriculum: area and language studies, degree programmes, teaching and learning process

Are there programmes which include options for area and language studies (including courses in intercultural communication and culture studies?) What is their impact?

How has the international dimension been integrated into the courses/units in the various disciplines? How effective have the integration efforts been?

What joint or double degree programmes are offered by the institution in partnership with foreign institutions? What is their impact on the curriculum and the students?

Does teaching include the use of examples, case studies, research, literature, etc., drawn from different countries, regions and cultures? To what effect?

To what extent is the "international classroom setting" applied, *i.e.* are students encouraged to study together and to interact with foreign students?

To what extent is instruction given in languages other than the primary language(s) of instruction of the institution?

What recommendations are made with respect to the future place of area and language studies in the institutional strategies and policies for internationalisation?

What measures are recommended to improve the international dimension in the curriculum?

What recommendations are made to improve the internationalisation of the teaching and learning process?

b) Domestic students

What are the quantitative goals (if any) for the number of students studying abroad annually? Are they being met and how effective are the mechanisms to achieve them?

Do students participate in international research projects and international networks. How? What is the impact?

What policies and support services are in place to encourage and support students to participate in international activities? How effective are they?

OECD 1999

Are students being informed and advised about international work/study/research opportunities? Are the mechanisms effective?

How are students being prepared for international academic experiences (including language and cultural preparation)? Is the preparation effective and what is the impact?

What recommendations are made to improve the opportunities for students to add an international dimension to their study?

c) Foreign students

What are the quantitative goals (if any) for the number of foreign students (both fee paying students and exchange students)? How effective are the measures taken to reach these goals?

What strategies does the institution have to attract, recruit and select foreign fee paying students? What are the objectives behind these strategies and how effective are these strategies?

What strategies does the institution have to attract and select (bilateral and multilateral programme) exchange students? How effective are they?

How is the level of academic success of foreign students monitored? How effective is it? How is the integration (educational and social) of foreign students with domestic students and with their local environment monitored? How effective is it?

How is social guidance and academic counselling for foreign students organised?

Does a difference exist in objectives, impact and attention between the strategies for foreign fee paying students and exchange students?

What measures should be taken to improve the strategies for recruitment, selection and integration of foreign fee paying and/or exchange students?

d) Study abroad and student exchange programmes

What is the range of programmes available for study abroad and student exchange? How effective are these programmes?

How effectively are study abroad periods integrated into the curriculum? Has the transfer and recognition of credits been arranged in an adequate manner?

To what extent have international work experience or internships been incorporated into the curriculum? What is the impact of these arrangements?

How are study abroad and student exchange programmes evaluated? In what way have the results of these evaluations been taken into account in the further delivery of these programmes?

What measures are recommended to improve the quality of the study abroad and student exchange programmes in the overall context of the internationalisation strategies and policies of the institution?

E. Research and scholarly collaboration

(Address those issues which are relevant to your institution and undertake a SWOT analysis on the international dimension of research and scholarly collaboration of the institution.)

Which collaborative agreements exist with foreign institutions/research centres/private companies for research? How effective are these?

What international/regional research and graduate centres belong to or are sponsored by the institution? What role do they play in the internationalisation strategies and policies of the institution?

To what degree is the institution involved in international research projects? How successful is it?

How actively involved is the institution in the production of internationally published scientific articles? What mechanisms are in place to stimulate the involvement?

What mechanisms are in place to stimulate the institution's performance in organising and benefiting from international conferences and seminars? How effective are these?

What support (internal and external) structures are in place for international collaborative research? How effective are these?

What mechanisms exist to guarantee that international research (and its outputs) is linked to internationalisation of teaching? What is the effect?

What opportunities and resources are made available to stimulate the international dimension in research? Are they effective?

What recommendations are made to improve the international dimension of research, as part of the strategies and policies of the institution?

F. Human resources management

(Address those issues which are relevant to your institution and undertake a SWOT analysis on the international dimension of human resources management of the institution.)

251

What mechanisms are in place to involve academic and administrative staff in international activities (at home and abroad)? Please distinguish between research, teaching, publications and development assistance. How effective are these mechanisms?

What mechanisms are in place to stimulate the presence of foreign academic and administrative staff members on campus (temporary/permanent)? How effective are they?

How are teaching and research of visiting staff being organised? How effectively are they integrated into the curriculum?

Do appointment procedures seek for staff from abroad? How effective are they?

How is selection and recruitment of new staff (academic and administrative) targeted at personnel who are internationally experienced/active? How effective is that policy?

Are there procedures for selecting staff for international education assignments (*e.g.* for teaching international programmes/to international groups/teaching in other languages)? How effective are they?

What mechanisms are in place to guarantee and stimulate that staff members possess the knowledge and skills required for teaching in international programmes and for other international assignments? How effective are they?

Are there mechanisms in place to guarantee that international teaching/research/development assistance experience counts toward promotion and tenure? If so, how effective are they?

What recommendations are made to improve the international dimension of the human resource management of the institution as part of its internationalisation strategies and policies?

G. Contracts and services

(Address those issues which are relevant to your institution and undertake a SWOT analysis on the international dimension of contracts and services of the institution.)

a) Partnerships and networks

What is the range of bilateral and multilateral collaborative agreements with foreign partner institutions for education? How active/functional are these?

What procedures exist for the establishment, management and periodic evaluation of partnerships and linkages? How well do these procedures function?

What is the relation between the policies and strategies at the faculty level and those at the central level? How effective is that relationship?

What measures are recommended to improve the partnerships and networks the institutions takes part in and their relation to the strategies and policies of the institution?

b) Out of country education programmes

Does the institution deliver educational programmes to students located in other countries. If so, what methods are used to deliver these courses (*i.e.* correspondence, partner institutions, www, satellite campus, franchise partners or brokers, etc.)? What are the rationales for such programmes?

Is there a process (internal/external) of the institution for the evaluation of such programmes, if provided? If so, what is the impact of these evaluations?

What are the institution's strategies to attract, recruit and select students and staff for such programmes and courses? How effective are these strategies?

What measures are recommended to improve these programmes and their relationship to the institution's overall internationalisation strategy?

c) Development assistance

What is the institution's involvement (as a contractor or partner) in development projects, how are they perceived by the faculty? What is their impact on the teaching and research functions of the institution?

What is the link between development assistance projects and other internationalisation activities of the institution?

What policies and procedures exist for the design, management and evaluation of development projects, and what is the effect of these procedures on the projects and on the institutions strategy for internationalisation?

What measures are recommended to improve the quality of the role of the institution in these activities and of the integration of these projects in the overall internationalisation strategy of the institution?

d) External services and project work

How active is the institution in external services (*e.g.* contract education, training, consultancy), and to what extent do these services include an international or cross-cultural dimension?

What is the impact of these services on the internationalisation strategy of the institution?

What measures are recommended to improve the quality of these services and their relationship to the internationalisation strategy of the institution?

Conclusions and recommendations

What are the main conclusions from the self-assessment on internationalisation?

What are the main concerns and challenges for the institution with regard to the further development of internationalisation?

What are the main recommendations to the institution for the further improvement of its international dimension?

Are the goals and objectives for internationalisation of the institution clearly formulated?

Are these goals and objectives translated into the institution's curriculum, research and public service functions and does the institution provide the necessary support and infrastructure for successful internationalisation?

How does the institution monitor its internationalisation efforts?

What specific topics or questions would you like to bring to the attention of the peer review team?

5.1.4. The self-assessment report

After the self-assessment exercise has been completed, the preparation of the self-assessment report is the next step in the IQRP. The report should be limited to a maximum 20-30 pages plus possible annexes. It would be most helpful if it followed as much as possible the general pattern of the self-assessment outline, with the caveat that not all the categories and questions in the outline may be appropriate or relevant for each institution. It is also important to stress that the self-assessment team may add issues not covered by the framework but considered relevant. Thus the self-assessment outline should be considered as a guide only, intended to introduce many of the areas and issues to be considered and to encourage the teams to undertake an analytical approach.

The self-assessment report will be much more than a description of the type and extent of internationalisation efforts; it is meant to critically assess and address ways to assure and improve the quality of internationalisation of the teaching, research and public service functions of the institution in the light of existing issues and forthcoming challenges.

The language of the self-assessment report will in part be guided by the make-up of the PRT. During the initial stages of the IQRP the secretary of the SAT will decide in collaboration with the secretary of the PRT the working language of the PRT site visit and also the language of the self-assessment report. If a language, other than the native language, is used for the SAT and PRT reports, it is assumed that the supporting documents, such as data annexes, can be in the institution's national language.

The peer review team members are to receive the self-assessment report at least one month prior to the visit. The institution will send one copy of the SAT report for each of the PRT members plus two additional copies for the IQRP-archive to the secretary of the PRT.

5.2. The peer review process

5.2.1. Membership of the peer review team

The peer review team (PRT) can vary in size but requires a minimum of three members and usually consists of three-four members; all must be external and independent of the institution undergoing the IQRP. The experts appointed to the PRT will have a general understanding of quality assessment and assurance, will have a particular expertise in the internationalisation of higher education, and will be knowledgeable and experienced in higher education.

The PRT chairperson with preference should be a senior academic with expertise in higher education governance and preferably the development and management of international relations/programmes of institutions of higher education. Knowledge of recent developments in the internationalisation of higher education globally is also essential. The expertise and experience of the other members should relate to the priority areas of the institution's aims and objectives for internationalisation. They should be knowledgeable in academic culture and governance. It is considered an additional asset to have a team member with prior experience in quality assurance review exercises.

The composition of the PRT is primarily international, but it may include one member from the institution's home country or a member with considerable experience in and knowledge of higher education in the country (but not related to the institution itself). At least one member of the PRT should come from another continent than the institution's home country. The first person is likely to be able to provide the PRT with insight in the national context, the second person is likely to provide the PRT with a perspective beyond the regional context.

One member of the PRT will serve as secretary and be responsible for organising the work of the PRT and for co-ordinating the preparation of its report. The secretary of the PRT is also the liaison person with the secretary of the SAT for the response of the PRT to the self-assessment report, and the preparation of terms of reference of the site visit (see 5.2.3).

The secretary of the PRT prepares a written agreement with the institution on the terms under which the self-assessment and peer review reports will be placed in the IQRP archives of IMHE. The following options are available:

- The documents will not be included in the archives.
- The documents will be included but permission for use by parties other than the institution has to be granted by the institution on each occasion.
- The documents will be included and permission is granted by the institution to IMHE to provide a copy of the documents upon request.

In the last two cases, the SAT secretary is responsible for providing two copies of the self-assessment and peer review reports to IMHE.

The institution will be responsible for all costs related to the peer review. It is important to clarify and agree upon all the financial aspects of the review, before individuals are invited to become members of the PRT.

5.2.2. Responsibilities of the peer review team

The task of the PRT is to examine:

- The goals for internationalisation of the institution and whether they are clearly formulated.
- How these goals are translated into the institution's curriculum, research and public service functions and if the institution is providing the necessary support and infrastructure for successful internationalisation.
- How the institution monitors its internationalisation efforts.
- The institution's capacity to change; and its autonomy in order to improve its internationalisation strategies.
- The adequacy of its diagnosis and proposals for change and improvement.

The PRT members will receive the self-assessment report at least one month prior to the visit. After thoroughly reviewing it, the PRT may provide general comments to the self-assessment team prior to the site visit. Then the PRT will pay a two- to three-day visit to the institution and produce a detailed report (20-30 pages) for the institution no later than two months after the site visit.

5.2.3. Design of the peer review process

Ideally the PRT meets once before the actual site visit to discuss the self-assessment report, finalise the terms of reference for the visit and agree on the division of labour among the team members. It is preferable that such a visit takes place at the institution where the IQRP is carried out, and includes also a meeting with the self-assessment team to discuss the comments on the self-assessment report and to prepare the programme.

It is acknowledged that in many cases for reasons of costs and time such a preparatory visit will not be possible. In that case, the secretary of the PRT will establish active communication with the other PRT members to receive their comments on the self-assessment report and suggestions for the terms of reference and the programme of the site visit. Also, in that case it is recommended that the secretary will pay a preparatory visit to the institution to discuss the comments on the self-assessment report and finalise the terms of reference and the programme with the SAT.

The PRT will have on site a half or one day planning meeting prior to the commencement of the official PRT programme.

Based on the initial review of the self-assessment report and discussions of the PRT, a decision will be made as to whether additional information is needed before the site visit. Prior to the site visit a list of specific issues to be addressed, individuals/groups to be met will be prepared by the PRT and forwarded to the self-assessment team.

The institution prepares a detailed schedule for the PRT visit, which may vary in length between three and four days. The team should meet key persons among selected administrative and academic staff, students and graduates, and, if possible, representatives of other bodies (both inside and outside the institution) responsible for, or involved in international activities. Where appropriate, it may be useful to visit the units where students or staff receive assistance and service as well as other related facilities of the institution. In some cases it may be appropriate for PRT members to visit locations and programmes of the institution in other parts of the world. The schedule includes also meetings with the self-assessment team, the leadership of the institution, chief academic and administrative staff responsible for international activities and related support services.

At the end of the site visit, the PRT meets with the SAT to comment on the site visit and discuss the plans for the preparation of the PRT report and its presentation to the institution. The PRT also meets with the senior leaders of the institution to give a brief report, oral and preliminary, on the visit.

5.2.4. The peer review team report

The major issues to be addressed in the PRT report are the following:

- Is the institution's self-assessment report on internationalisation sufficiently analytical and constructively critical?
- Are the strengths and weaknesses of the institution's international activities clearly articulated and the plans for improvements clearly presented and realistic?
- Is the institution achieving the aims and objectives it has set for itself?
- How do the institution's vision and goals relate to the development and sustainability of its international activities within the totality?
- What action is required of the institution in order to monitor progress and provide continuing impetus?

The PRT prepares a draft report and sends it to the chairperson of the SAT within two months after the site visit. The draft version of the PRT report is meant for review and comment before the final version is submitted. This provides the institution with

257

the opportunity to correct any factual errors and errors of interpretation. The institution provides feedback to the PRT within two weeks of the receipt of the draft version of the report. It is up to the PRT to decide whether to include the recommended changes in the report or not. Any required changes are made by the PRT and the final report is sent to the institution. The institution will receive five copies of the report. It is up to the institution to decide how many additional copies it will make for internal and external use. The institution has complete ownership of the report. The report is strictly confidential if the institution wishes to consider it as such.

The follow-up activities and other use of the PRT report are the responsibility of the institution. It is suggested that both the self-assessment report and the PRT report be made available at least internally. Given the self-assessment process has taken place with active participation by many individuals and groups in the institution, it is important that they are included in an open discussion or planning session about the comments and suggestions made in both the SAT and PRT reports. In other words, the use and follow-up to the reports is an integral part of the process of assessing, assuring and improving the internationalisation strategies.

6. Follow-up phase

The institution may add to the IQRP a follow-up phase, occuring one and a half to two years after the PRT report has been delivered. This is particularly important in those cases in which the IQRP is used to start a process for the development of an internationalisation strategy within an institution. As part of this follow-up phase the self-assessment team will write a document analysing the progress in implementing the recommendations made by the SAT and PRT and the internationalisation strategy. It will make recommendations for further actions. This report is the basis for a one- to two-day site visit by the PRT to give their views on the progress and the recommendations for further action.

The decision to include a follow-up phase in the IQRP preferably should be taken at the beginning of the IQRP and at latest at the end of the PRT visit.

7. Time-frame of the IQRP

Whilst this has to be sensitive to the particular setting of the institution, the following provides a broad template against which the institution may devise a specific schedule. The indicated length of the IQRP is approximately ten months and in the case of a follow-up phase another six months. Of the ten months, four months are needed for the self-assessment process, and in the follow-up phase two months.

Month 1	Decision to start an IQRP: appointment of the SAT, contact on the implementation of the IQRP and PRT assistance.
Month 2	Start of the self-assessment process, appointment of the PRT, dates fixed for PRT visit (signing of the contract).
Month 7	Self-assessment report ready and sent to PRT members.

Month 8	Preparatory meeting of PRT (half to one day on site), visit of the PRT (two to three days), decision on follow-up project and involvement of PRT.
Month 9	Draft report of PRT sent to the institution for comments (response in two weeks by institution).
Month 10	Final PRT report ready and sent to the institution.

In case of follow-up:

Month 31	Preparation of self-assessment follow-up report by SAT.
Month 33	Self-assessment follow-up report ready, self-assessment report sent to PRT members (includes terms of reference and programme of PRT site visit).
Month 34	Visit of PRT (one to two days).
Month 35	Draft follow-up report of PRT sent to the institution for comments (response in two weeks by institution).
Month 36	Follow-up report of PRT ready and sent to institution.

8. The use of the IQRP

Each institution is in principle free to use the IQRP guidelines, but should make reference to the intellectual property by IMHE in co-operation with ACA. For reasons of coherence, servicing and assessment, it is highly recommended that the institution which undertakes the IQRP, makes use of expertise in quality assurance of higher education by (inter)national bodies and agencies. IMHE, ACA and CRE co-operate in the implementation of IQRP in Europe. For information on assistance in the realisation of the IQRP at an institution, one may contact the CRE Secretariat in the European case and the IMHE Secretariat in other cases.

About the Authors

TONY ADAMS is Director of International Programmes at Mcquarie University in Sydney, Australia. Prior to that he was Dean of International Programmes at the Royal Melbourne Institute of Technology (RMIT). He is responsible for the development of Mcquarie's international strategy and its facilitation and implementation. He was a member of the RMIT Foundation Professoriate and in 1997 received the IDP Education Australia award for his contribution to international education. He is a member of the editorial board of the *Journal of Studies in International Education* and is author of several articles in this field.

JEROME BOOKIN-WEINER is Dean of International Education at Bentley College in Waltham, Massachusetts, United States. Prior to assuming his position at Bentley College, he served as Director of the Centre for International Programmes and Director of the Virginia Centre for World Trade at Old Dominion University in Norfolk, Virginia, 1976-87. At both Bentley college and Old Dominion University, Dr. Bookin-Weiner has been involved in building multi-dimensional international education programmes.

Dr. Bookin-Weiner was educated at Dickinson College in Carlisle, Pennsylvania, and Columbia University, New York, where he earned his master of arts in history and Ph.D., specialising in the history of the modern Middle East and North Africa. He also attended the Jacob Hiatt Institute of Brandeis University in Jerusalem, and the Bourguiba Institute of Living Languages in Tunis. He was a Fulbright Senior Research Scholar in Morocco in the summers of 1989 and 1990.

PAUL FOGELBERG studied at the University of Helsinki, Finland, where he obtained his doctorate in 1970. Having occupied different positions at the departments of geography of the Universities of Helsinki and Oulu since 1963, he was nominated professor of geography at the University of Helsinki in 1982. In 1990-92 he was Vice-Dean of the Faculty of Science, and in 1992-98 Vice-Rector of the university. He retired from his university positions in September 1998. Among his international commitments are: member of the directing group of IMHE/OECD as the representative of Finland, 1993-96; deputy member of the board of the International Association of Universities (IAU) since 1995; member of the board of the

European Association of Science Editors (EASE), 1982-97; and president of EASE, 1991-94. He chaired the IQRP self-assessment team for the University of Helsinki, and was a member of the IQRP peer review team for the University of Tartu.

MARIAN GELDNER is since 1989 Full Professor of Economics and since 1996 Vice-Rector for External Relations of the Warsaw School of Economics, Poland. His teaching and research fields are Microeconomics, International Management, Economics of International Business. In 1983-1984, Marian Geldner was Senior Fulbright Research Scholar at the Department of Economics, Rutgers, the State University of New Jersey, United States; in 1973-74, Visiting Research Fellow at the Department of Economics, University of Copenhagen, Denmark; and in 1971 a Visiting Fellow at the Centre of Contemporary European Studies, University of Sussex, Great Britain. He has over 10 years experience as trainer and instructor at numerous training programmes and seminars, and over five years experience of managing a private local consultancy practice in Poland. In 1989-95, he was President and Managing Partner of the Association of Consultants and Advisers Ltd., Warsaw. In 1987-89, he was on leave from Warsaw School of Economics to become UNIDO Consultant Chief Technical Adviser/Financial Analyst, managing an UNIDO executed project "Investor Advisory Assistance Service", for the Ministry of Finance, Khartoum, Sudan.

JANE KNIGHT brings both a researcher's and practitionner's perspective to the internationalisation of higher education. She is currently Head of International Affairs in the Office of the President at Ryerson Polytechnic University, Toronto, Canada. Previously Dr. Knight was acting Associate Director of Ryerson International, Director of the China Partnership Programme and led a university-wide task force to develop an internationalisation strategy. Prior work with UNESCO in Paris and a development NGO in India help her to bring policy and practical experience to the study of international education. Currently Dr. Knight is a member of the editorial board of the *Journal of Studies in International Education*. On the research front, she and Hans de Wit (University of Amsterdam) are leading an international project of the IMHE/OECD on quality assurance of the international dimension. They worked on a comparative study of internationalisation strategies in the Asia-Pacific Region which resulted in EAIE publication (1997). At the national level, Dr. Knight has conducted several national studies on the status and issues of internationalisation in Canada.

JOSEPH KOECH obtained his B.Ed. (Hons) and M.A. from the University of Nairobi, Kenya, and M.Ed. in Adult and Higher Education and Ph.D. in Educational Administration from the University of Alberta, Canada. Since 1978, he has taught in secondary schools, teacher training colleges and also served as Dean of students in a higher diploma teacher training college. He joined Moi University in 1988 as Senior Administrative Officer in the Administrative Division and from 1990 he has served as Principal Administrative Officer. Currently, he serves as Principal Administrative Officer (Human Resources). From 1996, he has been Supervisor of the MHO Central Services Project, a project funded by the Dutch Government between Moi University and two Dutch universities. His interests are mainly in higher education administration and inter-institutional linkages.

SALVADOR MALO is currently Vice-President for Planning at the Universidad Nacional Autónoma de México (UNAM). Salvador Malo has a long career in science and higher education and was a member of the Mexican Task Force Group for Collaboration in Higher Education in North America. With a first degree in Physics from UNAM and a Ph.D., also in Physics, from Imperial College, University of London, he worked for three years at the International Atomic Energy Agency in Vienna, Austria. Back in Mexico he did research on surface science for several years at Mexico's Instituto Mexicano del Petróleo, where he occupied several positions including that of Vice-President for Research. He later joined the Mexican Department of Education to initiate several programmes to promote science development in Mexican state universities, one of them being the well-known Sistema Nacional de Investigadores. At the UNAM, besides being a professor in its School of Sciences and, recently, in its Centre for University Studies, he has also held the position of Secretary-General, and of Vice-President for Administration.

GRANT McBURNIE is Executive Officer, International and Public Affairs, Monash University, Melbourne, Australia. He is involved in a range of international policy and operational issues including strategic planning, management of transnational education, student mobility, student recruitment and inter-institutional co-operation. As a member of the university's Off-shore Quality Assurance Committee, Dr. McBurnie has co-ordinated a variety of projects on university internationalisation, including programmes contributing to Monash winning the "Good Universities Guide University of the Year Award" for internationalisation of the student service. As a member of the university's Off-shore Quality Assurance Committee, he has worked with international teams reviewing degree programmes in Hong Kong, China, Malaysia, Singapore and Indonesia. His academic background is in social history, with a focus on twentieth century eugenics movements. Current research interests include international education and quality assurance in transnational education.

PETER OPAKAS holds a B.Ed. from the University of Nairobi, Kenya, an Advanced Diploma in Educational Administration and a Master of Education Degree from the University of Leeds, England. He has a wide experience in the administration of Kenya's education system, having served as a Graduate Teacher, Secondary School Headmaster in a number of secondary schools in Kenya. He has served as a District Education Officer in a number of Kenya's Districts of Turkana, Nyeri, Nakuru, Baringo and Kisii. Since 1991, Mr. Opakas has worked at Moi University in the Central University Administration, at present at the level of Principal Administrative Officer. His duties include amongst others staff recruiting and training. He has a wide experience in dealing with international staff and has travelled widely in East Africa. His current interest is in the area of the development of

263

international links between Moi University and other educational and related institutions.

MARJORIE PEACE LENN is the Executive Director of the Center for Quality Assurance in International Education and the Global Alliance for Transnational Education (GATE) located at the National Centre for Higher Education in Washington, DC. A consortium of higher education associations, the centre is dedicated to monitoring quality issues in the globalisation of the United States higher education and the globalisation of the professions, and provides assistance in the development and improvement of quality assurance systems throughout the globe. In 1996, the centre became the Secretariat of GATE. A former senior administrator at the University of Massachusetts/Amherst and Vice-President of the Council on Postsecondary Accreditation, the umbrella organisation for the accreditation of the 6 000 institutions in the United States, Dr. Lenn is published in several languages and speaks extensively to international and domestic audiences. Dr. Lenn serves on multiple boards and does extensive consulting directly with ministries and legislative organisations, and through such organisations as the World Bank, the Asian Development Bank (ADB), OAS, the UNESCO, the Council of Europe, AAU (Africa), UNDP, and others.

ROSAMARIA VALLE at present is Director-General for Educational Evaluation at the UNAM and member of the National Committee for the Evaluation of Social Sciences Programmes. A Ph.D. graduate from the Faculty of Psychology of UNAM, trained in clinical psychology at the Salpêtrière and Ste Anne hospitals in Paris, she was Head of the Psychology Department at the Penitentiary Services of Ontario, Canada. Back in Mexico she was Director of the School of Psychology at Anahuac University in Mexico City, and Head of the Educational Development Centre at the same school. At UNAM she has been Advisor to the Secretary-General, and is Professor of the Faculty of Psychology. Her areas of interest include children and adolescent mental health, school failure prevention, moral development and education, and educational evaluation.

BERND WÄCHTER is the Director of the Academic Co-operation Association (ACA) in Brussels. Earlier posts include the head of ERASMUS in the SOCRATESA & Youth Office in Brussels and the directorship of the European Division of the German Academic Exchange Service (DAAD) in Bonn, Germany. He also has worked for the British Council and a number of German higher education institutions. Bernd Wächter has published widely on European educational co-operation.

MARIJK VAN DER WENDE works as a senior researcher at the Centre for Higher Education Policy Studies (CHEPS) of the University of Twente, the Netherlands. Besides, she is associated to the Universiteit van Amsterdam, Faculty of Sciences, as a senior advisor on postgraduate programmes and international development. From 1992 to 1998, she worked at NUFFIC, the Netherlands Organisation for International Co-operation in Higher Education, as a senior researcher and co-ordinator for studies and training. She conducted a range of studies in the field of internationalisation of higher education and has been the leader of a number of professional training courses on this issue. In 1996, Marijk van der Wende received her Ph.D. from Utrecht University. The subject of her dissertation was: "Internationalising the Curriculum in Dutch Higher Education, an International Comparative Perspective", based on a study she carried out for the Centre for Educational Research and Innovation (CERI) of the OECD. She is a member of the editorial board of the *Journal of Studies in International Education*.

HANS DE WIT is since 1996 Vice-President for International Affairs of the Universiteit van Amsterdam, the Netherlands. He serves on multiple boards. In 1994, he was president of the European Association for International Education (EAIE). Currently, he is among other positions: Vice-Chair of the Board of Trustees of World Education Services (WES, New York), Member of the Board of Directors of the Council on International Educational Exchange (CIEE, New York), and Officer of the Dutch Foundation for International Cultural Activities. In 1995, he was visiting lecturer at the Department of Sociology of Boston College (United States). He is a consultant for the IMHE/OECD programme on strategies for internationalisation in higher education and internationalisation quality review. He was editor *of Strategies for Internationalisation of Higher Education – A Comparative Study of Australia, Canada, Europe and the United States of America*, EAIE, 1995. He was with Jane Knight co-editor of *Internationalisation of Higher Education in Asia Pacific Countries*, EAIE, 1997. He is the editor of the *Journal of Studies in International Education*, of the Council on International Educational Exchange.

DAVID WOODHOUSE is Director of the New Zealand Universities Academic Audit Unit, which is responsible for auditing the academic quality assurance and control procedures of New Zealand's universities. He is active internationally in quality assurance, providing advice and training on educational quality assurance in a number of countries. Currently, he is President of the International Network of Quality Assurance Agencies in Higher Education; edits the Network newsletter; is on the Board of the Global Alliance for Transnational Education; and is an Executive Editor of the international journal *Quality in Higher Education. Theory and Practice*. Before working in New Zealand, Dr. David Woodhouse was Deputy Director of the Hong Kong Council for Academic Accreditation, with responsibility for the quality of degree courses in Hong Kong, China. Before that, he was a faculty member in mathematics, computer science and computer education in universities in several countries, and was at various times head of a department and dean of a faculty.

KARIN WRIEDT RUNNE is full time professor in the Faculty of Psychology at the UNAM. She received her first university degree in psychology and did her graduate studies on higher education at the same university. She obtained a specialisation degree in Institutional Management, Planning and Evaluation of Higher Education, a programme sponsored by the National Institute for Public Administration (INAP) and the ANUIES. She taught several courses at UNAM and other public universities of Mexico. She is co-author of the book *The Future of University: UNAM 2025*. She worked in different programmes of ANUIES and of the National Institute for Adult Education and in the Faculty of Philosophy, the Open University System and the Dean's Assessors Co-ordination at UNAM. She works now in the General Direction of Educational Evaluation at UNAM.

Acronyms

AACSB	American Assembly of Collegiate Schools of Business
ABET	Accreditation Board for Engineering and Technology
ACA	Academic Co-operation Association
AIESEC	Association internationale des étudiants en sciences économiques et commerciales
ANUIES	Asociación Nacional de Universidades e Instituciones de Educación Superior
APEC	Asia-Pacific Economic Cooperation
AVCC	Australian Vice-Chancellors' Committee
BA	Bachelor of arts
BS	Bachelor of science
CBIE	Canadian Bureau for International Education
CEEPUS	Central European Exchange Programme for University Studies
CEMS	Community of European Management Schools
CIBER	Centre for International Business Education and Research
CIDA	Canadian International Development Agency
CIEE	Council on International Educational Exchange
CIMO	Centre for International Mobility
CRE	Association of European Universities
CUAED	Coordinación de Universidad Abierta y Educación a Distancia
DAAD	German Academic Exchange Service
DEET	Department of Employment, Education and Training
DEETYA	Department of Employment, Education, Training and Youth Affairs
DFAT	Department of Foreign Affairs and Trade
DIS	Denmark's International Study Programmes
EAIE	European Association for International Education
ECTS	European Credit Transfer System
EQR	External quality review
ERASMUS	European (Community) Action Scheme for the Mobility of University Students

OECD 1999

ESL	English as a Second Language
EU	European Union
EVALUE	Evaluation and Self-evaluation of Universities in Europe
FEANI	European Federation of National Engineering Associations
GATE	Global Alliance for Transnational Education
GATS	General Agreement on Trade in Services
HEQC	Higher Education Quality Council
ILO	International Labour Organisation
IMF	International Monetary Fund
INQAAHE	International Network of Quality Assurance Agencies for Higher Education
ISEP	International Student Exchange Programme
ISO	International Organisation for Standardisation
MBA	Master of business administration
MSA	Master of science in accountancy
NAFSA	Association of International Educators
NAFTA	North American Free Trade Agreement
NEASC	New England Association of Schools and Colleges
NUFFIC	Netherlands Organisation for International Co-operation in Higher Education
PRT	Peer review team
QAA	Quality Assurance Agency for Higher Education
RINAF	Regional Informatics Network for Africa
SAR	Self-assessment report
SAT	Self-assessment team
SEP	Secretaría de Educación Pública
SGH	Szkola Glówna Handlowa (Warsaw School of Economics)
TOEFL	Test of English as a Foreign Language
TQM	Total Quality Management
UKCOSA	United Kingdom Council for Overseas Student Affairs
UNAM	Universidad Nacional Autónoma de México
UNDP	United Nations Development Programme
UNFPA	United Nations Population Fund
UNIDO	United Nations Industrial Development Organisation
USAID	US Agency for International Development

OECD PUBLICATIONS, 2, rue André-Pascal, 75775 PARIS CEDEX 16
PRINTED IN FRANCE
(89 1999 10 1 P) ISBN 92-64-17049-9 – No. 50603 1999

w2c, manager, choose notice
next in selling prof choo cait